PAKISTAN

GLOBAL SECURITY WATCH
PAKISTAN

Syed Farooq Hasnat

PRAEGER

AN IMPRINT OF ABC-CLIO, LLC
Santa Barbara, California • Denver, Colorado • Oxford, England

Library of Congress Cataloging-in-Publication Data

Hasnat, Syed Farooq.
   Global security watch—Pakistan / Syed Farooq Hasnat.
     p. cm. — (Global security watch)
   title: Pakistan
   Includes bibliographical references and index.
    ISBN 978–0–313–34697–2 (hard copy : alk. paper) — ISBN 978–0–313–34698–9 (ebook)
1. National security—Pakistan. 2. Pakistan—Foreign relations. 3. Pakistan—Strategic aspects.
4. Pakistan—Politics and government—21st century.
I. Title. II. Title: Pakistan.
UA853.P3H387   2011
355′.03305491—dc22   2011013500

ISBN: 978–0–313–34697–2
EISBN: 978–0–313–34698–9

15 14 13 12 11   1 2 3 4 5

This book is also available on the World Wide Web as an eBook.
Visit www.abc-clio.com for details.

Praeger
An Imprint of ABC-CLIO, LLC

ABC-CLIO, LLC
130 Cremona Drive, P.O. Box 1911
Santa Barbara, California 93116-1911

This book is printed on acid-free paper (∞)

Manufactured in the United States of America

Contents

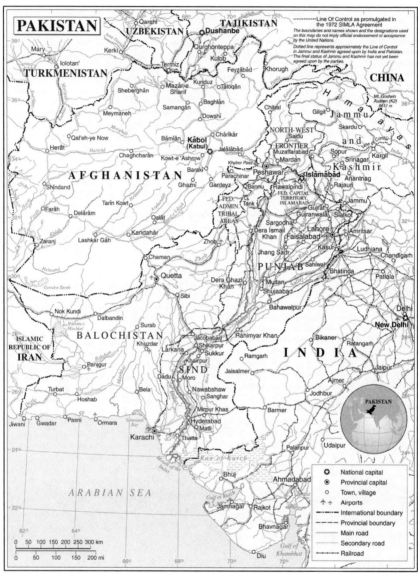

PAKISTAN

UZBEKISTAN

Qarshi

TAJIKISTAN

Dushanbe

Qurghonteppa

Kulob

Kerki

Mary

Iolotan'

Termiz

Feyzābād

Khorugh

TURKMENISTAN

Sheberghān

Mazār-e Sharīf

Kunduz

Tāloqān

Baghlān

Chitral

Gilgit

CHINA

Skardu

Mt. Godwin Austen (K2) 8611 m

Meymaneh

Samangān

Dowshī

Him**a**l**a**y**a**s

Jammu

Qal'eh-ye Now

Herāt

Bāmīān

Kābol (Kabul)

Chārīkār

Jalālābād

NORTH-WEST FRONTIER

Saidu

Muzaffarabad

Sopur

and

Srīnagar

Kargil

Line of Contr

Kashmir

Hariräd

Chaghcharān

Kowt-e 'Ashrow

Khyber Pass

Mardān

Peshāwar

Islāmābād

Anantnag

Rajauri

AFGHANISTAN

Shindand

Ghazni

Barakī

Parachinar

Gardeyz

Bannu

Rawalpindi

FED. CAPITAL TERRITORY, ISLAMABAD

Jammu

FED. ADMIN. TRIBAL AREAS

Tank

Gujrāt

Sargodha

Gujranwala

Siālkot

Farāh

Delārām

Tarīn Kowt

Qalāt

Dera Ismail Khan

Zhob

Lahore

Amritsar

Faisalabad

Zaranj

Lashkar Gāh

Kandahār

Jhang Sadr

Kasur

Ludhiana

Chandigarh

Chaman

Zhob

PUNJAB

Sahiwal

Bhatinda

Patiala

Quetta

Dera Ghazi Khān

Multan

Shujaabad

Sibi

Bahawalpur

Delhi

Nok Kundi

Dalbandin

Surab

Rahimyar Khan

New Delhi

ISLAMIC REPUBLIC OF IRAN

BALOCHISTAN

Khuzdar

Jacobabad

Shikarpur

Lārkāna

Sukkur

Bikaner

Ratangarh

Panjgur

Khairpur

Ramgarh

I N D I A

Jaipur

SIND

Dādu

Moro

Jaisalmer

Ajmer

Turbat

Hoshab

Bela

Nawabshaw

Sanghar

Jodhbur

Jiwani

Gwadar

Pasni

Ormara

Mirpur Khas

Barmer

Sonmiani Bay

Karachi

Thatta

Matli

Hyderabad

Palanpur

Udaipur

PAKISTAN

Ran of Kutch

Bhuj

Ahmadabad

A R A B I A N   S E A

Gulf of Kutch

Jamnagar

Rajkot

Bhavnagar

Gulf of Khambhat

Diu

○ 50 100 150 200 250 300 km

○ 50 100 150 200 mi

◎	National capital
◉	Provincial capital
○	Town, village
✈ ✈	Airports
---·--	International boundary
---·---	Provincial boundary
———	Main road
———	Secondary road
+++	Railroad

Map No. 4181 Rev. 1 UNITED NATIONS
January 2004

Department of Peacekeeping Operations
Cartographic Section

Preface

Pakistan has changed a lot since its establishment in August, 1947. The founding fathers envisaged Pakistan as a modern, democratic Muslim state. However, it could not sustain democracy because the bureaucratic-military elite displaced the divided political leaders and established their control over the affairs of the country. Right from the beginning, Pakistan assigned the highest priority to external security, neglecting societal development. Consequently, it could not address problems like rampant poverty, illiteracy, corruption, and poor government, which negated the essence of the establishment of Pakistan.

There are many reasons behind these failures and disillusionment. As a result of four military dictatorships in the country, the democratic process was derailed and institutions weakened. Even in the decade of democracy, (1988 to 1999) hardly any elected government was given a chance to complete its full tenure. The extended delays in the making of the Constitution for the new state were yet another reason for the failure of the construction of any viable institutions, nor were any solid traditions established for managing the country.

The Afghan war in the 1980s multiplied Pakistan's problems. It was during this period that the culture of militancy and bigotry was inculcated in the society by the military government of General Zia-ul-Haq. This played havoc with the social fabric of the country, badly disturbing its equilibrium. It also undermined Pakistan's global image because the international community started viewing the country as a hub and even a sponsor of terror groups. Pakistan's drift towards religious extremism and militancy have serious implications for the region, with global connotations. The most alarming aspect of this phenomenon remains in religious extremism, where sectarian intolerance and hatred was allowed to grow unchecked. This promoted killings, blasts, armed attacks and suicide bombings, in which thousands of Pakistanis have lost their lives.

Religious extremism and terrorism proliferated in Pakistan after 2002. The main security concerns of the Pakistani state continue to be external with India as the prime focus of worry and attention. However, internal security challenges have become very threatening. Internal security issues include the simmering unrest in Balochistan, sectarian and ethnic-related target killings in Karachi, and on a more serious scale, the growing militancy/insurgency in the tribal belt bordering Afghanistan are the major concerns. The most daunting menace for Pakistani society comes from the emergence of sectarian terrorist groups, often ignored by all governments, whether civilian or military. Moderate Muslims, who form a majority of the population, are under siege by a handful of bigoted and well-armed radical groups that either use *madrasa* students as "street power" or rely upon guns to intimidate those who do not share their perspective. These groups do not conform to the folk culture and beliefs of Pakistani society, but are influenced by the alien beliefs inculcated through charity money by some Middle Eastern countries, during and after the Afghan war in the 1980s.

The hope for Pakistan lies in designing policies which can pull the country out of the multiple crises caused by this culture of militancy and extremism. The first remedy is the continuation of the democratic political process, accompanied by the overwhelming task of rescuing the battered state education system. The second remedy lies in addressing the issues of poverty and underdevelopment, with an emphasis on the socio-economic development of the tribal areas. The elimination of insurgency does not simply mean a military victory or even suppressing militant groups. It actually means the induction of the people into the mainstream and promising them an assured future.

This book addresses various aspects of Pakistan's security concerns, especially those that arise from within Pakistani society. It is hoped that skillfully managing these societal tensions can bring a sense of balance and tranquility to the country.

CHAPTER 1

Strategic Concerns of Pakistan: An Overview

BACKGROUND

Pakistan's policymakers, especially those dealing directly with security affairs, perceived threats to Pakistan's territorial integrity from the early days of independence. The main threat came from its eastern neighbor, India and to a lesser degree Afghanistan intermittently became a security concern for Pakistan's strategic interests. These threats did not remain stagnant but changed patterns with the shifting developments—domestic as well as regional and international.

The promotion of definite goals and manifestation of territorial and nationalistic frontiers of a nation like Pakistan normally becomes a major reason of unease for the ruling elite. The priority of goals varies from state to state and from time to time, and the self-preservation or the security of a state, either to safeguard independent status or to maintain territorial integrity, remains the vital target for the elite irrespective of the time and situational factor.[1] Thus, circumstantial alterations do not affect the basic concerns of the policymaking elite. However, desired goals other than the security of national independence and territorial safeguards fluctuate according to the prevalent conditions and are not permanent.

The United Nations, which was established, among other things, to promote a system of collective security, could not come up to the prospects, and many countries like Pakistan found themselves vulnerable to external pressures and coercive means applied by stronger states. On the other hand, the concept of inter-state relations, as the most important component of world affairs, gave way to rapidly changing societies. In most cases, the demands and aspirations of the people could not be met by the inefficiency of bureaucratic structures, as well as the political parties. Those countries that failed to construct meaningful socio-economic and political structures were more prone to domestic instability than those countries that could. At times, internal weaknesses gave way to external pressures and interventions. Pakistan became a classical case where military frequently intervened, inflicting serious damage on the development of political institutions. This fostered a widespread disenchantment among the people of East Pakistan, leading in 1971 to the separate sovereign state of Bangladesh. A vicious civil war was fought and the ill-prepared and demoralized Pakistan army surrendered in large numbers to India, with which Pakistan's relations had been extremely troubled since independence. India took full advantage of the situation, and its military intervened on behalf of the large population of East Pakistan.

By the beginning of the 1970s, domestic insurgencies and upheavals gained ground in Pakistan and various parts of the world. The main emphasis of national security shifted from external threats to internal strife. The wavering societies, in turn, provided an opportunity for certain groups to cultivate their bases with the motive of achieving objectives elsewhere. A classic example is that of Afghanistan. Al-Qaeda and Osama bin Laden took advantage of a fragmented Taliban Afghanistan and established themselves there because the Afghan government had either a limited control over them or was hesitant to act because of complimentary benefits, deriving from their own weaknesses. Without the knowledge of the Kabul government, Osama planned his attacks on U.S. targets in the Middle East, Africa, and ultimately on the United States itself. Being a close neighbor of the Afghans, the fall-out of this action had direct long-term consequences for Pakistan.

The changing concept of security that began to take shape back in the 1970s is described as follows,

> It is made more difficult by the speed with which history is now moving. New problems and crises are replaced almost at once with still newer ones, and the cumulative effects of many years' events become hard to trace, and to the extent traced, often hard to remember fully, as one tries to cope with today's newspaper and this week's journals. Specialists in national security, who have a professional responsibility to remain *au courant* with ongoing events, are not immune from the difficulties of retaining a full perspective on the "endless crisis" within which we are now living.[2]

The security of a state can be perceived in a manner of ways. During the Cold War period (1949–1989), for the big powers, security requirements went beyond the sole concern for national territorial rights as seen in its rigid meaning. For example, the Russian invasion of Afghanistan in 1979 was seen as a security threat to the American interests. Likewise, in other parts of the world, the possibility of an American attack on Cuba was regarded as a security threat for the interests of the Soviet Union. In other words, regardless of the time frame or the constraints of the global system, the security perceptions of a state are relative phenomena. For smaller states, especially those of the developing group, the major concern about security considerations seldom goes beyond their territorial integrity.

Apart from the concerns of national integrity, the security goals or methods of a state differ according to its military might. Referring to Robert L. Rothstein's analysis, big and "small powers think and act differently and any analysis which fails to take that fact into account is bound to be simplistic and inadequate."[3] For the purposes of this book, the security concerns are confined, as reflected in the following paragraphs, to a militarily weak nation like Pakistan.

In the above paragraphs, a distinction is made between the security perceptions of the big powers and the developing nations. Even within the developing bloc, differentiation becomes inevitable on the basis of the strategic importance of nations which can be categorized into three main groups, relevant to the Cold War era but establishing one of the principles of security. In the first group, are those countries which are either located near the geographical boundaries of a big power or are in the vicinity of one of her staunch allies or adversaries. For example, "Turkey's strategic importance within North Atlantic Treaty Organization (NATO) derives from her key geographic position astride the role exist for the Soviet Black Sea Fleet and as a barrier between the Soviet Union and its client states in the near East."[4] Another important aspect of the geophysical situation of Turkey is that the U.S. "strategic (and tactical) defense effort relies upon Turkish cooperation and Turkish base concessions."[5] A similar analogy can be drawn with U.S. strategic interests in Afghanistan. In the second group, are those nations which are located in a tension-prone geographical area, and in the third group are those countries which possess vital natural resources such as oil. These three groups will form a category of strategically important nations while other nations will not fall into the same category. It should be clarified that the determination of strategic versus non-strategic developing nations is made in a global context. But if we confine ourselves to regional considerations, there will be hardly a nation which is not important in one sphere or another.

The pressures from the international arena are greater on countries enjoying strategic importance. Therefore, these countries would adopt such policies so as to ease pressure from various environmental factors. The pressure on the developing nations can even reach the extent of endangering their national security or political independence in the form of erosion of sovereignty. The switch from "strategic to non-strategic" or vice versa, varies in a time period, and changes with the factors that made them significant in the first place. Countries which are important for global politics today may not be so important tomorrow. Just three decades ago, countries like Oman, Bahrain, and Kuwait were not strategically as important as they are today. Similarly, the strategic importance of some of these countries will decline with the drying up of their oil wells in the coming decades.

We must not overlook the ambiguity of the concept that mixes the regime preservation with that of actual threat to the sovereignty of a state. Elite groups consciously or unconsciously associate the security of the state with their personal security and try to persuade the populace of their country that a removal or an erosion of the powers of the ruling elite would mean the deterioration, or even the destruction of their society. Therefore, it should be taken into account that "hopes, wishes, aspirations and dreams (of the Elite) are not the same as practical and concrete interests (of the Nation)."[6] In practice, the psychological rhetoric propagated by the elite is presented in such a manner that the population becomes unaware of the gravity of the genuine threats posed to the nation.

Donald E. Nuechterlein perhaps refers to such a situation when he writes,

> An interest is vital when the highest policy makers in a sovereign state conclude that the issue at stake in an international dispute is so fundamental to the political, economic and social well being of their country that it should not be compromised further, even if this results in the use of economic and military force.[7]

Still, the question to be pondered is the security of the "fundamental issues at stake." We would agree with Arnold Wolfers that the concept of national interest is perceived by different people in different ways[8] and thus, the ambiguities about the authenticity of the security interests of a country cannot be determined by the elite alone. Even if the sincerity of the national elite is accepted, the ambiguity regarding the perceptions of the policy may not be clear. A distinction has to be made between the real and imaginary fears about national security. Firstly, the imaginary fears might be based on historic experiences or incorrect readings of the designs of the adversary. Secondly, the ruling elite can raise a slogan of external threat so as to divert the attention of the people from their domestic problems. Thirdly, a minor threat can be deliberately propagated as a serious threat in order to deal with domestic deficiencies. Finally, even the element of rationality in the policies of the elite in a certain situation may not make them completely free from subjective thinking.[9] The argument can be summed up by quoting Robert D. Matthews,

> Any policy that serves to maintain a ruling elite in power or to favor a particular section of the population at the expense of the nation as a whole cannot be termed a policy of national security, unless it can be shown it is in the interest of the entire population that the present government stay in power or the privileged group continue to be favored. Similarly, a policy designed to preserve an alliance of nation-states as such, but which does not add to, and may even detract from the security of the individual nation(s), cannot be labeled one of national security.[10]

The burden falls upon the analysts and they alone should pass judgment on the genuineness of security threats to a nation. In the light of the above discussion, a clear distinction will be made between a threat to the elite themselves and the sovereignty of the nation. Our concern will be with the latter. The elite's interpretations regarding national security should be viewed with caution. A nation also faces security threats from internal forces. Internal strife can lead to outside intervention and thus endangering the territorial integrity of a state. As an example, the Pakistani establishment in 1971 mismanaged the internal situation to such an extent that it resulted in external intervention and thus, disintegrated Pakistan.[11]

After 9/11, the United States conceived its security threat from such non-state actors as al-Qaeda, arrogating to itself the right of preemptive strike, reaching targets beyond its borders, and searching for answers to the new threats to the homeland—real or imaginary. It became the basic objective of President George W. Bush to "hunt down" all "necessary evils" in the type of non-state actors, along with "fixing up" nations that, in his view, lacked democratic institutions. There were serious fears expressed that the Bush administration was vying for placement as an imperial power, with risky propositions, as opposed to promoting internationalism. At the time, it was expressed,

> The new course in Washington raises disturbing questions about the kind of international order—or disorder—the world will experience in the coming years. Will it be an era of American cooperation or of American dominance, of American multilateralism or unilateralism? Will the United States set a good example by staying within the boundaries of international law, or will it justify its own transgressions of international law by appealing to some higher good? Will the United States be satisfied with the modest and accustomed role of leader of a partnership of democratic nations, or will it strive, in effect if not in name, to assume the mantle of universal empire?[12]

This new concept of security and its "bits and pieces" underwent rapid changes to an extent that in terms of power and connections, it became difficult to signify the difference between the states and non-state entities. Moreover, it raised many questions, like the correlation of human rights with that of national security. It is pointed out that after the "end of the Cold War, human rights have become the dominant vocabulary in foreign affairs. The question after September 11 is whether the era of human rights has come and gone."[13] An apprehension was widely felt that this Republican President, in his effort to protect the national security of the United States, could not establish a balance between the measures taken to secure Americans and the erosion of the freedoms that are so well defined in the U.S. Constitution. According to Richard Falk,

> The sacrifice of human rights associated with the developments since September 11 can be assessed from at least three perspectives:
>
> – the heavy dose of cold water that has temporary extinguished the forward progress being made with respect to extending and deepening the reach of human rights as epitomized by the normative revolution underway in the 1990s;
>
> – the willingness of the citizenry to forego the vigilance required to protect constitutional liberties at home, being reduced to passivity by a combination of fears about future megaterrorist attacks with an uncritical patriotic fervor that presently endorses as beneficial virtually anything that the government seeks to do in the name of security and counterterrorism;

– the new geopolitics of empire-building that fosters alliances and submission, a
global game of power and control, that consigns matters of values and ethics than
opposition to the "evil" of terrorism, to inoperative status.[14]

A number of commentators have expressed similar reservations, maintaining
that the "overdose" of security measures would jeopardize the very basis for which
these measures are being taken. *The Washington Post,* expressing its frustration,
quoted in its editorial Mayor Anthony A. Williams of Washington, D.C.,

... the Mayor said in a statement: 'We cannot allow the symbols of American freedom
and democracy to be transformed into fortresses of fear.' That, however, is exactly what
U.S. security officials, in the name of fighting terrorism, are doing.[15]

Amid the fears expressed that the "over-concern" of national security will over-
take the matters of civil liberties, some have suggested that the new world order as
originally envisioned by George W. Bush, must adopt a balanced approach.
There has to be an equilibrium between a genuine or imaginary concerns for
security and liberties and that the "basic human rights may not be watered-
down under the pretext of combating terrorism."[16]

During a national crisis, governments tend to act in a repulsive manner as the
whole concept of national security is closely tied with that of patriotism. A real
test of the strength of a nation comes in its ability to adhere to its values and principles, while confronting unpleasant conditions. It is within these times that the
endorsement of a society is either vindicated, or flutters with the tide of panic
and confusion. In this regard, "there is a ... reason to distrust governmental
authority in relation to the protection of the rights of citizens. An authority or
discretionary power granted for one purpose is often used by those in
government for quite unrelated reasons."[17] In this case, the main responsibility
of preserving national security while balancing the rights of the citizens rests with
the people at large, or through their representatives. Thereby, reckless policies to
preserve national security can further aggravate the dangers of national and
international security, as being witnessed in the case of the United States and its
policies in Iraq and other places.

The efforts of a new U.S. attitude are felt far and wide. It is realized that the
world underwent little change after the events of 9/11. But, it is in fact the
United States that has undergone drastic transformations. On the one hand,
the United States emerged as the most powerful nation in the world; while on
the other hand, it is now exposed to global inequalities and conflicts that will
have serious bearing on the national security of U.S. society. A Japanese scholar
points out that this situation, "is likely to cast a complex shadow over American
diplomacy for a long time to come."[18]

On the other hand, the possibility of a strong international security system,
either through the collective security system expounded by the UN Charter or
by aligning with a big power, has not passed the test of history. The volley of

conflicts has not been arrested by the UN Security Council and alignment with a big power; in some cases, the latter become more of a liability and a cause of further tensions than an asset. There are varieties of causes for the ineffectiveness of security requirements through the above-mentioned means. The demand of this particular book does not warrant a detail study of the failure of either the UN collective security system or the ineffectiveness of relying on a big power. It is generally agreed that "(The United Nations) has not yet reached the point where it provides for any state's security, let alone that of the Small Powers."[19] In recent times, the United Nations in general and its Security Council in particular, operate under the influence of a sole superpower, the United States. A clear demonstration of that came during the Iraqi crisis of 2004, when the UN Security Council was ignored and this Middle Eastern country was attacked with full force, with long-term plans to occupy the land and its resources and, above all, make it an example for the "others" to follow.

The other option for the developing nations like Pakistan is to safeguard its territorial integrity and national sovereignty through self-reliance, i.e., to achieve within its own means a degree of security against any potential adversary. Still further, national security can come through regional security arrangements, executed by developing nations themselves and free from the big power influence.

The capability of a state to preserve its integrity and independence does not rely on military power alone, but depends on a variety of internal capabilities. The security complexities, even confined to the matters of territorial integrity and sovereignty of a state cannot be devoid of such multiple factors as those of economic and political rather the military capabilities; economic stability, political viability, and military capability are all intertwined together. Each one of these factors must support the other for the achievement of the desired favorable results. Military capability can be better achieved with the help of economic prosperity, i.e., the ability to buy arms or to even construct the armament infrastructure in the country. Correct political policies would enable the economic as well as military factors to operate in a more efficient manner. Similarly, a sturdier military posture to discourage external threats or influence can enhance the achievement of the political and economic pursuits. Military power might not be used in its real and practical sense as its mere presence in the background can suffice to gain the objectives. Military power is now considered to encompass a variety of factors. At the very basis of this consideration is the development of the studies of national security as explained here,

> The earliest studies of national security tended to concentrate on military problems, a reflection of the early conception of national security as being rather narrowly concerned with military matters. . . . (The) national security experts have increasingly turned to economic considerations and economic methods in their discussions. They have attempted to define and assess scientifically all the elements constituting of nation's economic potential for war.

Internal values are, of course, not merely economic, and national security makes serious demands upon political institutions as well. Although interest in this aspect of national security developed somewhere later, it is now one of the major areas of academic speculation.[20]

Likewise, as seen from the discussion of the above-mentioned authors, other authors have equally extended the concerns of security from merely a matter of war and peace and other Cold War-related issues like arms proliferation, military alliances, deterrence, and military strategy. James J. Wirth, while presenting a new agenda for the meaning of national security, considers that in the past "low politics" were not taken as seriously as they should have been. His "low politics" category includes, "the environment, the management of scarce resources, or efforts to constrain population growth."[21] Wirth argues that these elements of national security "were often perceived as a source of trouble, but rarely as a threat to national security."[22] The author further states,

The time has arrived to measure the cost of conflict by using more than just the immediate losses of blood and treasure. A global perspective requires strategies to consider the long-term environmental consequences of war and preparations for war . . . In other words, will low politics create changes in the international security environment that will force a significant transformation of strategy, military force structure, or doctrine? [23]

Taking a clue from the changing make-up of the world system, a belief system is gaining with firm conviction that the core of the security issue has shifted from inter-state conflicts to various domestic variables and tensions. There has been growing recognition of non-military factors that are widely discussed by various social scientists as well as strategists: "non-traditional security discourse . . . is not limited to intellectuals and academics . . . but is increasingly recognized by governments who continue to either explore or participate in a vast array of institutional arrangements."[24]

In support of the arguments of social scientists and military strategists, it is pointed out that since 1990, when a New World Order emerged, the intra-state conflicts occupied a dominant ranking in nearly 100 armed conflicts around the globe.[25] Jessica Mathews suggests that "a competing notion of 'human security' is creeping around the edges of official thinking, suggesting that security be viewed as emerging from the conditions of daily life—food, shelter, employment, health, public safety—rather than flowing downward from a country's foreign relations and military strength."[26]

If the concept of security is judged in terms of preserving the state institutions to its functional level, that of providing protection to its citizens, then various factors like economic development, viable political process, and the ability to deal with societal contradictions become an important part of the security concerns of a nation. This reflection is gathered from the views of various authors, as presented above. Those proficient in international security recognize that "soft power" is more effective than a demonstration of might, purely based on military considerations.[27] The example of numerous developments bears testimony towards that fact. It was the collapse of domestic structures that became the main reason for the demise of the Soviet Union, splitting it into pieces. Afghanistan, Somalia, Sudan, all went down because of the collapse of domestic structures rather than aggression from some outside force. Territorial integrity, the enshrined principle of national security, which was sincerely adopted by the UN Charter, no longer holds validity. Nations can disintegrate from within as well; among the long list of factors that have emerged is a cohesive force of national security, which a nation must take into consideration. In the following chapters, we will, for the purpose of the study of Pakistan's strategic interests, be dealing with three major forces, namely 1) political instability, 2) economic vulnerability, and 3) nation-building by analyzing various factors that are relevant to the society.

SECURITY AND DEPENDENCE

The impression of weak states is often closely linked with speculation of a strategy that is purely based on the principles of dependency. The weaker state's plight, like that of Pakistan, can be profoundly analyzed, suggesting that the notion that weak or small nations cannot survive without the protection of big powers is not accurate. Therefore, an attempt will be made to enumerate analytically the various causes of our suggested perception and thus bring out an assertion nearer to the realities of the contemporary era. Before we move ahead in our investigations, we will make an attempt to define the concept of a weak nation. One can maintain that a weak nation is a relative term. The strong powers are strong nations as compared to any other polity because they enjoy certain predominant factors for their power projection. Other nations do not possess these factors to that optimum level of estimation. Some of the components responsible for the enhancement of a country's power can be determined as a combined strength of nuclear capability, industrial advancement, economic strength, trained manpower, political vitality of institutions, demographics, and finally, the projection and the nature of their objectives to dominate the process of conflict resolution in their surroundings. These elements make big powers, along with some regional contestants, challenging contenders for the increase of influence in the regional as well as global context.

Yet, a careful observation would reveal such instances where possession of these potentials does not ensure the achievement of all national objectives. This is where a limitation can be imposed on these powers by the integrated will of a nation, however weak it might appear. Examples can be given of the U.S. experience in Vietnam in the 1960s, the loss of face by the Soviets in Afghanistan, the Soviet-Cuban set-backs in Angola and Mozambique, the U.S. failure to dominate the Persian Gulf region, the Indian debacles in Sri Lanka and Kashmir, the

Israeli setback in Lebanon, and the present U.S. wars in Iraq and Afghanistan. These are illustrations of the so-called "motivator's" restricted capabilities and demonstrate their limitations.

The examples noted above indicate that weak nations have been able to assert themselves as effective powers, both in military as well as political terms. They have been able to perform this feat through the manipulation of their diplomatic skills, regional or international influence, and national power utilization. The most important element, however, is the will of the people to resist external pressures. Therefore, the characteristics of a nation to be judged as weak or strong are a matter of the factual state of affairs of a given situation. Pakistan, in the above-mentioned context, has a chance to resist the external pressures and can remain an independent state free from foreign domination and above all, from dependency.

Economic dominance is one single component which still holds ground when calculated in terms of a strong or a weak nation's dichotomy. As a result of being beneficiaries of the gains of an unequal international economic order, economically powerful entities (like the Western economic bloc of Europe, the Group of 7, multinationals, etc.) thrive at the cost of other nations like Pakistan. Pakistani society has succumbed to pressures because of the weaknesses and lack of imagination of the ruling elite, both civil and military.

It has been viewed that some nations, ever since their inception, could not emancipate themselves psychologically as a result of their institutional inability and thus could not project the desired factors of a self-reliant competence. As a result, most of these countries, including Pakistan, remain tied to or have taken protection under the monetary "umbrella" of economically strong nations or multinationals. Pakistan, for example, became completely dependent on the whims of the World Bank, the International Monetary Fund (IMF), and foreign assistance. Such is the case with numerous other nations, who struggle under the massive burden of international debt with a major portion of their national wealth spent on debt servicing.

The concept of neo-colonialism arose as a result of powerful nations dominating the regional states, through the so-called legitimate process of extension of aid for the welfare and even survival of the weaker nations. This factor in itself is a major misperception for the weaker nations. Aid "donations" or debts may be telescoped by repeating the advertised saying that powerful countries, through their advanced industrial base and modern technology, multiply their gains by purchasing the cheap raw material of the smaller nations and then make them pay for the technologically advanced and sophisticated machinery and hardware for arms, etc. Weaker nations remain the consumers of advanced technology at a phenomenal price as compared to the price obtained for their raw material. The resultant interaction in the international monetary order manifests a one-way flow of assets to the industrially advanced nations without any solid compensation to the less industrially advanced nations. The phenomenon is made worse through protectionist tendencies of the industrially advanced nations. The present "North-South dialogue" or "East-West imbalance" has proved to give only lip service to appease the weaker nations' appetite for protest. The "aid" and "grants" in fact are the dues which otherwise should have flowed back to these weaker nations as compensation for the existing unjust economic order.

The donor countries have further compounded the problem of Pakistan by their infiltration into its national political, economic, educational, and other vital infrastructural institutions. The mechanism involved by the international monetary system can be seen as a glaring example. The conditions imposed from outside the country even lay down the activities for national pursuits in almost all the sectors of national projection. For example, Pakistan continues to remain indecisive with regard to the question of national priorities.

The crux of the problem of Pakistan's economic "enslavement" lies in non-sympathetic state machinery which gets enmeshed in external influence, an internal powerful minority faction, and the quest for the survival of minority groups as a part of the perpetuation of the status quo. The state machinery is powerfully utilized to project the cause of the vested interests, e.g., the corrupt politicians, army generals, and bureaucrats and symbolize it with the interest of the majority in the name of the economic prosperity of the country. Therefore, the strategy for survival lies in disentanglement from the removal of false economic remedies and setting the institutional base of the state machinery along the new lines of the popular will of the people. For such a possibility to happen, broad-based education throughout the Pakistani population is a must.

The contemporary world situation of detente and de-escalation of regional conflicts is conducive to shaking off the dependency syndrome and building anew the state infrastructure so as to formulate national policies in such a way that self-reliance becomes the cardinal policy option. But only those nations who decide to rely on their national resources and have their leaders manage conflicts with their societies will prosper under these conditions.

A NEW MEANING OF CONFLICTS

Increasingly, the perceptions and rules governing post-Second World War conflicts, border wars, and even total wars have changed. In various situations, the era of standing armies and the might of arms have become less relevant. Theorists and futurists of conflict can no longer rely upon the raw data of the armed forces as well the destructive capacity of arms. There are many more factors that must be scrutinized before we can come to an objective prediction. Tactics have changed and so has the focus of the theater of war. Urban guerilla combat, hit-and-run raids, suicide bombings, and even more so the battles being fought in front of cameras with night-vision technology, are the hard realities that will be considered in the future. Furthermore, it has been observed that low-intensity conflicts take a heavy toll on the developed economies. Apart from the tactics, the ideological nature of global conflicts particularly in the Middle East has received a new meaning. Muslims see the support for westernization of their societies as a reminder of the European colonial onslaught through their "civilizing mission." They perceive the agenda of "enlightened moderation" as nothing but a foreign instrument of dominance, especially when political institutions are made the exception to this rule. The West, in turn, views Muslim agitation as a threat to their "civilization" and "way of life," as repeatedly presented by Western politicians and media. In short, the rules of the game have changed.

The United States under President George W. Bush saw global conflicts in a changed perspective. The well-known Bush doctrine included the notion of a "preemptive strike," meaning that a country can be attacked and even destroyed if there is a suspicion that in the future it can pose a threat to U.S. interests. Using the pretext of Saddam Hussein's weapons of mass destruction, Iraq was attacked in March–April 2003. Even when it came to be known that there were no such weapons in Iraq, nor had Saddam any links with al-Qaeda, the justification to continue the conflict received other names like "regime change" and "establishing a democratic system." This all goes against the conventional wisdom, as established by the UN charter, that a country cannot resort to war unless attacked in actual terms and its national sovereignty therefore threatened.

MIT professor Noam Chomsky and co-author Professor Gilbert Achcar point towards the new implications of inter-state conflicts in their recent book, *Perilous Power*. The authors observe that firstly, religion is being used in the recent conflicts as a vehicle for political and economic interests. Secondly, fundamentalism is not confined to the Muslim combatant groups alone as,

> a powerful Christian strain of it exists in the U.S. that has enormous influence over right wing Republican-led governments as it did during the Reagan years and especially now under George Bush who believes his agenda is a God-directed messianic mission.[28]

The authors acknowledge that fundamentalism has become a global affair, spread over nearly all societies around the globe—a phenomenon that came into focus just over the last quarter century.[29] This view is supplemented by Reza Aslan in his book *No god but God*. He cites one of many examples where global conflicts are seen by the fundamentalists in the West, as the tension between good and evil. Aslan writes,

> When the Republican senator from Oklahoma, James Inhofe, stands before the U.S. Congress and insists that the ongoing conflicts in the Middle East are not political or territorial battles but "a contest over whether or not the word of God is true," he speaks, knowingly or not, the language of the Crusades.[30]

The author further explains,

> Over the last few years, however, as international conflicts have increasingly been framed in apocalyptic terms and political agendas on all sides couched in theological language, it

has become impossible to ignore the startling similarities between the antagonistic and uninformed rhetoric that fueled the destructive religious wars of the past, and that which drives the current conflicts of the Middle East.[31]

The changed perspective of conflicts requires that nations like Pakistan with huge defense budgets and a top-heavy army could reconsider their security options. As the examples of Iraq and Lebanon show, the new wars can be fought successfully, without the shining insignias of the elite class. Genuine requisites to protect a nation include the strength of people through their well-constructed civil institutions including that of viable economic structures, as well as the involvement by the people in the nation's decision-making processes.

HISTORIC LEGACY OF STRATEGIC INTERESTS

The main concern of Pakistan's national strategy is derived from the tensions and unresolved conflicts with India, emerging from the legacy of historic experiences. These conflicts, compounded by hostile perceptions about each other have further complicated the relations. The Muslim leaders of British India, struggling for a separate homeland, came in direct conflict with the Hindu leaders of the Indian National Congress, who regarded the partition of India as an inconceivable act. They believed that the creation of Pakistan would amount to the division of their motherland. The Muslims of British India had different views regarding the concept of Indian nationalism. They regarded themselves as a separate nation that had existed side by side with the Hindus, with its own separate features. They demanded that the British should leave India only after establishing a sovereign state of Pakistan. The new nation was to be established in Northwest India and in the Bengali majority areas of Southeast India. The final partition of British India, between the sovereign states of Bharat (India) and Pakistan in August 1947, was bloody and vengeful. The contradictions and tensions were the result of Muslims struggling for recognition as a separate nation while Hindu leaders insisted that the Muslims were part of a greater Indian nationhood.

Muslims had ruled South Asia for more than thousand years (711–1857). Their era was one of prosperity and justice, accompanied by a suitable base of the rule of law and an excellent system of administration. Even during the British rule, this complicated as well as cumbersome revenue system was maintained, with little modifications. In 1857, the British seized power from Muslims and as a matter of calculated policy began to persecute Muslims by using the twin weapons of vengeance and rage in collaboration with Hindus. The Muslim awakening in the post-1857 period was expressed through legal, constitutional, and educational channels. Options of diplomacy and statesmanship were applied as an effective weapon by the Muslim leaders of the South Asian region. The Muslim leaders were not only successful in curtailing the deterioration of the moral, spiritual, and political values of Muslims, but were also able to boost the spirits of their downtrodden classes.

Leaders such as Sayyid Ahmed Khan (1857–1898), Maulana Mohammad Ali and Shaukat Ali (1914–1922), Allama Mohammad Iqbal (1930 Allahabad Address), and Quaid-e-Azam, Muhammad Ali Jinnah outwitted their opponents, presented the Muslim case with precision, and were able to boost the status of the victimized classes. At the same time, these personalities fixed the directions of the common people and the elite alike, to regain a lost foothold in Indian society and eventually, in the global context.

In 1875, Sayyid Ahmed Khan, a renowned leader of the awakening Muslim struggle, set up a Muslim college, later to become a University in Aligarh (near Delhi), in which modern sciences of that time were introduced in the English language along with the Islamic traditions, as provided by Arabic and Persian literature. He believed that without modern education, the Muslim community in British India would fall prey to the dictates of the Hindu majority and would suffer further. In addition, the reformer made it clear that the Muslims by any definition were a separate nation and, therefore, had to pursue their aspirations in a manner that suited their interests. Maulana Mohammad Ali and Maulana Shaukat Ali motivated the masses and taught them to express their sentiments through mass demonstrations—a skill which came handy for the future struggle. In this way, Muslim expression moved from the offices and drawing rooms to the streets of South Asia. It gave the Muslim community power, with which they were not conversant in the past. Mohammad Iqbal, a poet-philosopher, through verses of revolutionary poetry, reminded Muslims of their strength and potential. The combined effect of the mentioned individuals and many others like them culminated in the personality of Muhammad Ali Jinnah, who gave a decisive conclusion to the Muslim rights in South Asia.

A lengthy conflict to reconstruct the status of the Muslims of South Asia resulted with a March 23, 1940 proclamation which clearly expressed the future course of action for the community. The Lahore Resolution stated that the Muslims of South Asia constitute a separate nation in its own right and, therefore, deserved a place where they would not concede to the Hindu majority so as to dominate the Muslim minority community in religious, economic, and political matters. Reflecting the sentiments of the Muslims of the South Asian region, Quaid-e-Azam, Muhammad Ali Jinnah said in his presidential address,

> Mussalmans [sic] are a nation according to any definition of a nation and they must have their homelands, their territory and their State. We wish to live in peace and harmony with our neighbours as a free and independent people. We wish our people to develop to the fullest our spiritual, cultural, economic, social and political life in a way that we think best and in consonance with our own ideals and according to the genius of our people.

The bitterness of the creation of Pakistan was reflected in the foreign policies of the newly independent neighbors. A foundation of mistrust was laid between

the leaders and peoples of both India and Pakistan, making it exceedingly difficult to come to any consensus.

Pakistan's security concerns with India remained paramount and consistent,
with Kashmir remaining a main irritant for adverse relations. Pakistan went to
war with India at least three times in 1948, 1965, and 1970. In addition, there
were border wars on Rann of Kutch in 1965 and Kargil in 1999. On a number
of occasions, both countries had a standoff where the forces of belligerent nations
came face to face. The most serious near-war situation occurred in 2002, when
the two nuclear powers of South Asia came to the brink of war. A major catastro-
phe was averted because of the underlining nuclear deterrent and diplomatic
maneuvering of the United States.

Pakistan has been suspicious of India for its designs to undermine its sovereignty and to destabilize it from within while India's low-intensity war in Kashmir posed a serious national security threat to that country. Indians accuse
Pakistan of supporting militancy in Kashmir while Pakistan regards it as a genuine indigenous freedom struggle of the Kashmiri people.

In the early years of Pakistan's independence, Afghanistan posed a moderate
security threat. Afghanistan's irredentist claim on Pakistan's territory adversarily
affected their relations. This particular Afghan threat to Pakistan's security faded
away with time and nearly concluded with the 1979 invasion of the Soviet Union
in that country. Thereafter, the security concerns of Pakistan towards its western
borders occupied a different dimension. A possible Soviet expansion and domination of the Pakistani border territories was not ruled out. It was only after the
events of September 2001 that Afghanistan presented a third security concern
for Pakistan. The ongoing activities of al-Qaeda in Afghanistan and the border
tribal areas of Pakistan gave international dimension to the security issues of
Pakistan. On the other hand, the reemergence of Taliban in Afghanistan and in
the tribal areas of Pakistan bore serious implications for both NATO (North
Atlantic Treaty Organization) and U.S. forces. U.S. strategists regard the presence of al-Qaeda and the Taliban in Afghanistan as a direct threat to the national
security of mainland United States.

The concept of regional security shifted as a consequence of the events of 2001,
with U.S./NATO military operations in Afghanistan. With that, the central concern for Pakistan's elite underwent a perceptional change regarding the traditional
military threat from India. India is no longer seen as a prime security threat
to Pakistan; it is the domestic instability of institutions combined with other
factors like the rise of militancy that have become prime factors in Pakistan's strategic concerns. This did not happen in a near-similar historic situation when
the Soviets occupied Afghanistan (1979–1988) and fierce battles were being
bought between the invaders and the Pakistan/U.S.-backed tribal guerillas in
Afghanistan. The Indian security factor nevertheless remained active, though in
the background.

INTRODUCTION OF NUCLEAR ISSUE IN THE GLOBAL
SECURITY PARAMETERS

On May 11 and 13, 1998, India conducted a series of five nuclear tests. On May 15, it officially declared itself a nuclear-weapon state. The Indian Prime Minister Atal Bihari Vajpayee stated that "India is now a nuclear power with a big bomb." Indian government and media had already created a frenzied environment where officials made repeated threats to neighboring Pakistan and China. Former foreign secretaries and chiefs of armed forces spoke on national TV and to the press, giving various forms of threats to Pakistan. A routine diplomatic expression gave way to an enormous explicit posture of military hegemony. As fallout of these "official statements," Pakistan felt insecure and vulnerable. It was felt that the form in which this nuclear episode took place left Pakistan with only one option—to demonstrate that it can deter as well as retaliate in case of a real nuclear threat from India. The old style "balance of terror" revisited with South Asian attire and mechanism. It was generally felt in Pakistan that the Indian bluff must be called, otherwise it was argued, get prepared to live as a subservient nation.

On the military front, the Bharatiya Janata Party (BJP) leadership made it clear that it was determined to cap its tested missiles with nuclear warheads. Minister for Science and Technology Murli Manohar Joshi warned that the BJP government would soon implement its declared policy. The minister is quoted to have said on May 12 that "Indian scientists will put a nuclear warhead on missiles as soon as the situation requires." The Indian leadership justified the nuclear tests on the basis of security threats. First, Pakistan was mentioned and then the Chinese concern was included as well. In reality, as the Chinese spokesman said on May 14, it is the Indian hegemony designs for South Asia which prompted it to go nuclear.

It is clear that the BJP never abandoned its election manifesto of acquiring nuclear weapons capability. There were two more promises that the Indian leadership made to its people. The first is to incorporate the held-Kashmir in the Indian Union and the second is related to "getting back" the "Pakistani-occupied Kashmir." Both of these election promises had serious security consequences for Pakistan. In his post-nuclear letter to President Bill Clinton and other world leaders, Prime Minister Vajpayee targeted Pakistan in half of his message. Kashmir and Punjab were mentioned as core areas of security threats for India and thereby, a rationale for the nuclear weapons. While looking at the track record of May 12 and 14, it was felt in Pakistan that there was no reason that Vajapee's government would not implement the other sections of their election manifesto, in letter and in spirit.

In post-nuclear South Asia, the security situation of Pakistan became grave. The Indians had collected a battery of guided missiles like Agni, with a range of 1,800 kilometers (1,118 miles), and Prithvi, already deployed on the Pakistan border, which can hit its target 250 kilometers (155 miles) away. At least two nuclear explosions conducted by India were of tactical nature, designed for the purposes of limited nuclear strike. It seemed certain that the Indian war machine was ready to be equipped with these weapons for field battles.

Pakistan found itself truly in a security impasse. If it were to test its nuclear device, enormous Western political, as well economic, pressures would be exerted upon the nation. But it was also felt that in real strategic planning, it was Pakistan alone that would plan for its security. Pakistani public opinion believed that the nation had been let down by Western nations in the past, and therefore Pakistan had to decide for itself and fight its own battle of survival.

In the circumstances, Pakistan had to take realist steps to preserve its sovereignty and independence. At least two visible options were before the policy makers. One option was to accept Western pressure and refrain from demonstrating its deterrent capacity. In this scenario, Pakistan would have received economic assistance and other financial relief in return. It was argued that in the 1950s and 1960s and again in 1980s, Pakistan did receive large economic packages but was unable to develop its infrastructure. The people of Pakistan were left to suffer and there was no reason to believe that this time it would be any different. In addition, it was argued that Pakistan would lose its independence and sovereignty and could become an Indian vessel state. Furthermore, it would be forced to sign the Comprehensive Test Ban Treaty (CTBT) and open up its nuclear installations for inspection, thus closing all security options for the future. Second, if Pakistan went nuclear, its security would be guaranteed by establishing a retaliatory capacity. It was felt that this would be a solid deterrent to desist Indians from venturing into Kashmir. Finally, a decision was taken by Prime Minister Nawaz Sharif that Pakistan would test its nuclear capability, as a response to the Indian initiation, so as to be in a better position to defend its national security interests. It was argued in Pakistani official circles that it could be hoped to persuade Pakistan's friends in the West to understand its security compulsions.

In a televised address of May 28, 1998, and later in a press conference, Prime Minister Nawaz Sharif informed the Pakistani nation of the reasons for the nuclear tests in these words,

> Pakistan today successfully conducted five nuclear tests. The results were as expected. There was no release of radioactivity. I congratulate all Pakistani scientists, engineers and technicians for their dedicated team work and expertise in mastering complex and advanced technologies. The entire nation takes justifiable pride in the accomplishments of the Pakistan Atomic Energy Commission, Dr. A. Q. Khan Research Laboratories and all affiliated Organizations. . . . Our security, and the peace and stability of the entire region, was gravely threatened. As any self-respecting nation, we had no choice left for us. Our hand was forced by the present Indian leadership's reckless actions. We could not ignore the magnitude of the threat. . . . Under no circumstances would the Pakistani

nation compromise on matters pertaining to its life and existence. Our decision to exercise the nuclear option has been taken in the interest of national self-defence [sic]. These
weapons are to deter aggression, whether nuclear or conventional.[32]

Pakistan's nuclear program soon got into trouble and it was seen as more of a
liability than an asset for the defense needs of the country. The confidence in
the safeguard of the nuclear-related material and technology was severely lacking,
as the war in Afghanistan against al-Qaeda and the Taliban received more serious
attention. It was admitted that the "Pakistani officials recognized that they had
not been sufficiently transparent to alleviate concerns regarding proliferation
threats from Pakistan and sought to convince the international community that
they have taken adequate measures."[33]

CLASSIFICATIONS OF STRATEGIC ISSUES

As defined in Figure 1.1, there are at least seven classifications of issues for
matters of strategic interest for Pakistan. The first three classifications are inter-
state conflicts, including wars as well as border armed conflicts. Most of these
conflicts were with India, related directly or indirectly with the main Kashmir
issue, while most of the others are a direct consequence of militant activities,
inside or outside the borders of Pakistan. Apart from India, Pakistan's two main
strategic concerns came from Afghanistan: first, after the Soviet occupation in
1979 and second, when U.S. and NATO forces took military action in that
country in the post-9/11 period. Pakistan could not escape the fallout of these
internationally related developments which posed a serious challenge to its
national security. A strong link was established between the international and
national strategic concerns. The classification of Pakistan's strategic concerns in
Figure 1.1 will help explain the challenges underwent by its security apparatus.
The details of this stratification will form a main theme of this book.

The first three classifications have been instrumental in the increasing flow of
arms in the region, in one form or another. In other words, the arms race with
India is directly linked with past as well as existing conflicts in the area. When
observed, the first five classifications lead us to many types of tensions, from distrust about a future apprehension to a legacy of a prior armed conflict.

Figure 1.1 indicates that the conflict pattern has maintained a regular consis-
tency. In no time from 1947 to 2007 has this pattern of conflicts relaxed. An
impression is therefore created that the primary security considerations of Pakistan
have either involved its neighbors or dissident groups within the country, rather
than big powers. However, when a superpower was involved in a conflict, like
the Soviet invasion and the U.S./NATO occupation of Afghanistan, its security
concerns became larger in scope in terms of human suffering and implications
for the regional community. The Soviet occupation of Afghanistan from 1978 to
1988 brought a devastation which even today has its ramifications for Pakistani

1. **Inter-State Wars:** Kashmir War, 1965; East Pakistan War, 1970.
2. **Border/Limited Armed Conflict:** Kashmir War, 1948; Pakistan Ariel Attack on Afghan Troops, 1961; Rann of Kutch War, 1965; Soviets Occupied Afghanistan, 1978–1988; Kargil Border War, 1999.
3. **Regional Border Tensions and Suspicions:** Paktoonistan claim by Afghanistan, 1947–1963; Indian Brace Track Military Exercises, 1987; Iran Taliban Suspicions, 1996–2001; Central Asian Taliban Issue, 1996–2001; India–Pakistan Military Standoff, 2002–2003.
4. **Security Related Issues:** U-2 Incident, 1960; Siachen Glacier, 1984–Ongoing; International Nuclear Proliferation Concerns, 2001–Ongoing; Links Between International Terrorist Agenda and Pakistani *Madrasas* and Sanctuaries, 2001– Ongoing.
5. **Regional Ethnic linked Pressures:** Indian Sikh Insurgency, 1980s; Kashmir Strife, 1989–2001; Afghan Civil War, 1989–1995; 1996–2001; Barbri Mosque, 1992; U.S./NATO Operations in Afghanistan, 2001–Ongoing.
6. **Internal Dissent:** Baloch Insurgency, 1973–1977; Sindh Riots, 1987–1988; FATA Insurgency, 2001–Ongoing; Baloch Insurgency (2), 2001–2008; Lal Masjid Crises, 2007; Swat Militants, 2007.
7. **Simmering Tensions:** Water and Refugee Issues with India, 1947–1960; Border Demarcation (Sir Creek), 1948–Ongoing; Biharis in Bangladesh, 1971– Ongoing; Potential Conflicts like Water, Mineral Deposits on Sea Borders.

Figure 1.1   Various Forms of Tensions/Conflicts: 1947–2011.

society. This can also be said of the U.S. occupation of Afghanistan from 2002 onwards.

Another point to be noted in Figure 1.1 is that a vast number of inter-state conflicts occurred either as limited wars or border conflicts/skirmishes or within the geographical boundaries, in the guise of insurgencies or civil wars. In other words, total wars which involve a deep penetration into an adversary's territory have been very few. Only two out of all the various conflicts can be regarded as total wars. In a large number of conflicts, insurgency movements, confined to Balochistan and North-West Frontier (NWFP) provinces have been predominant. This is in addition to the rise of militancy or a militant culture in Pakistani society, especially after 2001, and its consequences upon the creation of various militant groups. Most of these groups have aggressive national and regional agendas.

Like other members of the international community, Pakistan's security concerns are now equally with non-traditional players, i.e., along with nation states. In fact, a kind of a balance has now occurred between the traditional and non-traditional players. At least three non-state actors have been identified by Professor Hasan-Askari Rizvi that are relevant to Pakistan's strategic concerns. According to Professor Rizvi,

> a number of transnational and nongovernmental actors figured prominently at international level; the leading examples being the liberation, ideological and religious

movements which . . . (operate) across the territorial boundaries of states, multinational corporations, and a host of other nongovernmental bodies.[34]

A significant observation stems from the fact that because of the nature of conflicts, the use of nuclear weapons remains unlikely. The use of nuclear weapons against a dissident group or in a border war is self-defeating and therefore, its usage remains a remote possibility.

CONCLUSION

After more than nine years of General (retired) Pervez Musharraf's rule (October 1999–December 2008), Pakistan has seen quite the opposite of what the regime had boasted. During this extended unrepresentative term, the direction of his military government was uni-focused, i.e., the personal survival of Musharraf. This was achieved by manipulating the national consensus Constitution of 1973 and national political institutions. Musharraf solely depended on the support and encouragement from Washington and some Western European countries. Throughout Musharraf's rule, a vicious political victimization had been in the offing. As a result, it undermined the national political parties while ethnic groups with narrow agendas were sponsored and encouraged. This attitude hampered the growth of national cohesion and affected the stability of Pakistani society. The vacuum created by the impediment of effective national institutions, along with rampant corruption at the highest levels of the military and among the "cronies" of the regime, gave way to the destabilization of society. It created a culture of militancy, extreme bigotry, and feelings of deprivation among the Pakistan population. As a consequence, militancy gained strength in the otherwise tolerant and balanced Pakistani society. In short, Pakistan's security was compromised and the country was exposed to various types of challenges, both domestic and foreign.

In conclusion, a central factor may be mentioned. It can be agreed with Manfred Halpern, when he argues that,

> . . . international relations are. . . . being profoundly transformed mainly through internal politics. The balance of power, and the orientation, health and stability of the international system, are vitally affected by the success or failure of local elites in dealing with the social, political, economic, intellectual, and psychological modernisation [sic] of their countries.[35]

The pre-requisite for a successful strategic foreign policy and security is a political structure internally strong on all sides.

NOTES

1. See Robert Osgood, *Ideals and Self-Interest in America's Foreign Relations* (Chicago: University of Chicago Press, 1953), quoted in Fred A. Sondermann, "The Concept of the National Interest," *Orbis*, Spring (1977): 125. According to Robert Osgood, the "Survival or Self-preservation (are) defined in terms of territorial integrity, political independence, and maintenance of fundamental governmental institutions."

2. Richard Smoke, "National Security Affairs," in Fred I. Greenstein and Nelson W. Polsby, eds., *Handbook of Political Science*, Vol. 8 *International Politics* (Reading, Mass: Addison-Wesley Publishing Co., 1975) pp. 254–255.

3. Robert L. Rothstein, *Alliance and Small Powers* (New York & London: Columbia University Press, 1969), p.1.

4. Michael M. Boll, "Turkey's New National Concept: What it means for NATO," *Orbis*, Fall (1979), pp. 609–610.

5. Ibid.

6. Michael M. Boll, op. cit., pp. 609–610.

7. Donald E. Nuchterlein, "The concept of 'National Interest': A time for New Approaches," *Orbis*, Spring (1979), p. 85.

8. Arnold Wolfers, "National Security as an Ambiguous Symbol," *Political Science Quarterly*, December (1952), p. 481.

9. Klaus Knorr, "On the International Uses of Military Force in the Contemporary World," *Orbis*, Spring (1977), p. 26.

10. Robert D. Matthews, "National Security: Propaganda or Legitimate Concern?" in *Problems of Contemporary Militarism*, op. cit., p. 143.

11. See *Bangladesh Papers* (Lahore: Vanguard Books, N.D.).

12. David C. Hendrickson, "Imperialism Versus Internationalism: The United States and World Order," *Gaiko Forum, Japanese Perspectives on Foreign Affairs*, Fall (2002), p. 36.

13. Michael Ignatieff, "Is the Human Rights Era Ending?" *The New York Times*, February 5, 2002.

14. Richard Falk, *The Great Terror War* (New York: Olive Branch Press, 2003), p. 170.

15. "Fortress of Fear," ed., *The Washington Post*, August 4, 2004.

16. Sabine von Schorlemer, "Human Rights: Substantive and Institutional Implications of the War against Terrorism," *EJIL*, Vol. 14, No. 2; 2003, p. 280.

17. Richard Falk, op.cit., p. 171.

18. Kojima Akira, "Redefining the National Interest for a new Era: A New Paradigm for Diplomacy." *Gaiko Forum: Japanese Perspectives on Foreign Affairs*, Spring (2003), p. 3.

19. Robert L. Rolhstein, *Alliances and Small Powers* (New York & London: Columbia University Press, 1968), p. 42. The same is true of an alliance-system when a major power is the supporting partner. Pakistan's frustrating experience in an alliance with a major power is the best example of the ineffectiveness of allying with a big power so as to achieve security goals. See W. Howard Wriggins, "The Balancing Process in Pakistan's Foreign Policy," in *Pakistan: The Long View*, eds., Lawrence Ziring, Ralph Braibanti, and W. Howard Wriggins (Durham, N.C.: Duke University Press, 1977), pp. 314–316.

20. Morton Berkowitz and P.G. Bock, "National Security," in *International Encyclopedia of the Social Sciences*, ed., David L. Sills, Vol. 11 (New York: The Macmillan Co., 19), p. 41.

21. James J. Wirtz, "A New Agenda for Security and Strategy?" in Strategy *in the Contemporary World: An Introduction to Strategic Studies*, eds., John Baylis, James Wirtz, et al. (London: Oxford University Press, 2002), p. 310.

22. Ibid.

23. Ibid., p. 312.

24. Sridhar K. Khatri, "What is the 'New' Security Agenda for South Asia?," unpublished paper presented in Regional Seminar on *Non-Traditional Security in South Asia*; Kathmandu, Nepal; November 16–17, 2004, p. 3.

25. Jessica T. Mathews, "Power Shift," *Foreign Affairs*, January/February (1997), p. 51.

26. Ibid.

27. Kojima Akira, "Redefining the National Interest for a New Era: A New Paradigm for Diplomacy," *Gaiko Forum: Japanese Perspectives on Foreign Affairs*, Spring (2003), p. 7.

28. Stephen Lendman, Second of a five-part series analyzing and reviewing Noam Chomsky and *Gilbert Achcar's* book Perilous Power, http://www.populistamerica.com/perilous_power _part_ii

29. Noam Chomsky, Gilbert Achcar, edited with a preface by Stephen R. Shalom, Perilous *Power: The Middle East & U.S. Foreign Policy: Dialogues on Terror, Democracy, War, and Justice* (Boulder & London: Paradigm Publishers, 2006), p. 34.

30. Reza Aslan, *No god but God: The Origins, Evolution, and Future of Islam* (New York: Random House Trade Paperbacks, 2006), p. xxiv.

31. Ibid.

32. *Dawn*, May 29, 1998.

33. Kenneth N. Luongo and Brig. Gen. (Ret.) Naeem Salik, "Building Confidence in Pakistan's Nuclear Security," *Arms Control Today*, December (2007), http://www.armscontrol.org/act/ 2007_12/Luongo.asp

34. Hasan-Askari Rizvi, *Pakistan and the Geostrategic Environment: A Study of Foreign Policy* (Basingstoke, Hampshire and London: The MacMillan Press Ltd, 1993), p. 3.

35. Manfred Halpern, *The Politics of Social Change in the Middle East and North Africa* (Princeton, New Jersey: Princeton University Press, 1963), p. viii.

CHAPTER 2

Pakistan's Strategic Location

Some countries are located more strategically than others. Geographic location by itself can be a major factor in determining the strengths and weaknesses of a country. A country is also affected by what happens in its neighborhood or environment. The environment can either enhance the capabilities of a nation or reduce its capacity to maneuver. Equally important is the strategy, conduct, and the perceptions of the policy-makers, through which they deal with the prevalent variables. History also shows us that, at times, international convulsions and connections can have dramatic effects on the security of a nation, as well. A collapse or failure of a society can have serious repercussions on its neighbors, even more so if identical ethnic populations reside on both sides of the borders, where they may be in a minority. It is the combination of international, regional, and domestic factors that determine the strategic location of a nation.

The theories that relied upon land mass as a source of power and influence are not relevant in the present-day world of technology and communication. Theorists like Sir Halford Mackinder had advocated the "importance in world politics of nations that controlled great land areas."[1] The rapid process of de-colonization in the post-Second World War period changed the entire complexion of geopolitics and made the concepts of "heartland" and "hinderland" irrelevant.[2] Recent events have shown that even impoverished nations with small populations and geographic area can have large consequences upon regional and world politics. According to modern scholars, "geopolitics is only one aspect of the global environment that may influence foreign policy,"[3] as there are a variety of numerous attributes both external and domestic that have the capacity to determine the effectiveness of a country's behavior.

In the case of Pakistan, both criteria of validity, its geographic disposition as well as endeavors around its borders, make Pakistan a strategically significant country.

THE GEOGRAPHIC SETTING OF PAKISTAN

Pakistan encompasses 796,095 square kilometers (307,374 square miles) and is double the size when compared to the state of California. Pakistan is comparatively narrow in its width, which is approximately 500 kilometers (311 miles). For military strategists, this narrow width had been a concern, as it limited the maneuverability of the army in the advent of penetration by Indian forces, in case of a full-fledged war. Some military commanders presented a vague idea of meeting this deficiency by seeking a "strategic depth"[4] in Afghanistan. However, this concept is fiercely challenged by a large segment of strategic analysts, and should not be considered as part of a confirmed military strategy. Afghanistan's history is full of turmoil and tribal rivalries. The landscape is imposing and difficult to interact with the tribes. No matter how much weight this erroneous concept of strategic depth had, it gave way in the late 1990s when Pakistan acquired nuclear capability and a missile system which could hit its target as far as 1300 km (812 miles) inside India. Pakistan's deterrent capacity is being seen as an alternative, for seeking a "strategic depth."

It is now agreed that the concept of "strategic depth" became a strategic liability, especially when the army interfered in the affairs of Afghanistan in the post-Soviet era (1989–2001). In its editorial, a Pakistani newspaper writes that "the biggest crime to which many retired generals must confess, and then apologize for, is the policy of seeking "strategic depth" in Afghanistan because the consequences of this policy are now threatening to actually spell the end of Pakistan itself."[5] The second part of the argument might be an exaggerated opinion, but nonetheless this connection posed a serious security threat to Pakistan by providing an opportunity for the extremists in Afghanistan to spread their ideology and militant actions within Pakistani society. This erroneous concept was the result of various military dictators that ruled for more than half of Pakistan's history. It was the creation of a mindset whereby these military rulers thought that they had a final word, not only on the matters of security and strategy of Pakistan, but also on those of neighboring Afghanistan. The army generals were under the illusion that they alone had the solution to Pakistan's security needs.[6] This impression was largely dispelled when events have shown that every military rule brought with itself malfunctions of domestic institutions and that the internal and external security of Pakistan was furthered weakened. Afghanistan's President Hamid Karzai, while speaking to the army officers at Pakistan National Defense College, dismissed the Pakistani military's doctrine of a "strategic depth" and said that the real " 'Strategic Depth' concept was the one where both the countries build strong economic trade and bilateral relations, which could be of immense help to the neighboring countries."[7]

Pakistan's international border with Afghanistan, known as Durand line, is 2,430 km (1, 610 miles) in length. It came as a result of an agreement signed by British India and the Afghan ruler. As this boundary divides tribes which now live on both sides of the border, from time to time it has been a source of contention and tensions between the two countries. Nonetheless, the Durand line is recognized as an international border by the international community. A flexible cross-border policy is adopted both by Afghan and Pakistani border patrols for the tribes residing on both sides of the border.

The geo-strategic importance of Pakistan's geography goes back further in history than the country itself. The area gained its significance in various ways long before the creation of Pakistan in 1947. Two ancient cities of the Indus Valley civilization—Harappa and Mohenjo-daro flourished about 5,000 years ago (2600 B.C. to 1600 B.C.), along the banks of river Indus. These two cities were 600 kilometers (373 miles) away from each other, giving evidence that "Indus Valley civilization was more extensive than its contemporaries—Egypt's Old Kingdom and Mesopotamia's Sumeria."[8] Therefore, it represented one of the oldest and developed civilizations of ancient times. Enough evidence has been found to prove that the inhabitants of these two cities had trade relations with existing Middle Eastern civilizations. Taxila (500 B.C. to 10 A.D.) represents the Ghandara civilization and is on the fringes of the Pakistan capital, Islamabad; it was a meeting point of the important Silk Road trade route. Pakistan is regarded as a new state in an ancient land, where a variety of ethnic groups reside—a number of them have their ethnic kin in adjoining countries like Afghanistan, Iran, and India.

In many ways, the people and the elite of Pakistan owe their identity to the time of Muslim rule in what is now Pakistan. It started with Muhammad bin Qasim, who in 712 A.D. occupied the areas of what is today the Sindh province of Pakistan. In the northwest, he was followed by various Turkic rulers, who in 999, came from the present-day Central Asia. It was in 1526 that a stable Muslim empire was established under the Mughals, which was later replaced by the British Empire in 1858. The area that now comprises Pakistan "was gradually infused with an entirely new Islamic culture that included architecture, language, cuisine, and attire."[9] Islam in South Asia was introduced by the Muslim Sufis (Saints), followed by traders and artists, who spread all over the area. Iftikhar H. Malik, a scholar of Pakistani culture and customs writes that the "Islamic conquest and the commercial and cultural relationship with India resulted in the region's integration into a larger cultural and political zone, now under Muslim control."[10] This geographic landscape included present-day Afghanistan, Iran, and the Turkic countries of Central Asia. There are a number of tribes and other people of various ethnicities in Sindh, Punjab, and elsewhere who claim that they are the descendents of the Arabs.[11] A renowned Pakistan intellectual, Aitzaz Ahsan denies the Arab connections and is convinced that the areas that now constitute Pakistan have lineal links with the "Central Asian people, mainly by the saints and princes of Seljuk-Turk, Afghan, and Mongol [Mughal] stock. . . . [This area], retained unbroken politico-cultural links with central Asia for longer periods and more intimately than with any other peoples, including those of the rest of India."[12]

Today, with a population of 160 million, Pakistan is the fifth largest country in the world. It is strategically located at the crossroads of South Asia, the Middle East, and the Central Asian regions. Pakistan's important strategic location is sketched as follows,

> Pakistan occupies a most important strategic position, namely the frontier area between South Asia, the Southwest Asia countries bordering on the Persian Gulf, and the Central Asian Islamic tribal areas of Afghanistan, the . . . (Central Asia), and Xinjiang province in China. While Pakistan is usually identified as a South Asian state, it could just as reasonably be included in Southwest Asia. And indeed, as a general principle, Pakistanis have preferred to emphasize their ties with the Islamic states to the west rather than with the Hindu majority area in the subcontinent.[13]

The geopolitical location of Pakistan fits well in the overall strategic considerations of the Middle Eastern region in general and the Gulf sub-region in particular. Pakistan's role in the Middle East is of obvious importance particularly because of its situation at the entrance of the Gulf of Oman and the strategically vital Strait of Hormuz along with its coastline along the Arabian Sea and Indian Ocean. Pakistan's strategic importance is further enhanced by the borders it shares with two of the three world's major powers, the People's Republic of China, 523 kilometers (325 miles) and, 2,912 kilometers (1810 miles) of frontier with India—a country with ambitions to stretch its influence well beyond its territorial boundaries, both in economic and political fields.

Two of Pakistan's provinces have a close affinity with the Middle Eastern countries of Afghanistan and Iran. The most sensitive ethnic/administrative area, the Province Khyber-Pakhtunkhwa, (formerly known as the North-West Frontier Province or NWFP) has always been regarded by the Pakhtuns on both sides of the border as a province possessing a similar culture and ethnic stock (apart, that is, from the powerful uniting elements of a Muslim nationhood). Apart from various contradictions and opposing policies, the government in Kabul can not ignore the relationships between Afghanistan on one hand and Pakistan (in general) and the NWFP (in particular), on the other hand. These relations are heavily bracketed in economic, social, and security ties.

Balochistan, Pakistan's biggest province in terms of geographic dimensions, has similar tribal, ethnic, and linguistic ties with Iranian Balochistan. The border between the two countries is 909 kilometers (565 miles), and the coast of this province runs along the Arabian Sea.[14] As a result of a series of agreements in

1896 and 1905, the international border between Iran and the British Indian Empire was demarcated. On February 6, 1958, a boundary agreement was signed between the governments of Pakistan and Iran, for the purpose of clarifying previous such agreements. Pakistan signed its maritime boundary with Iran in 1997 which defined the continental shelf of the two countries as a result of lengthy negotiations which began in 1992. On the Arabian Sea, Pakistan's total coastline length is 1,046 kilometers (650 miles). Pakistan is a signatory to the 1982 UN Convention on the Law of the Sea; under the agreement, "Pakistan claims 200-nautical-mile exclusive economic zone, a 12-nautical-mile territorial sea, and a 24-nautical-mile contiguous zone for security, immigration, customs, and other matters."[15]

Pakistan's future developmental plans, as well as improvement of its naval facilities on the coast of Makran, require having regular coordination with the administrators and planners of Iranian Balochistan. For this, an understanding with the Iranian government became a necessary policy. Recently, the border crossing points between the two countries became a hotbed for human smugglers, narcotic dealers, and other criminals. Scarcely manned, the border in the post-9/11 period provided an opportunity for terrorist groups to take refuge among the tribes or to cross the Iranian border to escape arrest. For the first time, Pakistan started to see the border with Iran as its strategic concern. It is generally believed that although impoverished, the province of Pakistani Balochistan has tremendous potential in fulfilling the agricultural, mineral, industrial, and security needs of Pakistan.

The potential fifth province, consisting of the "Northern Areas," is also inhabited by the people who are closely linked with their ethnic cousins in Iran as well as in Turkey and Central Asia, especially Tajikistan. A strategic Karakoram highway links northern Pakistan with the Sinkiang Province of China. This all-weather road is 805 kilometers (500 miles) long taking 15 years to build by both the Pakistani and Chinese workforce and engineers. The road runs along the historic "Silk Route," travelled by the traders some 2,000 years ago. Amplifying the importance of this strategic link between the two countries, Pakistan's president remarked that, "Just as the Great Wall of China was regarded as an extraordinary accomplishment in ancient times, the Karakoram Highway will be considered a wonder of the present age."[16] He further added, "This achievement will also serve as an enduring beacon of light to Pakistani-Chinese friendship, to guide further generations."[17]

In contrast, the Pakistani and Indian Punjab, when compared, are full of opposing trends. The scripts of the Pakistani and Indian Punjabi language are entirely different; Pakistani Punjabi uses the Persian alphabet, while Indian Punjabi is written in Gurmukhi. In fact, in 1947, the pre-independent Punjab was divided on the basis of the "two nation theory," in which it was determined that the Hindus/Sikhs and the Muslims had so much diversity in their socio-cultural base that it was not possible to categorize them as a homogeneous group. The factors mentioned, along with past historical hostilities that have run deep since Independence, add another testimonial to the absence of common socio-cultural and security ties with this South Asian country on Pakistan's eastern border. The hatred created by widespread bloodshed, rape, and kidnappings during colossal migration at the time of the creation of Pakistan took decades to partially defuse the bitter past.

Located at the intersections of the Gulf Sea lanes and the Arabian Sea, Pakistan is conscious of its strategic responsibilities in the area. With the terror activities of non-state actors, and after the October 2000 bombing of the U.S. naval ship USS Cole in Aden by al-Qaeda, killing 17 sailors, Pakistan became more sensitive towards the procedures to monitor and patrol its 12-nautical-mile territorial limits in the Arabian Sea, which stretches along the coast of the Balochistan and Sindh provinces. It was reported that in 2004, Pakistan entered into an agreement with Admiral Sir Alan West, the First Sea Lord and Chief of Naval Staff for the British Navy, thus becoming the "eighth member of the task force conducting Operation Enduring Freedom."[18] According to this agreement, Pakistan allowed the coalition navies to supervise its 12-mile-territorial sea zone. The force was created, based upon a premise that drug dealers and terrorist groups like "Al-Qaeda and local militants in Pakistan linked to Al-Qaeda were involved in the smuggling of heroin and hashish to Europe, both by regular ship containers as well as through private launches."[19] It was expected that the Pakistani initiative would discourage the terrorist groups from making a sea-connection between the troubled Afghanistan and Pakistan tribal areas and countries of the Middle East and beyond.

Pakistan's much talked about seaport, Gwadar, has been in the process of construction since 2001, on the coastline in Balochistan province near the Iranian border. It was formally inaugurated by the Chinese Vice Premier, Wu Bangguo in March 2002. Gwadar port is a strategic spot for at least four reasons. First, it is situated at the entrance of the vital Strait of Hormuz, where much oil is exported to international oil markets. Oil tankers pass through this narrow passage which provides an opening to the sea lanes in the Arabian Sea and the Indian Ocean. Second, it is being developed with Chinese assistance; therefore the port will establish a trade link for China through the strategic "all-weather" Karakurum highway to the coast of Arabian Sea. Third, it will also provide the shortest and most convenient trade outlet to the sea for landlocked Afghanistan and the Central Asian Republics. Fourth, Karachi was increasingly under threat of a blockade in the event of a serious conflict with India, as it is located very close to the Indian border.

Because of Chinese involvement in the building of the Gwadar facilities, Indian strategists in particular are worried about this development. India feels that the Gwadar port will be helpful to the Chinese navy, and their operations in the Indian Ocean will be facilitated. The Indian navy, which desires to establish its domination in the area, will face tough competition in the presence of the Chinese navy. In other words, Pakistan's naval partnership with the Chinese would pose a strategic threat to Indian security in the Arabian Sea and the Indian Ocean, in the case of any future regional or global disputes. It is not only India that is alarmed by eventual Chinese access to the Indian Ocean; the United States is equally concerned by this project. A scholar of environmental sociology explains the concerns of India and the United States as the following,

> The port, by design or by default, also provides China a strategic foothold in the Arabian Sea and the Indian Ocean, although to the alarm of India and the unease of the U.S. sitting opposite the Strait of Hurmoz, through which 80% of the world's energy exports flow, the Gwadar port will enable China to monitor its energy shipments from the Persian Gulf, and offer it, in the case of any hostile interruption in such shipments, a safer alternative passage for its energy imports from Central Asia. Its presence on the Indian Ocean will further increase its strategic influence with major South Asian nations, particularly Bangladesh, Nepal, Pakistan, and Sri Lanka, which would prompt the Indians in turn to re-strengthen their Navy.[20]

Indian naval chief, Admiral Sureesh Mehta described the Pakistani port as having "serious strategic implications for India,"[21] and called it the linchpin of the Chinese strategy of a 'string of pearls.' He said that the Chinese intend to establish "bases and outposts across the globe, strategically located along its energy lines, to monitor and safeguard energy flows."[22] He further stated that Gwardar will be connected with the Karakoram highway, thus providing China a gateway to Arabian Sea.[23] Admiral Mehta's Pakistani counterpart dismissed the Indian concern by responding that Pakistan had every right to develop its country and make economic progress.[24]

THE MIDDLE EASTERN DEFENSE AND SECURITY FACTORS

Pakistan's cultural and emotional ties cannot be the sole factors of attachment with the Middle East. There are geostrategic variables as well that "propel [Pakistan] to play an active role in West Asian politics."[25] The armed forces of Pakistan are numerically the largest among the countries of the Middle Eastern region, perhaps with the exception of Turkey. Moreover, Pakistan's technological expertise in the manufacturing of arms is an added factor not only for its security needs, but also for other countries of the region.

The growing Indian arms industry, in particular its naval potential, competes with that of Pakistan for gaining influence in the Arabian Sea. In the strategic assessment of Pakistan, the Gulf nations will be affected by Indian naval expansion with its ambitious plans to exercise control in the Indian Ocean and the Arabian Sea. This may lead to a clash of interests between the Indian navy and those navies of the Gulf nations. Pakistani military strategists regard the increasing Indian economic potential, along with its growing military superiority, as a potential security risk that may penetrate the eastern flank of the Middle Eastern region. A clash of interests between the Indians and the countries on Pakistan's western frontiers has a very high rate of probability in the not-too-distant future. Stephen J. Blank of the U.S. Army War College writes that,

> India is determined to prevent any maritime or landward threat to it from the Gulf. . . . We can state that, for India, the Middle East and the Persian Gulf constitutes a vast strategic buffer, an outer ring, if you will, that cannot be allowed to become a base from which policies inimical to India's interests and security can be pursued with impunity.[26]

In any such conflict or tension, Pakistan will become a vital factor for the security of the Middle Eastern societies.

It has become a regular affair for the Saudi navy to hold joint naval exercises with Pakistan in the Arabian Sea, reflecting a close security-related understanding between the two nations. In January–February 2008, the ninth "Naseem al Bahr" naval exercise took place in the Arabian Sea. At that occasion, the Chief of Staff of the Pakistan navy highlighted the security requirements of Pakistan and the region in a post-2001 world. He was reported to express these concerns as,

> In the post 9/11 scenario, there has been a paradigm shift in the security calculus of the region. The asymmetric threat in the shape of trans-national terrorist networks poses a significant challenge for all the littoral states. In quest for vital energy resources, the Gulf region and Arabian Sea are under major focus of key world powers.
>
> He also stressed upon the need for bilateral and multilateral operations to develop and enhance better interoperability between the naval forces striving together for achievement of regional maritime security.
>
> During Naseem al Bhar-XI the units will be actively involved in exercise under multi threat environments along with host of other operations related to counter terrorism, convoy protection, anti-air, anti-submarine, mine counter measure and intelligence based operations.
>
> Both Pakistan and Royal Saudi Navies have come a long way and continue to maintain frequent interaction al all levels through joint seminars, sea exercise, officers' exchange programs and training.[27]

The strategic planners of Pakistan take a serious view of the increasing Indian–Israel cooperation, particular in the field of defense. In the 1980s, it was a household word in Pakistan that the Israelis, along with the Indian military strategists, had plans to damage the progress of the Pakistani nuclear program. However, to a certain level this "alarm" went away with Pakistan becoming a nuclear power in 1998. But even in later years, regardless of former President Pervez Musharraf's inclination towards Israel, suspicion about the close ties between India and Israel remained a component in the strategic planning of Pakistan.

All these factors, when combined, add strength to the notion that Pakistan cannot be ignored in any future regional or international alignments in the Middle East, especially in matters relating to defense and security. Pakistan's interaction with the Middle Eastern states in various fields of mutual interest has the potential to serve the common interests of all the countries of west Asia—which lies in

Table 2.1 A Comparison of Remittances by Pakistani Expatriates

July–December 2006 and July–December 2007 (in million dollars)

Countries	Remittances	
	July–Dec. 2006	July–Dec. 2007
Saudi Arabia	483.32	563.06
UAE	397.03	500.33
Bahrain, Kuwait, Oman, Qatar	358.58	457.21
United States	659.27	874.21
United Kingdom	218.67	227.23
European Union	74.89	88.99
Norway, Switzerland, Australia, Canada, Japan and others	374.92	354.18

Source: Dawn, January 18, 2008.

ensuring the security of the region from outside adventurers—and, at the same time discouraging any regional country from attempting to dominate the region.

Pakistan's second, equally important concern during the Cold War period had been with the promotion and rhetoric of "Arab nationalism." This nationalism inclined toward a rapport with racism, as demonstrated during the Iran–Iraq war (1980–1988). However, the post-Cold War era witnessed the delusion of Arab nationalism and policies on nationalist and realistic considerations started to be formulated by Arab nations. This Arab change of outlook made it easier for Pakistan to plan any future strategic relationship with these countries, on the basis of their separate national interests.

A large number of Pakistani technocrats and skilled and semiskilled workers are actively participating in developmental activities in these countries. With some, Pakistan has had a fairly long history of undertaking in the fields of finance, banking, defense, and security matters. Pakistan's economy relies heavily upon remittances from overseas Pakistanis, either investing in their home country or sending living expenses to their families. Pakistan also relies upon, to a certain degree, aid provided by the industrialized nations, especially the United States, and the European Union.

Table 2.1 shows that the remittances from the Middle Eastern countries, in particular the Gulf region, contributed considerably towards the economic security of Pakistan. These remittances had an impact on the society and made a positive difference in improving the quality of life for many people. This was especially important as during Musharraf's inapt dictatorial regime, domestic structures had decayed and became unable to start the economic engine of the country. Ordinary Pakistanis believe that the money sent by their relatives living in the Gulf made "a huge difference" in their lives.[28] It provided opportunities to improve the quality of life and provide educational and health facilities for many families.

The events occurring in the Middle Eastern nations cannot be overlooked by Pakistan, as they carry with them fallout that affects any foreign policy. Moreover, they can seriously threaten the security concerns of Pakistan either by the deteriorating security situation in Iraq or by any future U.S. military action against Iran. In the latter case, the Gulf region in particular will be destabilized and Pakistan's security will be directly threatened in a number of ways. The prominent way will be a sharp and hostile reaction from the people of Pakistan. An example of this reaction was witnessed when the United States attacked Afghanistan in 2002.

Regional and International Security Formations

Pakistan had two concerns in terms of overall geo-strategic placement at the onset of its independence. The first came from multiple unresolved disputes with India, which resulted into three wars, two border wars, and at least three military standoffs between the two countries. The most persistent and violent dispute remains that of Kashmir. At the time of partition of South Asia into the sovereign states of Pakistan and India, many questions regarding "national borders. . . .had barely been addressed or were highly contested."[29] That led to a series of tense negotiations to resolve these pending disputes. Most of the disputes were related to the boundary of East Pakistan (now Bangladesh). In what was known as West Pakistan (until 1971), the "Rann of Kutch" dispute was settled by the International Court of Arbitration, and such complicated border demarcation like "Sir Creek" is in the stage of intense deliberations. A major reason for continued tensions and competitive behavior originates from the psyche of the Hindu and Muslim communities. The mechanism of partition by itself had a great impact on the future relations between the two countries of India and Pakistan. These contradictions are explained as,

> This "operation," (partition) which is often described using the metaphors of surgery, was far from clinical. Partition played a central role in the making of new Indian and Pakistani national identities and the apparently irreconcilable differences which continued to exist today. We could even go as far as saying that Indian and Pakistani ideas of nationhood were carved out diametrically, in definition against each other, this time.[30]

On its northwestern border, the security concern for Pakistani strategists was the continuous pressures of Afghanistan, instigating the Pakhtun tribes to secede from newly established Pakistan. Some of the Afghan claims included areas that were well within the territorial boundaries of Pakistan. In later chapters of this book, a detailed account of these security concerns will be described.

The new world arrangements established under the charter of the United Nations, after the conclusion of the Second World War and the beginning of the Cold War, provided an opportunity for the Pakistani leadership to meet its security needs, through the Western-led alliance systems: the Central Treaty

Organization (CENTO, formally Baghdad Pact) and the South East Asian Treaty Organization (SEATO). From this period on, Pakistan's security requirements were fulfilled by the United States and Western Europe. Contrary to the requirements of the rigid Cold War ambiance, Pakistan established close ties with its northern neighbor, China. Chinese emergence in 1949 as an effective Asian power had provided an opportunity for Pakistan to establish friendly relations with a country which shared a strategic continuity with the northern areas of the country. In 1950, Pakistan became the third non-community country to recognize the new regime in communist China. It was reported that,

> at the Bandung Conference in 1955 Chou En-lai informed the delegates that Pakistan's then Premier, Mohammed Ali, had assured him that, although Pakistan was a member of SEATO, she was neither hostile to China nor in fear of aggression from her. Mohammed Ali made a distinction at the conference between Russia and China; the latter he refused to regard as imperialist, since it had no satellite.[31]

A border treaty with China was signed in 1963 and a leading Pakistani newspaper in its editorial expressed the optimism, on the conclusion of this border agreement as the following,

> The common equalitarian and fraternal aspirations of Islam in Pakistan and Socialism in China demand that the Frontiers Agreement should be followed by another fuller Commercial Treaty. Then may come a defensive-offensive Pact ... Sino-Pakistan interests are far more identical than either the Sino-Russian interests or the Pakistan-European and Pakistan-American interests.[32]

Article 6 of the Agreement refers to the final settlement of the Kashmir conflict. The Article says that after the settlement of the Kashmir dispute between Pakistan and India,

> the sovereign authority concerned will reopen negotiations with the Government of the People's Republic of China on the boundary ... provided that in the event of the sovereign authority being Pakistan, the provisions of the present agreement and of the aforesaid protocol shall be maintained in the formal boundary treaty to be signed between the People's Republic of China and Pakistan.[33]

It was after the 1962 border war with India that relations between the two nations solidified. Many changing events demonstrate that Pakistan's ties with China were based on a long-standing, permanent, and strategic basis. For a number of years, Pakistan adopted a precariously delicate balance between its Western ally, the United States and China. China, until the beginning of 1970s, was regarded as an enemy country by the United States.

Within a short span of nearly two decades, i.e., since the end of the Second World War, a series of developments has engulfed international politics. These changes not only transformed the world's attitude towards "alien" societies, but they also infused new perceptions of the functioning of the global interactions. The Soviet Union collapsed along with its Eastern European allies and the United States emerged as a sole superpower. The post-Cold War era (1990–2001) presented a new set of principles or "value system" for the international community. The concept of territorial security gave way to economic development and states were judged on the performance of their financial strengths, democratic institutions, and respect for human rights. Private entrepreneurship was regarded as a useful tool of development than the state-controlled economies. Numerous military dictatorships were replaced by "new democracies," while others struggled to transform their institutions towards the new concept of security, which was no longer judged on military might but on economic prosperity, and the strengthening of democracy. Those states which failed to meet the "New World Order" criteria were categorized as "failed states."

The New World Order advanced through gradual processes as is witnessed in a variety of developments. These unfolding of events occurred on two fronts: at the international level and at the regional level. The decline of the United Nations became apparent as the permanent members of the Security Council looked towards the sole superpower, the United States, for the initiative to tackle regional security issues. But the United States was unable to solve numerous conflicts, prominent of them being the plight of the Palestinians and the Kashmir conflict.

The realization of the limited capabilities of strong global, or even regional powers where they could not translate their military proficiency into an effective policy objective to achieve their purpose began to be witnessed as they ventured from one regional situation to another. The list is extensive. The U.S. experience in Vietnam; the Soviet failures in Afghanistan, and the U.S. calamities in Iraq and Afghanistan are examples of the limitations of military capacities. In Afghanistan, the Soviets failed on two accounts—first, to establish an effective military base as well as political control and second, to engage in institutional building on the patterns of their desire. The Indian experience in Sri Lanka, first against the Liberation Tigers of Tamil Eelam (LTTE) and then, its differences with Colombo, is yet another example. The Indians failed in diplomatic maneuvers as well as in military strength. They failed to bring the two conflicting parties to the negotiating table and at the same time, failed to control the violent activities of the LTTE and had to ultimately withdraw. Scholars of inter-state relations believe that there have been a number of conflicts and crises that have "local and regional dynamics which could not be regulated by the super-powers, although they have at times supported one side or another to protect and promote their own interests."[34]

In the post-Cold War era, the most important phenomenon was the emergence of new economic power centers in countries which were underrated until the mid-1960s. These centers effectively countered the military might of their neighbors as the mere presence of these economically developed countries generated enough pressure to deter their adversaries. An example can be found in the Korean situation in which North Korea, with more military strength, unsuccessfully threatened South Korea because the latter had undertaken gigantic programs for economic development. At the other end of the spectrum, from 1989 onwards, the otherwise stable but economically weak Eastern European countries began to fall, one by one, like a house of cards.

This development has set an example for the future to replace the economic and political power centers with those based on purely military strength. Another example that can be presented is that of Taiwan. The People's Republic of China would have assimilated that country had it not matured into a vigorous economic power. The case of Singapore supports the concept still further that economic strength can become more than an alternative for a military power. Located near to Pakistan, Dubai has emerged as a model of economic development, is an example of a society where the free market economy was given a chance to establish. The Dubai-model of economic security compensates to a great degree for its deficiency in military capabilities.

After establishing its credentials, an economic power center like Japan has been effectively active in its mission of becoming a peace-keeping force. In the Japanese involvement of the Gulf Conflict of 1989–1990, in which the economic as well as military centers of the country merged, the economic power center proved to be more effective. Encouraged by its economic effectiveness, there was even a proposal of sending Japanese troops to Kuwait, but the Japanese Parliament voted down the proposal. This demonstrates a trend where an economic power center could involve itself in peacemaking efforts and thereby, become an active partner in a conflict-solving situation. In the Cold War era, these duties were performed exclusively by militarily powerful nations.

It was in this changing world that Pakistan struggled to establish democratic culture in its society and to build institutions around it (1990–1999). It was recognized in Pakistan that the country had to readjust its economic and political-military interests. Unexpectedly, in October 1999, the Pakistani army staged a coup and took control of the country. The military takeover once again derailed the fragile democratic process. It was also contradictory to the "value system" of the New World Order. With the events of 9/11, the global system underwent a drastic change. The international strategic landscape therefore changed abruptly for Pakistan's strategic concerns. Once again, a new set of rules were designed by the sole superpower, the United States with the apparent objective of combating international terrorism. For the Bush administration, security concerns became more important than democracy and human rights.

Whatever was achieved during the period 1990–2001, it was undermined by an act of a non-state actor. This suited President Musharraf's dictatorial rule as he rushed to pledge allegiance to the policies of President George W. Bush, no matter if it served Pakistani national and strategic interests or not. Such was the urgency of Musharraf to legitimize his military regime that he even gave a blanket support to U.S. military policies. And the legitimate requirements of the U.S.

security needs were not taken into account; no effort was taken to strike a balance between the security of Pakistan and the level of support for U.S. global interests. The security of Pakistan came under unprecedented threat when the war in Afghanistan involved Pakistani tribes near the Afghan-Pakistan border which challenged the basic structure of the country. Musharraf's unconditional support to Bush administration put Pakistan's relations with its traditional allies like Iran and China under pressure. Moreover, regional organizations like the Economic Cooperation Organization (ECO) and the Organization of Islamic Conference (OIC) were undermined by Pakistan.

The source of the 9/11 attacks on the U.S. mainland had originated and been planned from Pakistan's western neighbor, Afghanistan. The military establishment of Pakistan had close ties with the Taliban and other militant groups and therefore, came under tremendous pressure to change its policies towards its "allies" in that country. Pakistan was also expected to support the U.S. military operation against militant groups in Afghanistan. As in 1979, Pakistan once again became a frontline state. This time it was with a difference—Pakistan became a state which was on the defensive and under tremendous international pressure. The Pakistani military establishment became a prime suspect in the harboring of international and regional terrorist activities and was held responsible for nuclear proliferation, as well.

RELATIONAL PATTERNS AND PAKISTAN'S SECURITY

Pakistan's security can be appropriately assessed still further by looking at the frequency of factors that connect Pakistan to other countries. Interaction between countries can either be friendly or hostile. We will be in a better position to understand the geo-strategic location of Pakistan, if we understand Pakistan's contacts and more so its frequency of external acts with its strategic environment. In order for this to occur, typologies of relationships have to be constructed. In this portion of the chapter, we are not so concerned with geographic affinity or continuity. It is rather a calculation of Pakistan's frequency of contacts that determine the strategic interests of its security and strategic placement. It will also tell us about the preferences of Pakistan and the countries with whom it interacts. This exercise becomes more relevant in a world where boundaries have become much closer, due to communication and military technology. In today's world, Iraq is in closer proximity in relational terms, to the United States than to its neighbor Syria. For decades, Pakistan's relational links have been with the United States rather than with Iran or Sri Lanka. Conversely, it is the strategic concern that forces the United States to have more interaction with Afghanistan than with its closer neighbors in North and South America.

In this part of the chapter, we will deal with the types of environments the policymakers of Pakistan encounter while executing its strategic foreign policy options. A clarification must be made of the term "environment," as hinted above. Apart from the close geographical setting, there are other variables which can account for the environment, as they have the required capacity to influence the foreign policymaking process.[35] However, we will confine ourselves to the criteria based upon the frequency and degree of foreign interactions. The distance of Pakistan from the regional as well as global actors, according to our analysis, becomes less of an influencing factor. Nonetheless, events have a large bearing of influence on the security concerns as well its implications if they happen on the borders of Pakistan.

As the theory of adaptation goes, an entity can only survive and flourish if it adapts to its environment or alternatively, has enough capacity to change its surroundings according to its own requirements. The question of adaptability therefore remains the key to Pakistan's security. The manner in which it is achieved and the methods adopted could vary, according to the circumstances of different countries. Nations adapt to enhance their military capabilities so that they can acquire a better bargaining leverage with environmental forces. However, smaller countries like UAE, because of their particular circumstances, are able to rely more on their diplomatic and financial maneuvering, rather than on making attempts to gain in military strength. Countries with different requirements can combine both factors so that their weakness in military capability can be bridged by diplomacy and institutional strengths. The basic condition remains that environment should first be identified based on objective security interests of a nation. The following arguments are relevant to our proposition as follows,

> Vital interests cannot be defended by detachment and dissociation, but nor should they be defended by embracing the status *quo or* unattractive regimes. What is required is an enhanced reputation for decisiveness and credibility in defense of a country ... and a diplomacy that is persistent, selective and modulated.[36]

In order to obtain the desired security objectives, the policymakers of Pakistan are expected to understand with clarity the number of actors that form a component of Pakistan's strategic surroundings. Moreover, it becomes vital to read the signals coming from the external environment, in its proper perspective. This is important as it can help to effectively manage security threats, may they be in a "simmering" stage. Such understanding is also essential to secure enough time to prepare for the confrontation of any security threats.[37]

If we look back at history, we observe that Pakistan's perception of its potential adversaries and friends has been dominated by an unrepresentative establishment consisting of the military and the bureaucratic structures. Devoid of the national consensus, these structures fail to reflect the genuine desires of the population in their foreign policy preferences. In our scrutiny, we will base our findings on the actions taken by the ruling elite, but at the same time, we will point out the misperceptions of the foreign policymaking apparatus. In other words, the environmental considerations of Pakistan's foreign policy would be taken as the basic concern. As mentioned before, this will be based on the frequency and kind of interaction with the regional and international actors.

The above observations are made while keeping in view that there has been a lack of understanding about how to establish strong ties with Pakistan's natural allies. Because of the lack of representative institutions, the people-at-large have had no role in the formation of foreign policy in Pakistan. Therefore, vested interests like the bureaucratic structures with their ties to such organizations as the World Bank (WB) or the International Monetary Fund (IMF) are common. The military, along with the feudal and newly emerging class of industrialists, play a dominant role in the execution of a country's foreign policy—thus shifting Pakistan towards ties that do not fulfill the genuine wishes of and benefit the majority of the people. Seldom have these policies obtained the national interest of Pakistan. Since the decisions are non-representative, vested interests become dominant. In such circumstances, the genuine security requirements are overlooked, thus exposing the country to external dangers. It is a known fact that a state which is unable to control vested interests from encroaching upon its foreign policy endeavors can be regarded as weak.[38] It should be clarified that we are dealing with those pressure groups which have their own institutionalized interests, as opposed to such pressure groups as civil society, which represents the general will of the people.[39]

The shifting of environment also occurs where a nation has no control over the circumstances. In this situation, necessary shifts and adjustments become inevitable in order to move away from potential dangers. The external environment of Pakistan has been in a state of flux quite frequently, thus requiring a degree of appropriate alterations in its policy orientations. The fluctuations in the global setting, caused by the decline of the bipolar global system in the mid-1970s, were the first turning point. The second turning point came with the loss of East Pakistan in 1971. The third turning point was the emergence of the economic potential of the Gulf countries from 1973 onwards. The fourth turning point took place in 1990, with the collapse of the Soviet Union and Eastern Europe, giving way to a "New World Order." The last turning point, the 2001 agenda of the Bush administration to fight a "war against international terror," posed one of the most serious challenges to Pakistan's security. The following description of events partly explains the mentioned changes,

> There has been change in the nature of the major issues, e.g., the Cold War has turned into a detente and the North/South conflict, which had started on the issue of anti-colonialism still continuing about Southern Africa, has largely shifted to economic growth; there has been change in the salience of issue-areas—the gravity of international conflicts has moved from security to economics, resources and eco-politics—and the major danger spots which have gradually shifted from Europe to the Middle East and Africa. . . .[40]

Explaining the various mechanisms of the environment in the world system, as mentioned above, gave way to more flexibility in the regional mechanism in the early 1960s, thus allowing small and weak nations to pursue their policies in a somewhat unrestricted manner. However, there are some analysts who still believe that the big powers, in the form of "military or industrial power," dominated world politics and that the role of the "Third World (was) negligible."[41] Our argument is that those militarily weak nations which enjoyed the support of their people and wanted to pursue independent policies, succeeded in making their societies viable enough to prevail over the pressures of international demands. However, nations which depended on the financial or arms assistance of the big powers had to compromise their independent character.

The foreign policymakers of Pakistan instead adopted a "submissive policy." Pakistan did not take full advantage of the "new reality" of the situation of detente and the ruling elite continued to pursue the status quo. Evidence to this effect was given when the outdated alliance system in the form of CENTO was carried well into late 1978. The loss of East Pakistan in 1971 and the American-indifference towards Pakistan's security should have been a powerful enough catalyst to quit CENTO, but this action never materialized. In reality, it was the Islamic Revolution in Iran (1979) and its consequences which saw the collapse of this outdated alliance; otherwise, the policymakers were still not ready to quit CENTO. On the other hand, SEATO gradually became ineffective and ultimately collapsed as the People's Republic of China and the United States began to develop a new understanding of cooperation. Moreover, the emergence of the Gulf region in 1973 should also have been another reason to leave the U.S.-backed alliance system. However, it can be accepted that "half-baked" efforts were made to establish close contacts with the western neighbors of Pakistan. Such relations were based upon the principles of limited gains, in the form of foreign exchange remittances from the Pakistanis working in that area and grants to purchase military equipment. No long-lasting planned strategy was adopted to establish links with Pakistan's natural allies.

In other words, alternative security understanding should have been predicted in the first place, with planned and necessary adjustments made. The role of Pakistan should not have been that of a silent spectator; it should have been more aware of the changing circumstances in its regional, as well as global milieus. James N. Rosenau, narrated a policy of adjustments as follows,

> ... The political organism is always experiencing both continuities and change, and thus it is always in motion, slipping behind, moving ahead, holding fast, or otherwise adjusting and changing in response to internal developments and external circumstances.[42]

In the case of Pakistan, it is less of an adjustment that adhering to policies based on a certain presumptions.

The proposition that Pakistan is a militarily weak nation and, therefore, cannot freely exercise its foreign policy goals, is disputed by some analysts of foreign policy. There are a variety of factors which can compensate for lacking military strength. For example, apart from the skillful use of diplomacy, which we have already mentioned, there are such factors as participation of the masses (India is a good example), effective leadership, and economic and social advancement of a state. These elements, "often enable small states to exercise influence totally disproportionate to the rank and status accorded by the objective elements of power."[43]

A degree of attention, either as a matter of option or imposed from external surroundings, is the core of the formulation of the environmental types of Pakistan's security. The physical presence of a security threat, as well as the means to avoid it, should be taken in a similar conceptual meaning. The consideration of neighbors, as being the vital factors by themselves, will be accepted with reservation. However, at the same instance, the importance of geographical continuity cannot be overlooked. We agree with J. D. B. Miller when he writes,

> Neighbours [sic] have traditionally been important to any state, because of the high incidence of communication with them through trade and travel; the possibility of quarrels over disputed borders; the problem of what kinds of restrictions are needed in order to ensure that neighbours [sic] do not gain too much advantage from one's own situation; the effects of having similar or divergent ethnic stock; and so on. In a sense, neighbouring [sic] states always matter, even though they may not matter most.[44]

Miller's statement can be partially disputed when judged in the context of Pakistani situation. For example, with India or Iran, Pakistan does not maintain either trade or travel to a degree which a neighboring situation demands. However, even the absence of such relationship can pose security concerns, as the absence of normal conditions have the potential of creating security related tensions. Because of the lack of understanding of each others' perceptions, small issues can lead to bigger conflicts.

A study done in 1985, relating to a specific time period (1978–1985), showed the frequency of Pakistan's external foreign policy environment.[45] During this time, the Soviets were in occupation of Afghanistan, threatening Pakistan's security. India, on the other hand, adopted a policy where on numerous occasions it voted to justify the Soviet occupation in Afghanistan at such international forums as the UN General Assembly. At that time, Pakistan was squeezed between security threats coming from the northwest and east of its borders.

This study divided Pakistan's foreign activities into areas of conflict and cooperative conduct. The data was constructed on Pakistan's actions or statements towards the external environment in the mentioned period. It also contained statements and actions channeled towards Pakistan. The statements were carefully chosen and were representative of an official policy. Speculations of newspapers and electronic broadcasts on various aspects of foreign policy were omitted.[46]

As Tables 2.2 and 2.3 show, it was determined from the study that, in spite of the fact that during this period the Soviet invasion In Afghanistan was attracting the focus of the Pakistani policymakers, the conflict-related 228 frequencies in the Afghan example is 12 interactions, lower than 240 frequencies in the Indian

Table 2.2 Pakistan's Interaction with Environment of Immediate Attention

| | Number of Frequencies (December 1979–December 1985) | | | | | | | |
| | Conflict | | | | Cooperative | | | |
Country	Dec. 1979–Dec. 1981	1982–1983	1984–1985	Total	Dec. 1979–Dec. 1981	1982–1983	1984–1985	Total
Afghanistan	87	32	109	228	45	23	25	93
India	88	50	102	240	45	47	46	138
United States	06	05	01	12	49	31	29	109
China	00	00	00	00	36	30	18	84
Saudi Arabia	0	00	00	00	26	15	12	53
Iran	01	00	01	02	19	16	23	58
Turkey	00	00	00	00	08	10	15	33
Total	182	87	213	482	228	172	168	568

Source: Author's Calculation from *Daily Dawn*, December 1979 to December 31, 1985.

example. On the other hand, we note that the Indian conflicts in 1984–85 was nearly doubled of those in the previous two years (1982–83). This can be attributed to increasing Indian hostility to divert its domestic problems such as the Sikh insurgency in the Indian Punjab. Moreover, the Indian leaders were determined to take advantage of the politically weak structures in Pakistan, as well as its occupation with the Afghan crisis. The Afghan-related rise in conflicts in 1984–85 is attributed to the Afghan *mujahideen's* increasing pressure to which the Kabul regime retaliated by bombarding refugee camps in Pakistan.

Table 2.3 Percentage of Interactions in the Immediate Environment

| | Year-wise and Total Interactions (December 1979–December 1985) | | | | | | | |
| | Conflict | | | | Cooperative | | | |
Country	Dec. 1979–Dec. 1981	1982–1983	1984–1985	Total	Dec. 1979–Dec. 1981	1982–1983	1984–1985	Total
Afghanistan	47.8	36.7	51.1	47.3	19.7	13.3	14.8	16.3
India	48.3	57.4	47.8	49.7	19.7	27.3	27.3	24.2
United States	03.2	05.7	00.4	02.4	21.4	18.0	17.2	19.1
China	–	–	–	–	15.7	17.4	10.7	14.7
Saudi Arabia	–	–	–	–	11.4	08.7	07.1	09.3
Iran	00.5	–	00.4	00.4	08.3	09.3	13.6	10.2
Turkey	–	–	–	–	03.5	05.8	08.9	05.8

Source: Author's Calculation from *Daily Dawn*, December 1979 to December 31, 1985.

The results of the study in Tables 2.2 and 2.3 further indicate that Pakistan had a fairly low percentage of interaction, i.e., 5.8 percent with otherwise trustful and reliable friends like Turkey and Iran, which accounted for 10.2 percent in the cooperative field while Saudi Arabia had 9.3 percent of cooperative interactions. The data confirms the propositions made in the beginning of this chapter. During this period efforts were made to normalize relations with India. Most of the cooperative gestures were initiated by Pakistani President Zia-ul-Haq. That is the reason why we see a surprisingly high percentage of 24.2 cooperative interactions with India. Fifty percent of the conflict interaction with India indicates that they did not respond favorably to the President. It is also worth noting that India opposed Pakistan on all matters which were of vital security concern. For example, India opposed military aid from the United States and the nuclear capability of Pakistan, in particular. Most important of all, during this time, the Indian leadership occupied part of the Siachen Glacier just east of the Line of Control between Pakistan and India. Apart from the Pakistani President's gestures of friendship, there was reciprocal activity in fields such as facilitating railway traffic as well as an improvement of telephone systems which attributed to the positive category of relationship.

The contacts with China in this period of research remained constant with 14.9 percent of the total cooperative actions, while not a single case of conflict interaction was noted. The United States acquired a 19.1 percent of cooperative actions due to its policy of supporting Pakistan against the Soviet invasion in Afghanistan. On the other hand, Afghanistan's fairly high cooperative interactions with Pakistan accounts for the Afghan leaders' repeated statements of having direct talks with Pakistan. Moreover, the regular meetings in Geneva led the cooperative percentage of interactions to a higher level.

Based on the above-mentioned study, as stated in Tables 2.2 and 2.3, we can divide Pakistan's relational environment into three categories. These environmental categories are determined with regard to the security options of the policymakers of Pakistan. These categories are essential as they provide a guide to preparing a strategy and executing foreign policy options. The categories are as follows:

1. Immediate Attention Type
2. Normal Circumstantial Type
3. Distant Relational Type

The first category consists of those actors which directly or indirectly affect the vital concerns of Pakistan's security either to maintain its external postures, according to its military and economic interests, or to adopt internal developmental programs, without interference from big powers and multinational corporations. The mere presence of external actors does not influence the policy orientation of Pakistan's security. But, once set in motion to pursue certain goals, the external actors create a situation which requires immediate attention. The Immediate Attention Type environment not only includes situations which pose a security threat, but would also incorporate factors which, if pursued, would not allow the emergence of the security threat in the first place.

We can divide this first category, Immediate Attention, into the following five sub-divisions:

(i) the Russian occupation of Afghanistan; (ii) the United States as a supplier of arms and economic aid; (iii) the historical mistrust with India; (iv) the regular pattern of understanding with the People's Republic of China; and (v) the sharing of security concerns with such Middle Eastern nations as Saudi Arabia, Iran, and Turkey.

(ii) The Soviet occupation of Afghanistan in December 1979 and the continuous presence of Soviet troops focused Pakistan's attention towards its western environment. Afghanistan has been a source of tension because of its Pakhtunistan policy since the independence of Pakistan in 1947. However, it never became a serious threat for Pakistan's security and thus, remained in the second category of the Normal Circumstantial Type. In March 1978, Afghan President Daud Khan visited Pakistan among speculations that the future would witness closer ties between the two culturally and religiously similar countries. But Daud's assassination in April of the same year changed the situation for the worse as far as Pakistan's defense interests were concerned. The Soviet invasion "dramatically transformed Pakistan's geo-strategic situation." All of a sudden, Pakistan faced the specter of Soviet troops virtually everywhere along the thirteen-hundred-mile frontier.[47] The presence of large number of Afghan refugees on Pakistani soil, along with the resistance activities of the Afghan freedom fighters, further aggravated the security environment with Afghanistan. The policymakers of Pakistan since December 1979 were forced to focus their attention entirely towards Afghanistan. Afghanistan became an Immediate Attention Type environment for Pakistan. It was with a total reliance on the United States that the new situation was confronted. Pakistani society faced a variety of security challenges for which there were no existing political institutions. Whenever a nation is in a crisis situation, a mass involvement of its people can become a useful tool to defuse the impact. As history has repeatedly shown, the involvement of the people can become a powerful force to balance the deficiencies in the defense structures. Moreover, skillful diplomacy also becomes a factor in order to avoid the harmful fallout of national security threats.

(iii) The United States provided Pakistan with $3.2 billion in aid from 1981 to 1987. This figure also included a credit for military purposes. The U.S. grant intended to strengthen Pakistan's strategic posture against the Soviets in Afghanistan. "It was a step toward easing this problem, but it could not solve it."[48] It was this substantial U.S. involvement in Afghanistan that made the United States a part of the first category of Pakistan's security environment. With the United States becoming an integral part of the Immediate Attention Type, more security hazards were created for Pakistan. As West German scholar, Dieter Braun wrote,

> The Soviet Union does not lack leverages for propagandistically accusing Pakistan of being an accomplice of the U.S. In this connection, it is constantly asserted that Pakistan ceded to the U.S. military rights on its territory, which are a threat to the Soviet Union ... Numerous contacts between the two armed forces suggest that consultations are taking place concerning contingency planning. The same holds true for Pakistani and Western suspicions with regard to Indo-Soviet military cooperation ... In this domain, the Zia/Junejo government must act with particular care.[49]

A sizeable part of Pakistani public opinion was of the impression that the U.S. involvement in Afghanistan crisis should have been limited to humanitarian help for the refugees and moral pressures on the Soviets to withdraw from Afghanistan through the United Nations. Ultimately, it was the resilience of the Afghan fighters and American military assistance that forced the Soviet troops to leave Afghanistan.

(iii) India's desire to be a mini-superpower in the South Asian region has been obstructed by the refusal of Pakistan to become a subordinate state. This can also be said for other countries of the region. To give an example of the Indian thinking about their hegemonial objectives, Sarbjit Johal wrote,

> As the dominant military power in South Asia, the Indian government has several capabilities to punish, coerce, or influence Pakistan. These capabilities have steadily increased since independence, and even though the Pakistan military has revitalized since 1979, India's present capabilities are much greater than Pakistan's. India's armed forces number I.I million men, a significant total, globally as well as regionally.[50]

The long history of differences of Pakistan with India on vital issues, along with the reality of three major wars between the two countries, has created hurdles in any move to normalize relations with that country. In recent years, former President Musharraf made a series of attempts to appease the Indian leadership, but without any positive results. In fact, the mutual suspicion between the two countries is such that drifting India towards the Normal Circumstantial Type remains a distant possibility, at least for the near future.

(iv) Pakistani ties with the People's Republic of China have been consistent since their development from 1962. China has proved to be a reliable friend and its policy towards Pakistan has been devoid of any hegemonial designs. The Chinese factor in the first category of the environment category is in Pakistan's favor as far as its security interests are concerned. This is contrary to some other actors prevalent in the same category. China has been a security help since the 1965 war against India. For all other practical purposes, China became a security asset for Pakistan.

(v) Between 1971 and 1979, Pakistan concentrated its efforts to establish close ties with Iran, Turkey, and Saudi Arabia, along with other Middle Eastern countries. This policy was considered to be strategically correct as Pakistan was able to establish a series of friendly neighbors along its borders. In other words, these countries became a first preference environment for Pakistan's security and it moved nearer to its accepted external surroundings. After 1979, attention was diverted towards India, mainly to normalize relations. General Musharraf's single-focus foreign policy ignored Pakistan's close historic links with Iran, Turkey, and Saudi Arabia. Pakistan's foreign policy options towards the Gulf nations in particular and the Middle East in general should have been on the basis of economic and cultural commitments. These commitments should have been conducted on a people-to-people level giving boost to both trade and other business interests. Instead, the Pakistani focus has relied solely on government-to-government relations, which are not strong enough for permanent foundations. A cohesive understanding which is indispensable for better relations has not been given a fair trial in the past.

The Normal Circumstantial Type consists of those countries which, in an indirect manner, have a minor role in the ultimate security options of Pakistan. They include the development of economic relations with Japan, South Korea, and Taiwan;[51] the development of economic relations with all its variations, including sanctions from the Western European community; the establishment of communication with the regional and international Muslim community; and the understanding to coordinate on regional issues, with the countries of South Asia, other than India, are some of the prominent examples which fall within this category.

The Distant Relational Type includes those global actors which in normal circumstances do not occupy a prominent position in the security oriented foreign policy of Pakistan. Multinational corporations such as OPEC, developments in Africa, the tense situation in South East Asia, and the unfolding of events in Latin America are included in the environment of Pakistan's foreign policy, occupying the least important position.

NOTES

1. *The World Book Encyclopedia*, Volume 8 (Chicago: World Book, Inc., 2007), p. 106b.

2. In early 1990s, Sir Halford Mackinder presented a theory of heartland when describing inter-state relations. According to Mackinder, "This heartland covered 'Euro-Asia,' and it was vital that the democratic nations control that area." *The New Encyclopedia Britannica*, Vol. 5, 15th ed. (Chicago: Encyclopedia Britannica, Inc. 2002), p. 193. Another scholar, Nicholas Spykman, "argued that it was also important (for imperial powers) to control what he called the *Rimland*. The Rimland consisted of Western Europe, the Middle East, and southern and eastern Asia." *The World Book Encyclopedia*, op.cit. p. 106b.

3. Charles W. Kegley, Jr., and Eugene R. Wittkopf, *World Politics: Trend and Transformation* (Belmont, CA., Wadsworth, 2004), p. 67.

4. Some planners in the Pakistan military had thought that friendly Afghanistan could provide the Pakistani troops a cushion, in case of the Indian onslaught. The reality that Afghanistan

comprises of highly complicated tribal structure and is extremely difficult to pacify, for any such eventuality, was ignored.

5. "What the generals must apologise for," editorial, *Daily Times*, February 01, 2008, http://www.dailytimes.com.pk/default.asp?page=2008\02\01\story_1-2-2008_pg3_1

6. A renowned scholar Eqbal Ahmad complains about the military's concoction of this term by arguing, "In his letter to Zarb-i-Momin, the Taliban publication, Mr. Azam Tariq, leader of Pakistan's violently sectarian Sipah-i-Sahaba Party, is ecstatic over his ideological brothers' recent victories. His ecstasy is shared by Pakistan's national security managers, but for non-ideological reasons. The attainment of 'strategic depth' has been a prime objective of Pakistan's Afghan policy since the days of General Zia ul Haq. In recent years the Taliban replaced Gulbadin Hikmatyar as the instrument of its attainment. Their latest victories, specially their capture of Mazar Sharif, the nerve centre of northern Afghanistan, brings the Pakistani quest close to fulfillment if, that is, such a thing as "strategic depth" does exist in the real world. Unfortunately, in any meaningful way, it does not. In military thought it is a non-concept unless one is referring to a hard-to-reach place where a defeated army might safely cocoon. Yet far from improving the tenuous notion of 'strategic depth,' the Taliban's victory is likely to augment Pakistan's political and strategic predicament. The reasons are numerous, and compelling." Eqbal Ahmad, "A mirage misnamed strategic depth," *Al-Ahram* Weekly on-line, August 27– September 2, 1998, http://weekly.ahram.org.eg/1998/392/foc12.htm, M. P. Bhandara, a member of Pakistan National Assembly gives near similar arguments against the concept of 'Strategic Depth.' He writes, "The myth of our military establishment in the 1990s was that Afghanistan provided "strategic depth" for the ultimate defence of Pakistan. The enactment of the myth led to our coopting the Taliban as our closest allies: a bunch of illiterate fanatics without any scruples. The "strategic depth" theory implied that if India were to overrun Pakistan, the Pakistan armed forces would retreat to the rugged hills and warrens of Afghanistan to fight a rearguard action to reclaim the motherland. It was never clear to anyone how the Pakistan armed forces, sans the navy for obvious reasons, could save Pakistan from remote Afghanistan if it could not save it from its own soil.

But such is the power of the myth that "strategic depth" theory was at one time part of our military doctrine." M. P. Bhandara, "Myths Ending in Wars," *Dawn*, June 22, 2003.

7. *The Nation*, February 17, 2006.

8. John Keay, *India: A History* (New York: Atlantic Monthly Press, 2000), p. 10.

9. Marian Rengel, *Pakistan: A Primary Source Cultural Guide* (New York: PowerPlus Books, 2004), p. 27.

10. Iftikhar H. Malik, *Culture and Customs of Pakistan* (Westport, Connecticut and London: Greenwood Press, 2006), p. 32. Professor Malik states "After the early Arabs, most of the Muslim rulers of India were of Turkic stock, but, once in India, they adopted Persian both as a literary and court language. Of course, Arabic remained the language of the Muslim classics and the medium of prayers, but it was Persian that overtook all other languages. By this time, Sanskrit had become too elitist and was confined to a few Hindu ecclesiastic circles and . . . Persian emerged as the lingua franca.", ibid.

11. Apart from the Syeds, Pashtuns, Baloch, and tribes in the Punjab, as Arrains and Awans claim an Arab lineage. See Aitzaz Ahsan, *The Indus Saga and the Making of Pakistan* (Karachi: Oxford University Press, 1996).

12. Ibid., p. 89.

13. Francis Robinson, ed., *The Cambridge Encyclopedia of India, Pakistan, Bangladesh, Sri Lanka, Nepal, Bhutan and the Maldives* (Cambridge: Cambridge University Press, 1989), p. 249.

14. *Facts about Pakistan*, rev. ed. (Islamabad: Ministry of Information and Broadcasting, Government of Pakistan, 1988).

15. *Country Profile: Pakistan*, Library of Congress–Federal Research Division, February 2005, p. 6, http://lcweb2.loc.gov/frd/cs/profiles/Pakistan.pdf

16. William Borders, "A Strategic New Link on the Roof of the World," *The New York Times*, January 28, 1979.

17. Ibid.

18. Massoud Ansari, "Sea How They Run," Newsline, April 2004, http://www.newsline.com.pk/Newsapr2004/newsbeat1apr.htm

19. Ibid.

20. Tarique Niazi, Gwadar: "China's Naval Outpost on the Indian Ocean," *The Jamestown Foundation*, Vol. 5, Issue 4 (February 15, 2005), http://www.jamestown.org/publications_details.php?volume_id=408&issue_id=3232&article_id=2369262

21. *The Hindu*, January 22, 2008, http://www.hinduonnet.com/holnus/002200801221612.htm

22. ZEENEWS.COM., January 31, 2008, http://www.zeenews.com/articles.asp?aid=419623&sid=NAT

23. *The Hindu*, op. cit.

24. *Dawn*, February 3, 2008.

25. Syed Mehtab Ali Shah, "West Asia: Its Problems and Emerging Pattern," *Pakistan Horizon*, 41, 1 (January 1988), p. 94.

26. Stephen J. Blank, "Natural Allies? Regional Security in Asia and Prospects for Indo-American Strategic Cooperation," *The Strategic Studies Institute*, U.S. Army War College, September, 2005, p. 37.

27. "Pak-Saudi joint Naval exercise 'Naseem al Bahr' commences today," *Pakistan Defence*, 22 January, 2008, http://www.defence.pk/forums/naval-forces/9346-pak-saudi-joint-naval-exercise-naseem-al-bahr-commences-toady.html

28. "Pakistan: Remittances–the impact on Communities," *UN Office for the Coordination of Humanitarian Affairs*, 18 May, 2005, http://www.irinnews.org/report.aspx?reportid=28611

29. Yasmin Khan, *The Great Partition: The Making of India and Pakistan* (New Haven and London: Yale University Press, 2007), p. 4.

30. Ibid., p. 9.

31. *Dawn*, April 24, 1955; *Statesmen*, Delhi, April 30, 1955; *Pakistan Times,* April 24 and 29, 1955. as quoted in W. M. Dobell, "Ramifications of the China-Pakistan Border Treaty," *Pacific Affairs*, Vol. 37, No. 3. (Autumn, 1964), p. 283. "Upon his return from signing the Demarcation Agreement at Peking, Foreign Minister Bhutto lauded the settlement as awarding Pakistan some 750 square miles of land affording salt and grazing ground, access to all passes along the Karakoram Range and control of two-thirds of K-2 mountain.A few days later he added that three-quarters of the peak of K-2, including the summit, remained with Pakistan," *Indian Express,* report from Karachi, March 8, 1963; *Dawn,* March 12, 1963, as quoted in Ibid.

32. *Pakistan Times,* March 20, 1963, as quoted in Ibid., p. 291.

33. *Sino-Pakistan Frontier Agreement 1963*, http://www.kashmir-information.com/Legal Docs/SinoPak.html

34. Hasan-Askari Rizvi, *Pakistan and the Geostrategic Environment: A Study of Foreign Policy* (Basingstoke, Hampshire and London: The MacMillan Press Ltd, 1993), p. 3.

35. Harold and Margaret Sprout, "Environmental Factors in the Study of International Politics," ed., James N. Rosenau, *International Politics and Foreign Policy: A Reader in Research and* Theory (New York: The Free Press. 1969), 41–56.

36. Shahram Chubin, "The United States and the Third World: Motives, Objectives, Policies," ed., Christoph Bertram, *Third World Conflict and International Security* (London: The Macmillan Press,1982), p. 87.

37. Gerald Segal, *The Great Power Triangle* (London: The Macmillan Press, 1982). p. 153.

38. Stephen D. Krasner, *Defending the National Interest: Raw Materials Investments and U.S. Foreign* Policy (Princeton, New Jersey: Princeton University Press, 1978), p. 56.

39. In democratic societies, the policies are formulated after thorough debate by various factions of the society. But there the pressure groups are not monopolized by one group. In fact, the government in democratic societies on occasion compromises with the opposing views. In non-democratic countries, the opposing opinions are not accepted with an open mind.

40. Joseph Frankel, *International Relations in a Changing World* (Oxford: Oxford University Press, 1979), p. 200.

41. Etie Kedourie, "A New International Disorder," eds. Hedley Bull and Adam Watson, *The Expansion of International Society* (Oxford: Clarendon Press, 1984), p. 355.

42. James N. Rosenau, *The Study of Political Adaptation* (London: Frances Printer, 1981), p. 1.

43. Agrippah T. Mugomba, "Small Developing States and the External Operational Environment," *The Year Book of World Affairs,* 1979, Vol. 33, p. 212; Published under the auspices of the London Institute of World Affairs.

44. J. D. B. Miller, *The World of States* (London: Croom Helm, 1981), p. 50.

45. See, Syed Farooq Hasnat, "Environmental Typologies of Pakistan's Security," *Pakistan Horizon.* Vol. XL (1987): 51–64.

46. Only the statements of the head of state, head of government, Minister of Foreign Affairs, Minister of Internal Affairs, and Minister of Finance were included in the data.

47. W. Howard Wriggins, "Pakistan's Search for a Foreign Policy after the Invasion of Afghanistan," *Pacific Affairs* (Summer, 1984), p. 285.

48. Henry S. Bradsher, *Afghanistan and the Soviet Union* (Durham, N.C.: Duke Press Policy Studies, 1983), p. 254.

49. Dieter Braun, "Pakistan's Balancing Act—Factors Determining its Foreign and Security Policy," translated from *Europa*—Arc/n'v, Bonn, No. 15/1985 (10 August, 1985), p. 3.

50. Sarbjit Johal, "Regional Cooperation and Indo-Pakistan Relations," *South Asian and Middle Eastern* Studies (Villanova), Vlll:2 (Winter, 1984), p. 39.

51. For details of Pakistan economic relations with at least one country—Japan, see R.G. Sawhney, "Pakistan-Japan: Growing Economic Relations," *Strategic Analysis* (New Delhi) IX:6 (September, 1985), pp. 557–564.

CHAPTER 3

Domestic Security Issues: Challenges of Building Stable Institutions

BACKGROUND

This chapter deals with the institutions and events that had or continue to have serious imprints on the national security of Pakistan. It has already been spelled out in Chapter 1 that the security of Pakistan cannot be confined exclusively to military matters. Vibrant societies with an ability to manage tensions and conflicts, within the realms of their perimeters, contribute towards the security of a nation. And so do the strength and viability of the institutions that secure together various segments of a society. The collapse of the Soviet Union repeatedly presents evidence and a phenomenon that in order to achieve stability and security, non-military domestic variables play a large role. Unmanaged societies and decay in their structures can cause societal collapse with devastating consequences; they also weaken the ability of a nation to withstand external pressures. For a vibrant and secure society, stable socio-economic and constitutional/political institutions provide a framework to manage divergent agendas as presented by different sectors of a society. Most important of all, secure societies have an inbuilt "conflict-management" mechanism which can be represented in the laws of the land, with precedents established over an extended period of their history, or in the construction of institutions in their respective spheres. In sum, non-military variables, especially the democratic process, keep nations together while dictatorships become a factor of disengagement.

In other words, the capability of a state to preserve its integrity and independence does not rely on military power alone, but depends on a variety of internal capabilities. Even the matters of territorial integrity and sovereignty of a state cannot be devoid of such factors as economic and political rather the military capabilities; economic stability and political viability are all intertwined together. Each one of these factors must support the other for the achievement of the desired favorable results. Military capability can be better achieved with the help of economic prosperity, i.e., the ability to buy arms or to even construct the arms' infrastructure in the country. Correct political policies would enable the economic as well as military factors to operate in a more efficient manner. Similarly, a stronger military posture to discourage external threats or influence can enhance the achievement of political and economic pursuits. Military power might not be used in its real and practical sense; its mere presence in the background can suffice to gain objectives. Military power is now considered to encompass a variety of factors. At the very basis of this consideration is the development of the studies of national security as explained below,

> The earliest studies of national security tended to concentrate on military problems, a reflection of the early conception of national security as being rather narrowly concerned with military matters. . . . [The] national security experts have increasingly turned to economic considerations and economic methods in their discussions. They have attempted to define and assess scientifically all the elements constituting of nation's economic potential for war.
>
> Internal values are, of course, not merely economic, and national security makes serious demands upon political institutions as well. Although interest in this aspect of national security developed somewhere later, it is now one of the major areas of academic speculation.[1]

Taking a clue from the changing complexion of the world system, it is believed that the core of the security issue has shifted from interstate to those factors that were not relevant as they have emerged recently. There has been growing recognition of non-military factors which are widely discussed by various social scientists as well as strategists. It is no longer that a "non-traditional security discourse . . . is not limited to intellectuals and academics . . . but is increasingly recognized by governments who continue to either explore or participate in a vast array of institutional arrangements."[2]

In support of these arguments, it has been pointed out that since 1990, when a New World Order emerged, intra-state conflicts occupied a dominant ranking in nearly 100 armed conflicts around the globe.[3] Jessica Mathews suggests that "a competing notion of 'human security' is creeping around the edges of official thinking, suggesting that security be viewed as emerging from the conditions of daily life—food, shelter, employment, health, public safety—rather than flowing downward from a country's foreign relations and military strength."[4]

If the concept of security is judged in terms of preserving state institutions to their functional level, providing protection to its citizens, then various factors like economic development, a viable political process, and the ability to deal with societal contradictions become important parts of the security concerns of a nation. This is a reflection we gather from the views of various authors as presented above. An expert on international security recognizes that "soft power" is more effective than a demonstration of might, purely based on military considerations.[5] The examples of numerous developments bear testimony towards that fact. Apart from the collapse of the Soviet Union, the countries of Afghanistan, Somalia and Sudan all declined because of the collapse of domestic structures, rather than from aggression from some outside force. Territorial integrity, the enshrined principle of national security, which was sincerely adopted by the UN Charter, no longer holds validity. Nations can disintegrate from within as well. There is a long list of non-military factors that have emerged as a cohesive force of national security, which a nation must take into consideration. In this chapter, we will, for the purpose of the study of Pakistan's security, be dealing with three major issues: 1) political instability, 2) the establishment of a civil society, and 3) the weakening of the federal system. Each of these has a considerable impact on the national security of Pakistan.

Pakistan's history demonstrates that sturdy civil institutions and the supremacy of the constitution provided strength to Pakistan's security, while prolonged military rule made Pakistan more unstable and vulnerable to internal and external pressures. In 2007–2008, Pakistani society became prone to militancy, especially in the North-West Frontier Province (NWFP) and Balochistan provinces, mainly as a reaction to the highhanded policies of the military regime of General Pervez Musharraf. Musharraf had relied on military might to suppress the grievances of the people of Balochistan province and the areas on the Pakistan-Afghanistan border. Of all the military rulers of Pakistan, he lacked sufficient understanding of the civil values of the Pakistani society. Thereby, Musharraf was insensitive to the centuries-old traditions, culture, and infrastructure of the tribes and families of the land, which now form Pakistan. His harshness and callous policies gained him scores of personal enemies all over the country. On every account, .he failed to create a base of peace and stability and exposed Pakistan to more security risks. By the time national and provincial assembly elections were held on February 18, 2008, Pakistan had already exploded with suicidal attacks, targeted exclusively towards the military and police. General Musharraf had also become a direct target of hate by the civilian population of Pakistan.

One way to look at the domestic issues of Pakistan's national security is to examine whether it has the ability to conform to the requirements of a civil society. This becomes relevant as for more than half of its history Pakistan has been subjected to military coup d'états. The intelligence agencies belonging to the military, in particular, played a pivotal role in suppressing the institutions of democracy in Pakistan. In fact, Inter Services Intelligence (ISI) and Military Intelligence (MI) became notoriously effective in engineering the rigging of various elections, according to the preferences of each military dictator. These tactics were seen at their "best" in the elections of 2002, where General Musharraf used all the means to achieve the desired results. He was successful in establishing the Pakistan Muslim League (Q) through which he presented a civilian face, for more than eight years of his military rule.

Four phases of history can be identified where political process and participation was minimized by military dictators and civil liberties were curtailed: 1958–1969 (Field Martial Mohammad Ayub Khan); 1969–1971 (General Yahya Khan); 1977–1988 (General Zia-ul-Haq); October 1999–2008 (General Pervez Musharraf). In all, the people of Pakistan had to undergo the agony of five extra-constitutional martial laws. Musharraf has the distinction of imposing martial law twice, once against the elected government of Prime Minister Nawaz Sharif and the other against his own government in 2007. Each military ruler was responsible for the decay of Pakistani society in general, and the impediment of political structures in particular. The dictatorial periods cover more than half of Pakistan's 60-year history as a nation. This does not imply that Pakistan has been devoid of any experience of a political process. There have been interims of democratic process, which were either for a short period of time or were supervised by the military. At times, the democratic forces, consisting of various political parties, lawyers, students, and other segments of civil society, have clashed with the dictatorial rule. The mass movements against General Ayub Khan (1969) and General Musharraf (2007–2008) were consistent, and spread over a large segment of the society. And in spite of a brutal suppression by the rulers, these movements were self-sustaining.

The army's repeated coups were in violation of the wishes of the father of Pakistan, Muhammad Ali Jinnah. On June 14, 1948, while addressing army officers, he made it clear that the army must avoid politics and strictly adhere to their oath that directs them to "owe allegiance to the Constitution."[6] But all the army coup leaders, poorly educated and trained, gave their own version of building the national institutions and on all accounts, they failed miserably to achieve their targets. At the end of every Marital Law, Pakistan found itself grasping for remedies to re-establish the damaged national institutions. At the start of every democratic rule, repeated military interventions made the politicians "re-learn the ways of democracy. Unfortunately, the class monitors were the army and bureaucracy—two institutions that had known little else than autocratic rule for the most part."[7]

The people of Pakistan have time and again bounced back to establish democratic institutions, but the political leadership has failed to translate the will of the people into a meaningful conclusion. For example, the political elite could not make enough effort to eliminate state repression in one form or another. In the fragile democracy that existed in Pakistan at regular intervals, political parties were weak and democratic culture was almost non-existent. As a result, the remnants of repressive tendencies continued. Although, "through an alteration of incentives and the very functioning of the process by which policies are enacted, democracy makes the political system more accountable to constituents and decreases the likelihood that repressive behavior (especially the most lethal forms) will be used."[8]

The frequent collapse of a civil rule in Pakistan is not unique. Seventy examples can be cited during the twentieth century where various societies had a "democratic breakdown."[9] According to Robert Dahl,

> ...some democracies did weather their gales and hurricanes, not just once but many times. Several, as we saw, even overcame the dangers arising from sharp cultural differences. And some emerged with the democratic ship of state even more seaworthy than before. The survivors of these stormy periods are precisely the countries we can now call the older democracies.[10]

Pakistan can be categorized as a country where its civil society was able to stage a comeback, more than once, to establish democratic institutions.

Under normal circumstances, the evaluation and promotion of a civil culture helps to promote particular tendencies, upon which democratic institutions can be built. Another argument put forth is that Pakistani society lacks a political culture, based upon the norms of democratic principles, and therefore it could not attain its maturity.[11] A strong correlation exists between democracy and a certain kind of political culture. The habits and traditions of a people develop in an extended period of time, which forms the basis of a particular political system. There is a near-unanimous opinion in Pakistan that political process was not given enough space and time to establish itself into a workable and stable democratic institution. An extended uninterrupted time period is required for certain habits to gain ground. Traditions are established with repeated processes of trial and error while lessons are learned through practical applications of ideas and policies. It is, in this way, that societies gain maturity which in turn strengthens the state. In Pakistan, the frequent interruptions by military rule negated the basic principles of stability and the elements of institution-building.

For more than sixty years, Pakistan has been a battleground between democratic forces and military/dictatorial rule supported by a group of political opportunists. The latter believes that non-military institutions of Pakistan, like education, health, economy, and above all, democracy are the best solutions for the strengthening of the state and society of Pakistan. A vigorous debate has been going on in Pakistan, where a minority still believes that military security, i.e., the strengthening of military establishment, serves the purposes of national security. Meanwhile a large majority disagrees and believes in a state where military is only part of the security establishment. They are convinced that it is only through democratic institutions that Pakistani society, as well as the state, can meet its requirements of being a secure state. Kaiser Bengali, a respected economist, supports this argument. He points out that since 1977 (General Zia-ul-Haq's military takeover) Pakistan has turned into a "national security state." Bengali perceives that since national security has become a main preference of the ruling establishment, "development is no longer the main objective of the state and 'national' is being increasingly defined narrowly from the perspective of the military. Whatever the military thinks is national security is national security, and to the military, the military is national."[12]

The father of the nation, Muhammad Ali Jinnah, had clearly declared that Pakistan shall be a welfare state. While giving a presidential address on August 11, 1947 to the Constituent Assembly of Pakistan at Karachi, he promised that Pakistan will be a state for the "well being of the people, and especially of the masses and the poor."[13] Building on Jinnah's vision, Barrister Aitzaz Ahsan, a leading civil rights activist, argues that in order to legitimize its rule, Pakistan military changed the nature of the Pakistani society, thus moving away from the wishes of the founding fathers. It made Pakistan vulnerable and weak. He elaborates as follows,

> In my opinion, the father of the nation, Quaid-e-Azam, Muhammad Ali Jinnah and his companions had desired a welfare state–a social welfare state. (This idea was reflected in his various speeches and specially his speech of 11 August 1947.) In 1958 the army took over the affairs of the country. Even in those times when most of the developing nations were under the army rule, this action in Pakistan was without any legal and moral justification. It is the lack of legistimacy that forces the army to craft news ways to justify their rule, and the character of the state was modified in a discrete but specific manner. The welfare state was transformed into a national security state.
>
> We did a lot for the sake of national security by giving sacrifices, by accepting poverty and sufferings, as according to the policies of this new definition of a national security state. We were told that wars are necessary for the security of the state. Now, we all know that 1965 war against India was initiated by the military establishment. We also initiated [the] Kargil war, (by Musharraf, a military dictator). For the sake of the creation of a security state we turned our neighbors into enemies. One institution (army) became so prominent and powerful that the people were forced to submit to its wishes. We created a culture in which the head of the army became so daring that he terminated of the Judges of the higher courts (on November 3, 2007). For more than five months some of these 60 Judges were under arrest, along with their families.[14]

MALFUNCTION OF A POLITICAL SYSTEM

There is a long list of explanations that can be attributed to the problems of institutional-building in the polity of Pakistan ranging from the failure of elevating the literacy level to the development of a civil culture of the masses. During the lengthy tenures of the military rule, cosmetic organizations in the shape of representative bodies were established. These fell short of the requirements of any society, with the ambition of transforming itself into a modern, democratic, and stronger nation.

Before we move on to identify the instruments of the political system of Pakistan and the causes of the unstable political system, we will review those initial developments in history that became responsible for the "derailing" of the political process for decades to come. The instability of the Pakistani political system can be ascribed to the unnecessary and long delays in constitution-making and the untimely death of Pakistan top-level leaders in the early stages of the creation of Pakistan.[15] Both of these factors are directly intertwined. The death of such towering personalities like Quaid-e-Azam Muhammad Ali Jinnah and Prime Minister Liaquat Ali Khan encouraged petty bickering for leadership within the ruling Muslim League. As a consequence, an important task of institutional-building by providing a constitutional framework was brushed aside as a secondary preference.

Another element which greatly accelerated the unstable conditions was the introduction of bureaucratic personalities in the central decision-making bodies, which again can be directly attributed to the leadership vacuum in the political parties. Ghulam Muhammad, a civil servant, became the Governor General of Pakistan in October 1951, and another civil bureaucrat, Chaudhry Muhammad Ali, who was a Secretary General to the Government of Pakistan, became Finance Minister in 1955. General Iskandar Mirza, another ex-civil officer with an undemocratic mindset was elected the first President of Pakistan in 1956.[16] Muhammad Ali was a gentleman and an honest person but "his fate proves the general rule that a man who spent all his life in the ordered world of civil service rules and traditions makes a weak politician."[17] According to Asaf Hussain, a noted writer on Pakistani politics, from 1951 onwards, "the political system of Pakistan was under complete bureaucratic control."[18] Once firmly entrenched in politics, there was no going back for the bureaucracy.

The most serious blow to the already fragile political process, however, was the Martial Law of 1958, just before the first general elections were going to be held. It was widely speculated that the elections would bring the Pakistan Muslim League back into power, which would, in turn, become a source of national integration. It was also expected that the government formed following the first general elections after independence would commence a system of democratic political process and participation. The scrapped elections could have sorted out the contentious issues presented within Pakistani society and within the provinces. These frictions lingered for decades to come. Ten years of Ayub Khan's rule, i.e., from 1958 to 1968 was apparently a period of "stability" and "economic take-off," but the consequences which this decade generated for the future were so disastrous, that it became nearly impossible to cure the wounds inflicted by Ayub's policy of discrediting politicians and the political parties. The whole body-politic of Pakistan was thus damaged. While analyzing the institutional bases of power in Pakistan, Angas Maddison writes,

> In Pakistan, political power has been concentrated on the bureaucratic-military elite who were the successors of the British Raj. In the 1950s, they functioned with a parliamentary façade of politicians and ministers drawn largely from landlord interests, but there was no genuine general election in Pakistan before 1970, and the government has been a

military dictatorship since 1958. The main beneficiaries of independence have been . . .
the bureaucracy and military themselves who have enjoyed lavish perquisites and have
grown in number. . . .[19]

The above assessment made more than three decades ago was true even in
2008. The civilian/military bureaucracy not only maintained its tendency to gain
political power, but became the single most "effective political organization."
This condition certainly proved to be harmful for the development or even the
minimum working of political process and building of the institutions. Many
developed or developing democratic societies around the world provide evidence
that civilian/military bureaucratic organizations do not help to solve tensions and
disputes in societies. The management of conflicts cannot be solved and ultimately such nations become more insecure and vulnerable.

The national and provisional elections of 1970 and 1977 and the consequences,
thereafter, indicated a clear phenomenon. The lesson of the two elections is that if
the real results of political participation are tampered with, or if its final conclusion
is frustrated, then the result will be disastrous. In 1971, power was not handed over
to East Pakistan-based Awami League under Sheikh Mujibur Rahman, although it
got the majority of the seats in the National Assembly. While in 1977, elections
were rigged beyond tolerable proportions by the Bhutto administration. In other
words, in both instances a normal channel of political process was not allowed to
operate. The result of the will of the people was not allowed to meet its logical con-
clusions, as was required and expected. The weakening of the procedures of political participation and political process further prompted the already entrenched
military/bureaucracy to take control of the Pakistani polity. There cannot have
been a more domestic security threat to Pakistan than the impediment of
democratic institution-building and involvement of the people of all provinces
and areas. Without their participation, the state of Pakistan faced numerous
domestic security threats and the basic issues of dissention could not be solved
either by five Martial Laws or by the authoritarian rules of military dictators. Without the conviction of involvement by all provinces and areas, Pakistan, as history
demonstrates, could not achieve even the basic criteria of domestic security.

It is understandable that when military takes over, it establishes its own system
and that the political participation of the people remains extremely low. In
the case of Pakistan, a comprehensive political process could not find a suitable
place even when the democratically elected governments were in place. Still, in
the highest arena of political participation, which is the electioneering process,
where the involvement should be expected to be highest, it remained less than
expected. The exception was the 1970 elections.

In July 1977, Zulfikar Ali Bhutto's government was replaced by an extensive
and brutal Martial Law imposed by Bhutto's handpicked Chief of Army Staff,
General Zia-ul-Haq. The Martial Law became a source to derail the democratic
process in the country, with serious negative consequences. The fact remains,

Table 3.1 Phases of Political Participation in Pakistan: 1947–2011.

Nature of the Regimes	Years	Level of Participation
Parliamentary	1947–1958	High/Medium
Martial Law	1958–1962	Low
Presidential (Controlled Democracy)	1962–1969	Medium
Martial Law	1969–1971	Low
Parliamentary	1971–1977	High
Martial Law	1977–1985	Low
Presidential/Parliamentary (Controlled Democracy)	1985–1988	Medium
Parliamentary	1988–1999	High
Martial Law	1999–2002	Low
Parliamentary (Controlled Democracy)	2002–2008	Low/Medium
Martial Law	March 3–Dec. 15, 2007	Low
Presidential/Parliamentary (Struggle for Power)	2008–present	High/Medium

Source: Author's Observations.

however, that Bhutto's government fell far short of peoples' desires. His policy of nationalization was a complete disaster and as promised by the Pakistan Peoples Party (PPP)'s election manifesto, most were unable to improve their economic status. The Parliament under Prime Minister Bhutto was dominated by landlords and the representatives of the popular sentiments were set aside. Lawrence Ziring describes Bhutto as "predetermined by upbringing and temperament to be a domineering manager of people, never their true representative."[20]

By the time the next general elections (on party basis) were held in 1997, people had lost faith in the delivery capacity of the political parties and in the successive governments that were formed, not on the basis of efficiency and honesty, but on personal expediency.

The voter turnout in Pakistan, as seen in Table 3.2, in the last six national and provisional elections was less than 50 percent. In fact, after the 1990 elections, the percentage of voters dropped from 45.5 percent to 35.9 percent in 1997, while in the elections of 2002 the voter turnout was 41.8 percent. It should be noted that in 2002 elections, the voting age was reduced from 21 to 18, thus a large part of the younger population became eligible to take part in the electoral process and, as a result, the total number of registered voters increased from 54,189,534 (1997) to 71,358,040 (2002). Theorists of political participation have prescribed a number of reasons for the lack of interest of the Pakistani people in the political process of a society. According to Robert A. Dahl and Bruce Stinebrickner, one of the reasons that people refrain from taking part in the political process and especially in elections, is that they lose hope, either in the system or that they believe that their conditions could not be improved with the change of a regime.[21] They argue that,

Table 3.2 National Elections (1988–2008): Voter Turnout and Civilian Prime Ministers

Election Years	Turnout as % of Electorate	Prime Minister
1971	68.7	Zulfiqar Ali Bhutto
1988	43.1	Benazir Bhutto
1990	45.5	Nawaz Sharif
1993	40.5	Benazir Bhutto
1997	35.92	Nawaz Sharif
2002	41.8	Mir Zafar Ullah Khan Jamali
2008	45	Syed Yousaf Raza Gillani

when people expect high rewards from an activity; they may be willing to overcome great obstacles and incur high costs to gain them. But when they believe the rewards are going to be low or nonexistent, even modest obstacles and costs are enough to discourage them. In either case, the more things that stand in the way of political participation, the less participation there is likely to be. Why bother to climb over a fence if the grass is not greener on the other side? And why risk arrest and injury or even death to break through police lines set up to prevent people from demonstrating in a particular location unless high rewards for doing so can reasonably be expected?[22]

The theoretical presumptions of the above-mentioned scholars can safely be applied to Pakistani voting behavior, as successive political governments mentioned in Table 3.2 failed to fulfill the aspirations of the voters and instead, used either their influence to amass wealth, or to take privileges for themselves and their families. These are the reasons that whenever the Pakistani military staged a coup or when the governments (1988–1999) fell in quick succession, there was no visible public reaction. In the dismissal of nearly all these governments, serious charges of corruption and administrative malfunctions were levied. However, in ultimate analysis, the burden of fault lies with the repeated intervention by the military in Pakistani politics, based on the self-interest of army generals. The democratic culture and the strengths of democratic institutions were never allowed to solidify due to frequent military interventions. It has been analyzed that,

Military rule needs to be justified by those who impose it. One reason often cited is the ineptitude or downright venality of the political leadership. It is true that many of our political leaders have failed to govern efficiently for the public good, have relied on autocratic manipulation of their parties, ignored their constituencies, indulged in petty palace intrigues and have been far from honest in their dealings.

But it is repeated military intervention that is at the root of our inability to produce a cadre of credible political leaders and workers. In the crippling, stultifying Zia ul Haq era, military rule was presented to us swathed in folds of religiosity and ideology.[23]

The political process in Pakistan presents a complex scenario in which different forms of political representation have been introduced. It is interesting to note that the military regimes narrowed the base of representation at the national level and encouraged grassroots representation through non-party local bodies to reduce the strength of various national political actors in 1979, 1983, 1987, 1991, and 2000. The civil regimes focused more on party politics, thus encouraging representation at national level through various political parties. In the absence of elected assemblies, local governments became the only popularly elected bodies. However, these bodies failed to replace democratic institutions at the provincial and national level. Although they were designed to compensate for the lack of electoral bodies, on all accounts, they failed to do so.

During the military rule of Zia-ul-Haq, Prime Minister Mohammad Khan Junejo, who was handpicked by Zia, was considered apparently a "weak" leader. To the pleasant surprise of the Pakistan civil society, he tried to assert his authority as a civilian parliamentary leader. This brought him in conflict with the military leader on a number of occasions. His stance to expose the corrupt practices of the army, as an institution in general and the Zia regime in particular, was applauded by the civil society. While "Zia ul Haq's main interest was to keep the new civilian arrangement under his tutelage and protection and advancement of the interests of his constituency, i.e., the military,"[24] Junejo operated under a tense situation, where army-civil relations came under extreme pressure. Apart from a variety of sharp differences between the khaki and the civilian leadership, there were at least two main issues that heightened Zia's dissatisfaction against his own Prime Minister. Professor Hasan-Askari Rizvi mentions that these were the disagreement on the peace accord on Afghanistan and the Prime Minister's resolve to investigate the destruction of the ammunition depot at Ohjari that involved some senior army officers for their alleged involvement.[25] It was pointed out by various critics of public opinion that the general in charge of the depot was responsible for the cover-up of the pilfering that took place in the arms transfers for the Afghan fighters.[26] Hasan-Askari Rizvi sums up the end of the civilian political setup by a military dictator is these words,

> Zia-ul-Haq came to the conclusion that the civilian government was not heeding his advice and that it was also ignoring the interests of the military. He is reported to have said that the military "needed patrons not prosecutors." On 29 May 1988 . . . (he dismissed the Junejo government). . . . the troops took control of important government installations in Islamabad, including the Prime Minister's house, radio and television stations. Such a drastic step was taken at a time when there was no political or economic crisis in the country and Junejo had just returned from a visit to China.[27]

Zia's legacy left the Federation of Pakistan weak and political institutions struggling to rehabilitate themselves. His unique style of governance had intensified religious-sectarian and ethnic divides that undermined societal cohesion and harmony. The subsequent civilian organizations from 1988 to1999 and beyond had to confront these gigantic issues of diverseness and other security risks in the country.

A basic characteristic of the Pakistani political scene remains that in order to gain legitimacy, even the harshest of military regimes accepted the utility of some kind of manipulated and controlled electoral representation to legitimize their rule, domestically as well as for the international community. For example, the elections of 2002 held under the Martial Law regime were tempered and were a "carefully managed transition from military to civilian rule."[28] However, the "awakening" of the civil society during the mass movement of 2007–2008, showed that military rule has been detested and never accepted by the people of Pakistan. This encouraged those who believed in the true spirit of democracy and the peoples' participation in the Pakistani political process.

Scholars like Mohammad Waseem argue that even when political parties had the chance to form governments; their structures were too weak to compete with that of a well-entrenched establishment. He notes that "the establishment is vastly more resourceful than public office holders in terms of institutional potential for access to information, talent and finances."[29] On the other hand, in spite of repeated models of weaknesses, politicians failed to construct their political parties on mature grounds. Personality remained the pivot, around which the party was supposed to operate, but time and again it proved to be fragile, but no lessons were learned.

MUSHARRAF: HIS DECLINE AND THE RISE OF CIVIL SOCIETY

When the army under General Musharraf staged a military takeover in October, 1999, the major political parties led by Benazir Bhutto and Nawaz Sharif had lost public support because of charges of rampant corruption and misrule during their administrations. At least, people were not inclined to take to the streets to oppose Musharraf. During the decade of democratic rule (1988–1999), the two main parties, the Pakistan Peoples Party (PPP) of Benazir Bhutto and the Pakistan Muslim League of Mian Muhammad Nawaz Sharif, were at opposite ends of the political spectrum. It was no secret that each conspired with the military to stage the overthrow of its opponent. Taking advantage of the shortsightedness of both political leaders, the army had its heyday behind the scenes. General Musharraf took advantage of the ongoing political intrigue and public apathy and eventually exiled both leaders, although for different reasons.

Musharraf, who had ruled Pakistan for nearly nine years without much resistance, suddenly found himself in the middle of a crisis in early 2007. The government mishandled an otherwise routine judicial matter right from the start. First, on March 9, 2007, the Chief Justice of Pakistan's Supreme Court, Iftikhar Muhammad Chaudhry, was suspended. Next, the order was hurriedly withdrawn since it contradicted the spirit of Pakistan's Constitution.[30] Then, the Chief Justice and his family, along with numerous judges of the higher courts, were virtually put under house arrest, which provoked sharp condemnations from across the country. On July 20, 2007, a thirteen-member Supreme Judicial Council dismissed the reference of General Musharraf and reinstated Chief Justice Chaudhry. He soon became a

symbol of resistance against Musharraf's dictatorial rule. A mass movement supporting Justice Chaudhry was spearheaded by lawyers and supported by opposition
political parties and civil rights groups.

In the months before Musharraf imposed his second Martial Law on
November 3, 2007, the higher court under Chief Justice Chaudhry showed its
strength when it dealt with habeas corpus issues and other matters that linked
the government to corruption. In the past, the military governments easily
intimidated Pakistan's high courts. Notable among the court decisions that went
against the regime was the issue of missing persons. At the time, it was feared that
many Pakistani citizens were being handed over to U.S. intelligence agencies
without providing valid evidence that they were involved in any unlawful acts.
General Musharraf writes in his memoir that for every person handed to the
U.S. administration, his regime received a large financial reward. The details of
the amounts received were not disclosed in his memoir.[31] The second decision,
which irked the military government, was the court's nullification of the sale of
the Pakistan Steel Mill, which was to be sold to a private party known to the
Prime Minister, at a much cheaper price than its market value.

The Supreme Court's new attitude put Musharraf on edge ahead of the
announced 2007 elections, which were important for his survival as Pakistan's
leader. The court had other number of contentious issues to decide that also made
the military leadership nervous: Can the president be elected twice by the same
assembly? Could the president remain in military uniform and still be president?
Should the two exiled leaders Bhutto and Sharif be allowed to take part in the elections? There were also questions about the transparency of the elections and the dual
nationality of the hand-picked Prime Minister Shaukat Aziz.

With the threat of an independent judiciary, Musharraf removed the Chief
Justice, but he miscalculated the resilience of the judge who refused to resign.
Musharraf also miscalculated the level of widespread public support for this
opponent of his military rule. Street protests also exposed the vulnerability of
his creation, the ruling Q League (the Pakistan Muslim League, Quaid-e-Azam).

This was the first time in Pakistan's 60-year history that a mass movement was
launched without the leadership of political parties. The politicians had followed
the dictates of the public mood and the legal community. This was also the first
time that the army as an institution became the target of public resentment. Previously, it was individual military personalities who were singled out for criticism. The large public demonstrations and the involvement of various sections
of the civil society sent a message that Pakistan was not, politically "fragmented"
along the lines of moderates and fundamentalists, as Musharraf had claimed.
Subsequent events illustrated that the real contention was between those pushing
for democratic reforms and those who supported the continued military rule.

Initially, the Musharraf regime thought public resentment would fizzle, mainly
because of the summer heat and the political apathy that had prevailed for the

last eight years. Instead, with every passing day, the situation worsened for Musharraf. Unprecedented public support for the judge and opposition to the government was apparent on May 5, 2007, when Justice Chaudhry was showered with rose petals and welcome slogans by millions of supporters, as he journeyed from Islamabad to Lahore. The trip, which usually takes about five hours, took more than 26 hours as he greeted supporters along the way. Many had waited overnight to greet their new "symbol of resistance."

On May 12, 2007, when the Chief Justice visited Karachi at the invitation of Sindh High Court Bar Association, an ethnic group, the Muttahida Qaumi Movement (MQM)—a staunch supporter of General Musharraf—blocked the judge from addressing the lawyers gathered there. Karachi erupted; after three days of riots, 48 people had died and more than 150 were injured. On May 16, General Musharraf gave his full backing to the MQM and showed no sympathy for the killings. The Karachi carnage further weakened his military rule, as well increased the tensions in already-stressed Pakistan.

In the process, the military damaged its reputation as a professional institution. During the events of 2007, there was a clear signal that army had lost its ability to perform professionally even against under-equipped tribes of Northwest Pakistan. Nearly 300 Pakistan army soldiers, along with their nine officers surrendered in August 2007, without firing a shot. The army personnel also gave away their 17 military trucks.[32] Further, the army's performance during a 2007 raid on the Red Mosque (Lal Masjid) in Islamabad also exposed its lack of professionalism and ability to perform better in a battle-like situation. The army and its generals also received a setback during an extensively prolonged civil movement to restore the judiciary. The army as an institution came under severe criticism by the protesting political parties and members of the civil society. It was targeted for supporting General Musharraf and his henchmen. Army personnel were forbidden by their officers to visit places outside their prescribed stations in army uniform. This humiliating restriction further depressed the army as an institution, especially the lower ranks. A message circulated that any weaknesses in the democratic organization cannot compensate for a military rule. Fed up with corrupt, incompetent, and inapt military rulers, the people in Pakistan had started to believe that even a "worse democracy was far better than a best form of military rule." As Prime Minister Yousaf Raza Gillani writes in his memoirs,

> Because of the personal character of some people in the army this institution is becoming controversial. Repeated interventions has not only affected its professionalism as an institution but also hindered the process of democracy, repeatedly. No matter how sincere the army might be, it is not within its jurisdiction to run the government. It is necessary that the army must adhere to the oath taken under the constitution, and confine to the protection of the borders.[33]

The Pakistani people had kept their hopes alive, even though they were forced to "re-learn democracy over and over and over again."[34]

The events of 2007, as presented in Table 3.3, highlight the challenges and turmoil that confronted Pakistan during this time. As the Table demonstrates, Pakistan was confronted with twin factors of political instability and threats from militant groups. Musharraf's misrule of 8 years and his desire to prolong his rule brought him in direct confrontation with the political forces as well as with the higher judiciary. This confrontation destabilized Pakistani society, but at the same time, it provided opportunities for civil society to recover in an effective manner.

Table 3.3 Year of Turbulence and Conflict, 2007

Date	Events	Remarks
March 09	Chief Justice of Supreme Court Iftikhar Muhammad Chaudhry suspended by General Musharraf, referring his case to the Supreme Judicial Council.	Lawyers around the country boycotted the courts and staged demonstrations, citing the act of Musharraf as extra-constitutional and vindictive.
May 12	More than 50 killed in Karachi riots. It was alleged that the pro-Musharraf ethnic party Muttahida Qaumi Movement (MQM) was behind the killings, when large number of people attempted to meet the suspended Chief Justice at the airport.	The Chief Justice had come to address the Sindh High Court Bar, where he had gone to celebrate the 50th anniversary of establishment of the *Sindh High Court Bar Association*. He could not leave the airport building and returned back to Islamabad on the next flight. General Musharraf, while addressing a rally in Islamabad the same evening, appraised the acts of MQM.
July 10	Red Mosque (Lal Masjid) and adjoining Jamia Hafsa girls' *madrasa* stormed by the army in Islamabad, in which 50 militants and eight troops were killed.	The Red Mosque, located in the center of Islamabad, had become a center of activity by the extremist forces of the Deobandi sect, with connections with the Taliban and other sectarian terror groups of Punjab province. In spite of blatant militant behavior for years, General Musharraf ignored their actions.
July 20	Supreme Judicial Council reinstates Chief Justice Chaudhry.	The Supreme Court in a 10/3 judgment reinstated the Chief Justice, stating that Musharraf's order was illegal. But the Chief Justice once again stood disqualified when on November 3, he was not asked to take a new oath of office, as required

(Continued)

Table 3.3 (Continued)

Date	Events	Remarks
		by the extra-Constitutional act of Musharraf, as Commander-in-Chief of the Army. During this period, relations between the Chief Justice and the President remained strained.
Sept 10	On his return to Pakistan, Nawaz Sharif is arrested at Islamabad Airport and "deported" to Saudi Arabia.	The former two-time Prime Minister was physically manhandled and forcefully put in a plane for Saudi Arabia. He had returned after Supreme Court's ruling in August that he could return legally to Pakistan. He returns, once again on November 25, after Benazir Bhutto starts her election campaign.
Oct 19	Benazir Bhutto returns to Karachi after extended self-exile. A series of bomb blasts kills at least 139 people at her welcome processions and many more are injured.	Benazir in a statement said, "The attack was a message sent by the enemies of democracy to all the political parties of the country. It was intended to intimidate and blackmail all the political forces and elements working for democracy and human rights. It was a warning not only to me and the PPP but to all political parties; indeed to the entire civil society."
Nov 03	State of Emergency imposed by Musharraf in the name of the Chief of Army Staff, and he issued a Provisional Constitutional Order, which replaced the country's Constitution.	The justices of the higher courts were ordered to take an oath under the new order or they would stand dismissed. The Chief Justice, along with several other judges of the Superior Courts, were removed from service and many of them underwent house arrest. It was an extra-Constitutional act, which is considered as a fifth Martial Law imposed in Pakistan. TV and radio stations were taken of the air. Countrywide protests and marches start.
Dec 03	Nawaz Sharif is barred from taking part in the coming elections by the Electoral Commission.	The decision was based on his previous conviction by Muharraf's court.
Dec 26	Benazir Bhutto assassinated after she returns from an election rally in Rawalpindi.	Pakistan Muslim League-N leader Nawaz Sharif announced a boycott of the forthcoming elections, a decision which he took back. The Pakistan Peoples Party decided to participate in the forthcoming elections.

THE ASSASSINATION OF BENAZIR BHUTTO AND 2008 ELECTIONS

Pakistan has had so few national elections in its 60-year history that every exercise to elect the national and provincial legislatures becomes exceptional. These relatively rare events were not only a mechanism for a change of government, but also a means for putting the political process back on the rails and redefining the provisions of the 1973 Constitution, which had been shredded by four Martial Laws. General Musharraf declared Martial Law twice, ironically once against his own government and on both occasions had distorted the Constitution, to suit his requirements for an extended rule.

The February 2008 elections in Pakistan were exceptional as they took place in demanding circumstances. Of these circumstances, the December 27, 2007 assassination of Benazir Bhutto was clearly the most dramatic and arguably the most revealing. Following her assassination, electioneering came to an abrupt standstill and the elections themselves, originally scheduled for January 8, 2008, were postponed to February 18 of the same year.

The Ministry of the Interior's controversial explanation of Benazir Bhutto's brutal murder spawned its own set of consequences, deepening the distrust of the Musharraf government. In fact, the vast majority of Pakistanis rejected the official explanation. The government's subsequent revised explanation—including President Musharraf's suggestion that it was her own fault that she had been shot—fueled more confusion and outrage.[35]

In a December 2007–January 2008 Gallup International poll, more than 48 percent of Pakistani respondents blamed the government for the assassination while only 17 percent believed that militant groups were responsible for her removal from the political scene.[36] Benazir's husband, Asif Zardari called for a UN inquiry modeled after the inquiry into the assassination of former Prime Minister of Lebanon Rafiq Hariri—an idea the Musharraf government opposed.

Neither the fears of Musharraf and his supporters nor the suspicions that they might rig the elections were misplaced. During her last days, Benazir Bhutto (along with Nawaz Sharif) had generated a healthy political process and had electrified the people, much to the chagrin of the establishment. It had seemed that Pakistan was on track to re-establish its institutions and to revive the constitution in its original form. Musharraf admitted in a U.S. *CBS* television interview that he was shocked—and no doubt unnerved—when Bhutto returned to Pakistan to contest the elections. In fact, the establishment had wanted to keep Bhutto and Nawaz out of Pakistan so that they could entrench the "King's Party" in the Parliament with a comfortable margin, ideally securing a two-third's majority that would preserve Musharraf's hold on power and policy prerogatives.

Fearing that his handpicked party would not be able to obtain a two-thirds or even a simple majority in the parliament, Musharraf panicked and took a number of steps to solidify his position. These steps included the imposition of

Martial Law of November 3, 2007, the dismissal from service of Supreme Court justices who objected to his extra-constitutional decrees and their placement under house arrest (along with their families), the gagging of the media, a brutal crackdown on civil society, the abrogation of legal provisions standing in the way of his becoming President while simultaneously holding the position of the Army Chief of Staff, and hurriedly packing the Supreme Court with individuals who condoned these acts. By the time Musharraf lifted Martial Law and removed his army uniform, he had acquired all the necessary powers to manipulate the elections and to impose himself as President for another five years. On the contrary It was widely believed that the Q League was on the verge of being routed by the time when the Bhutto assassination took place. Leaders of the Q League were no longer even addressing public meetings and were confined to a few places in Punjab.

In contrast, Benazir Bhutto, who was a national figure and a representative of all the provinces of Pakistan, had managed to achieve a reasonable understanding with former Prime Minister Nawaz Sharif, the leader of the Pakistan Muslim League (PML-N). It was expected that both the major parties would form a coalition government after the elections. Clearly, Musharraf had other ideas. On the eve of the Bhutto assassination, the U.S.-brokered "deal" between Musharraf and Bhutto lay in tatters, as trust between these two contrary personalities no longer existed. In this respect, the Bush administration totally misread the dynamics of Pakistani politics. Nor, apparently, did the aAdministration understand that Bhutto derived her support from the people, who in turn disliked, and even hated Musharraf for his dictatorial rule. By pushing Bhutto to become the civilian face of a military dictator, the Bush administration exposed her to various risks in Pakistan. And as subsequent events have proved, Washington had little or no leverage, either with the military dictator or on the domestic dynamics of Pakistan.

The national elections of 2008 had a number of repercussions for the national security of Pakistan. On a number of occasions, just before her assassination, Bhutto had stated that although she had strong evidence the elections would be rigged, she would participate in them so as not to leave the field open for the government party. All of the political parties, with the exception of those few which support Musharraf, expressed their apprehension about the impartiality of the elections. They further believed that free elections could not be held while Musharraf was at the helm. Nonetheless, the circumstances surrounding the elections, if not the elections themselves, were illuminating. The pressure of the civil society was so tremendous that the elections could not be "satisfactorily" rigged (apart from the pre-poll rigging) and the ruling party (PML-Q) was routed in the elections. (See Figure 3.1 for details of the party position in the National Assembly of Pakistan.)

Political forces opposed to Musharraf and his policies were able to form governments at the center and in all four provinces. Musharraf, who vouched that

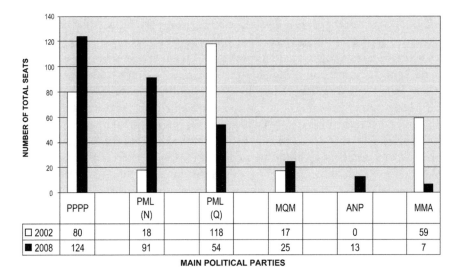

Figure 3.1 A Comparative Study of 2002 and 2008 National Elections Party Position.

Source: http://www.ecp.gov.pk/GE/2002/National.pdf; http://www.ecp.gov.pk/Misc/PartyPosition/NAPosition.pdf.

he would leave if rejected by the people stayed on, monitoring carefully the weaknesses of the newly democratic governments. Fears were expressed that if not removed through impeachment by the new parliament, he would certainly sabotage the new political dispensation. He had acquired sufficient powers by amending the constitution several times in the past and his handpicked judiciary could further support him in his actions against the elected parliament.

As in the past, the post-election skirmish between the presidency and its supporters and the newly elected political parties revealed that the conflict in Pakistan, contrary to many accounts in the Western press, was not between the "liberal" and the "orthodox" segments of society, but between the democrats and the dictatorial establishment. And, as a symbol of democracy and freedom, Benazir Bhutto did cast a huge shadow over the elections of February 18, 2008, no matter how they were pursued by the establishment.

Finally, on August 18, 2008, General Musharraf was edged out of office. His departure was not a result of any voluntary goodwill gesture nor did he resign, respecting the huge mandate of the people against his rule, in the February 18 national and provincial elections. He left because he could not withstand the charges of impeachment, ranging from violating the Constitution to gross misconduct. Behind the scene, moves were made to implicate him in the murders of various political personalities and a bloodbath in Balochistan and the Federally Administered Tribal areas (FATA region). He was also charged with handing over Pakistani citizens to foreign intelligence agencies, in lieu of financial rewards without enough proof of their involvement in terrorist activities. Another charge that Musharraf could have faced, if he had resisted the impeachment process, was that of squandering the national wealth by his government and close friends. In the end, the former commando of the Pakistan Army proved to be not as resilient as he had posed throughout his nine years of dictatorial rule. Notwithstanding Musharraf's vulnerability, it was the ultimate victory of the new political dispensation; the decisive victory belonged to the people of Pakistan. The otherwise ambitious army opted to stay neutral, when their former Chief of Staff underwent a series of humiliating experiences. Given the experience of the previous few years, a strong feeling existed in the army that due to frequent meddling in politics, it has compromised its professionalism and that a lack of discipline and commitment had entered its ranks.

The February 2008 elections gave a stunning defeat to Musharraf's handpicked party. The results of the elections were taken as a vote of non-confidence against the dictatorship and a victory for the democratic forces. During his tenure, Musharraf took great pains to advocate, inside and outside the country, that the people of Pakistan are not skillful enough to deserve democracy and that a system of his choice was the only solution for Pakistan.

After Musharraf's removal, a difficult task of putting the 1973 Constitution on the right track challenged the ruling coalition. Equally important was the issue of establishing political institutions in their respective spheres. The Constitution had been disfigured by Musharraf, first through the seventeenth amendment of December 2003 and then when he imposed his second Martial Law on November 3, 2007. Contrary to the desires of the founding fathers of Pakistan, a presidential system replaced the parliamentary institutions, giving overwhelming powers to the office of the president. The parliament, which is directly elected by the people, became a subordinate entity, operating at the whims of the indirectly chosen president, who in this case was also the chief of staff of the armed forces.

Democratic institutions are not established casually nor does political culture develop in a decade. It takes generations to entrench democratic traditions and norms in a society. Although more than half of Pakistan's history has been occupied by the rule of military adventurers, along with dictatorial rules, the people of Pakistan also waged magnificent popular movements to root out dictatorial regimes, as already mentioned in the first half of this chapter. The history of Pakistan presents a mixed bag of autocracy and a great desire among the people to democratize their society, according to the wishes of the founding fathers.

The dilemma of Pakistan has been that long spells of dictatorship uprooted democratic institutions and the process of institution-building was blocked. A political culture that is necessary for the functioning of democracy could not find its roots. As a result, whenever a dictatorial rule ended, the effort to create appropriate institutions were started anew. In fact, the whole fabric of democracy was required to be built again, confronted by numerous difficulties and obstacles. As the experience shows, the complete removal of the remnants of dictatorship remains a gigantic task. Some of the "unprincipled" politicians also play a part in the impediment of democratic institutions and the development of democratic traditions.

By the end of 2008, Pakistan was faced with a similar pattern of a post-dictatorial era. Without going into the details of the self-interests of some politicians and their apparent and hidden ties with the Musharraf regime, an immediate restoration to democracy was unlikely. There are a number of reasons for this prediction. Asif Ali Zardari's election as president will likely have a series of negative consequences. Firstly, as the co-chair of the ruling party (Pakistan Peoples Party), the balance of power was slanted against the parliament and the prime minister. There is a little chance that Zardari will voluntarily surrender the powers of that office, as according to the real spirit of the 1973 Constitution. Secondly, Zardari will not restore the judiciary to its original shape as it was on November 2, 2007, thus weakening a balance between various institutions of the state. Thirdly, his message after the 2008 elections that Musharraf will not be blamed for his heinous crimes against democracy and the people of Pakistan, points towards his "soft spot" for the former dictator for obvious reasons.

PROVISIONS FOR DECENTRALIZATION: THE SYSTEM OF FEDERATION IN PAKISTAN

In certain countries, federation or decentralization is created purely on the basis of administrative divisions, while in others, a country is decentralized on the criteria of either racial or linguistic considerations. Being a multiethnic country, Pakistan carries both criteria, namely the establishment of a provincial organization based on ethnicity as well as provinces further divided into divisions and districts. The latter divide is for administrative efficiency. In a classical sense, the federation has to have a legal/constitutional backing. It is the constitution that determines the division of power and its functions between the central authority and the provinces. However, a successful operation of the system in letter and spirit depends upon political will more than anything else. In the case of Pakistan, prolonged tenures of military rule hampered the functioning of a true federal system, giving encouragement to movements of dissention in the smaller provinces, like Balochistan, Sindh, and the North-West Frontier Province (FWFP). The dissatisfaction of the ethnic Balochi and Sindhis populations in particular, is based upon the fact that they are convinced that they are being kept away from the mainsteam of decision making and are being suppressed by the larger province, the Punjab. These perceptions became a main basis of insurgency and agitation, which in turn threatened the national security of Pakistan in a number of ways.

Table 3.4 Division of Population According to Provinces/Units, 1998

Province/Unit	Population	Density per sq. km.
Punjab	73,621,290	183
Sindh	30,439,893	99
North–West Frontier Province (NWFP)	17,743,645	112
Balochistan	6,565,885	6.9
Federally Administered Tribal Areas (FATA)	3,176,331	91
Northern Areas	870,347	20.7
Pakistan-controlled Kashmir	3,271,000	252

Source: Population Census Organization, Government of Pakistan, Islamabad, http://www.statpak.gov.pk/
depts/pco/statistics/pop_by_province/pop_by_province.html; http://www.ajk.gov/site/index.php
?option=com_c

Like the early colonial history of the United States, Pakistan at the time of its inception, inherited the existing provinces in British India: Bengal,[37] Punjab, Sindh, and the North-West Frontier Province (NWFP). Both the Bengal and Punjab provinces were divided on the basis of Muslim majority districts. Balochistan acquired the status of a province in 1947 (unlike other provinces it was headed by a Chief Commissioner). During the British rule, this area consisted of a combination of various tribal areas and princely states.[38]

BASIS OF THE FEDERATION

The Constitution of 1973 establishes a system of federation for Pakistan. According to Article 1 of the Constitution:

1. The Republic and its territories.—(1) Pakistan shall be a Federal Republic to be known as the Islamic Republic of Pakistan, hereinafter referred to as Pakistan.

1[(2) The territories of Pakistan shall comprise]
(a) the Provinces of Balochistan, the North-West Frontier, the Punjab and Sindh;
(b) the Islamabad Capital Territory, hereinafter referred to as the Federal Capital;
(c) the Federally Administered Tribal Areas; and
(d) such States and territories as are or may be included in Pakistan, whether by accession or otherwise.

As Table 3.4 explains, Pakistan is divided into four provinces which are uneven in its population spread. The provinces are comprised of four dominant ethnic groups which roughly correspond to the provinces: Punjabis in the Punjab, Sindhis in Sindh, Balochs in Balochistan and Pashtuns in NWFP. Apart from the recognized four major groups, there are other ethnic identities which have further complicated the ethnic balance, within some of the provinces. These ethnic minorities include the Mahajars or Urdu-speaking refugees from India, who are now nearly 50 percent of the population of Sindh and mostly reside in urban areas. This upset of the ethnic balance in Sindh province has created resentments and tensions, leading to political consequences. Apart from Mahajars in Sindh, there are such sub-ethnic groups as Makranis of Balochistan and the Khas and Kafirs of Chitral (FWFP).[39]

In Pakistan, the provinces were inherited with centralized political and administrative institutions from the British colonial rulers. These institutions were left, hardly amended, as they were at the time of the independence (1947) or were even further centralized. Although from the very beginning, it was agreed that the country would be a federation, (and in this regard, suitable provisions were made in various constitutions) but as experience shows the central government maintained strong indirect control over the federating units.[40] These policies contradicted the basic principles of a federation. The efforts and consequences to gain more control at the central government level is described below, which also directly relates to Pakistan:

> Many governments in Third World countries had become more centralized during the 1950s and early 1960s, after receiving independent from colonial regimes. They ... first turned their attention to nation-building and thus invested heavily in programmes for economic development. Both processes seemed to require and legitimize centralized management. But, over time the modest and sometimes negative consequences of central planning and administration became apparent.[41]

With time, the Pakistani ethnic composition intensified and became more complex. For example, with the rapid increase in population, the province of Punjab became too unwieldy to be justified as a manageable and effective single administrative unit. Furthermore, the province has various linguistic compartments, based on colloquial differences. Saraiki-speaking Punjabis, living in the south of Pakistan, regard themselves as a separate linguistic entity. The northern Punjab goes with the identity of Pothohar Plateau, while the central Punjab has its own characteristics.

In the Sindh province, the divergence of Sindhi-speaking and Urdu-speaking populations reached ugly proportions as witnessed in the riots of 1972 (which took serious turns in subsequent years), and as a consequence, a quota for government services was reserved on the basis of urban-rural divisions, which in fact was a recognition of the existing ethnic/linguistic divide in the province.

In Balochistan, the Pashto-speaking tribes constitute nearly half of the population. The rest of the province is further sub-divided by Makaranies and Brohies, i.e., apart from the Balochi-speaking residents of the province. The anthropological composition in NWFP province has its own controversies in Hindko-speaking people on the one hand and the differences in racial and ethnic characteristics of the population of Hazara region of the province, which are non-Pashtuns, on the other hand. Not to be ignored is the adjoining semi-autonomous tribal belt under the federal/provincial control, with cultural, political and strategic fallout on the province as well on Pakistan as a whole. Therefore, it did not come as a surprise when in the early 1970s, with the advent of new political dispensation under the

1973 Constitution, that the provinces had a chance to adopt their respective provincial language, but both Balochistan and NWFP choose Urdu as a compromise.
As explained here,

> Urdu was not seriously opposed at the provincial level in Baluchistan and NWFP
> because these provinces were not linguistically homogeneous. In NWFP, demanding
> Pashtu as a provincial language would have led to conflict with Hindko speakers, and
> indeed, tensions arose between the two linguistic communities in the 1970s. Baluchistan
> was even more heterogeneous . . . of which 41 percent was Pashtu speaking. . . . To call
> for Baluchi as a provincial language would have entailed recognizing Pashtu, to say noth-
> ing of Brahvi.[42]

With the demographic balance altered, the original shape of the respected provincial societal composition moved away from the rudimentary structures.
Though mild, there have been demands to readjust the intra-provincial structures. For example, the Siraki, south of the Punjab province, has hinted for a separate provincial status; while the population of Hazara in NWFP feels
uncomfortable when Pashtun nationalism is advanced. The Pashtuns of Balochistan have established their own political dynamic which is different from that of
the Baloch tribes. It is recognized that the shifts in the location of various ethnic
groups can be seen in a core-periphery (majority/minority) relationship, where
"the very location of the core and the periphery may shift over time, affecting
the roles of the peoples living in each."[43] The minority or less effective ethnic
group in an intra-provincial context can establish an alliance with nationally
based majority ethnic groups, thus enhancing its power base. In this way, it can
share in the benefits of the national government.[44] A typical example is when
the Muttahida Quami Movement (MQM), which had a "periphery" status in
Sindh, joined with the Punjab-based national government of Nawaz Sharif in
the 1990s for political and economic gains.

Apart from the provincial organization, there are 7 federally and 12 provin-
cially administered tribal areas. These administrative units are called Agencies
which are headed by a political agent, who is member of the bureaucracy, usually
belonging to the civil service of Pakistan. Tribal areas are fairly autonomous in
conducting their affairs especially in matters of justice. The laws governing the
tribal areas are particular to each tribe, and the Pakistani courts have no jurisdiction over the areas. The Northern Areas is a unique component of the state of
Pakistan, consisting of former Gilgit and Baltistan Agencies, bordering Afghanistan
and the Peoples' Republic of China. This area was under the administrative control
of the Ministry of Interior, States, Frontier Regions, and Kashmir Affairs. This area
for years was in the category of "no-man's land," waiting for its defined status.
Finally, the new political set-up of Gilgit-Baltistan (GB) was established in
August 2010, with a promise to become a full fledge fifty province of Pakistan.[45]
Ethnically the Northern Areas are inhabited by Shina- and Burushaski-speakers
with Balti people in the Baltistan sub-division of the area.

Previously, the 1962 Constitution (abrogated in March 1969) had centralized the federal system by adopting a strong presidential system of government. During the Ayub era (1958–1968), the central government was powerful to its maximum extent in administrative as well as financial matters. Moreover, the central civil service of Pakistan became virtually the masters of the destiny of the people of Pakistan.[46] The above described state of affairs can be summed up as follows,

> The federal principle was seriously compromised by the Constitution of 1956. Whatever was left of it was destroyed by the Constitution of 1962. The demand for the dissolution of One-Unit was a demand for both the restoration of autonomy and the revival of federation in a democratic environment. The 1973 Constitution had met the demand by conferring the residuary powers on the provinces in addition to the power to legislate on a large number of subjects in the concurrent list.[47]

According to the 1973 Constitution, Articles 141–152 establish the institution of the Federation System in Pakistan. Articles 153–174 were included in order to make the center-province relations and inter-provincial relations more viable and effective.

The Constitution of 1973, unanimously framed by the elected National Assembly, tried to establish a balance of legislative powers between the center and the provinces, at least in theory. Federalism being the most contentious issue received the most attention during the debate preceding the adoption of 1973 Constitution. It is no surprise that the "most strenuous battle was over the extent of the powers of the provinces and of the federation,"[48] especially when the constitution-making took place in the aftermath of the violent secession of an important province of East Pakistan. It was understood at the time that a workable federal system, agreed by all the provinces, could reduce friction between various ethnic populations of the provinces and that it could guarantee national security for Pakistan. It was also intended that the example of East Pakistan should not be repeated. In fact, more powers have been given to the provinces as has never happened before in the constitutional history of Pakistan. However, in case of inconsistency, the Constitution gives the benefit to the center. But this is relevant in the case of Concurrent Legislative List, which both the center and provinces share. The residuary power remains with the provinces.

Another important aspect of the system of federation in Pakistan is the establishment of Senate. Article 50 says that there shall be a Parliament consisting of two Houses to be known as the National Assembly and the Senate. The National Assembly is elected on the basis of population, while the Senate equally represents the provinces. There is also a representation from the Tribal Areas. Although Money Bills originate only in the National Assembly and are not required to transmit to the Senate, in all other legislation, the Bill must be passed by the Senate. The Senate acquires a unique position that it remains a continuous body when a provision is made.[49] It also forms part of the Electoral College for the election of the President, who according to the Constitution, is symbol of the unity of the federation.

APPLICATION OF THE FEDERAL SYSTEM

When it came to the practical application of the federal provisions, the trends of centralization became substantially obvious. The central government, even during Prime Minister Bhutto's time, who was the main architect of the system, allowed provincial autonomy only if the provinces went along with the policies of his central government. National integration could have been achieved with more success if relevant constitutional provisions were applied and given a fair chance to function.

The problem of adjusting ethnic aspirations along with the difficult task of nation-building is widespread and is not confined to Pakistan alone. There are very few societies which can be regarded as ethnically homogeneous. In Pakistan, there is increased realization that ethnicity is not an artificial phenomenon. It is an accepted reality and the assumption that ethnicity can be weeded out or made extinct due to the competence of a centralized system has now been accepted as a null hypothesis. It is assumed that if a political system fails to create a balanced and viable system of federation, it can become an agitational phenomenon. The negative fallout, if allowed to grow, can lead to the disintegration of the political system and the country itself,[50] as witnessed in the case of East Pakistan. The succession of that province was, in fact, a failure of the system of federation. There has to be a justifiable autonomy for the provinces, as provided by the Constitution in letter and spirit.[51]

The extended tenures of military dictatorships, with a strong central government, as mentioned in the beginning of this chapter, not only created a sense of alienation among the smaller provinces, but also violated one of the basic characteristics of the Constitution, which was agreed in 1973 by a unanimous consensus of all the ethnic population of Pakistan. During military rules, in particular, in violation of the wishes of the founding fathers, the country for all practical reasons had become a unitary system.[52]

The demand for provincial autonomy still remains strong, although with some exceptions. With the highhandedness of Musharraf's regime towards ethnic minorities in Balochistan and the FATA areas, a realization grew stronger among mainstream political parties that it was not possible to govern without inducting all the provinces and areas of Pakistan in the central decision-making processes. The promises of the February 18, 2008 electioneering helped to reduce violence as a means of achieving provincial autonomy, especially in the volatile Baloch areas of Balochistan province. The elections of 2008 and the political balance which they established, provided an undertaking that necessary measures will be provided in the laws to correct the imbalance between the federal and provincial governments. Furthermore, the federal government that came into being as the result of these elections was dominated by Pakistan Peoples Party, with a power base in the smaller province of Sindh. Punjab's dominant political parties in the present dispensation have been sidelined in the formation of the federal government.

Pakistan has come a long way from the times when any demand or even mention of provincial autonomy (as according to the Constitution) or rights for the minority ethnic communities was taken as treason, an "anti-Pakistan" gesture. This is a departure from the mindset where the "elite of Pakistan viewed regional and linguistic identities as inherently dangerous and as undermining the 'national project'."[53]

CONCLUSION

This chapter dealt with political/constitutional institutions, while the next chapters will analyze various domestic armed conflicts and tensions. All of these developments put together have been a cause of serious security concerns for Pakistan in recent years. The elements discussed in these chapters are intertwined with considerable consequences for each other. Workable political process with widespread participations by all the ethnic components can manage tensions and conflicts. Freely elected legislative bodies provide a forum for dialogue and discussion between various stakeholders. In the dictatorial eras of Pakistan history, differences of opinion were suppressed and opinions were throttled. This resulted in the eruption of violence and the tendencies of separateness became more chronic in the smaller provinces. Even within a province, like Sindh, intra-provincial ethnic conflicts were allowed to fester and as a result, civil institutions were severely weakened.

The strength of the Constitution in its relation to solve ethnic issues cannot be measured unless the document is applied, in letter and in spirit. If the Constitution has any shortcomings or deficiencies, there are provisions to make amendments as and when suited to the new requirements. Commenting on the viability of the Constitution, which carries the blueprints of the governance in all its manifestation, including the federal system in Pakistan, a noted scholar on Pakistan writes,

> Constitutions can be simply words printed on paper, or they can be "cornerstones of a nation," embodying within the words the philosophy, and a plan of action to carry out that philosophy, of a group of people organized for political purposes into a nation-state. The proof of the latter can only be found one time, in which the people at large and their representatives in the government and the opposition adhere to the spirit as well as the letter and cooperate to work for the nation under the rules of the game laid out in the basic law.[54]

The Constitution functions more appropriately if it is subjected to the balancing perceptions of divergent political factors, power-groups, and ethnic minorities. The emphasis on the interaction of these groups towards a workable compromise is required from political leadership.

National integration, which is integral part of the national security, can only be achieved if various ethnic groups are provided with an equal opportunity to participate in the political process of the country. In other words, a politically-correct ethnic balance provides a harmonious environment for the functioning of the democratic and federal system. It can ease ethnic tensions, which in turn will help achieve the much required national security of the country.

NOTES

1. Morton Berkowitz and P. G. Bock, "National Security," in *International Encyclopedia of the Social Sciences*, ed., David L. Sills, Vol. 11 (New York: The Macmillan Co., 19), p. 41.

2. Sridhar K. Khatri, "What is the New Security Agenda for South Asia?," unpublished paper presented in Regional Seminar on *Non-Traditional Security in South Asia*; Kathmandu, Nepal; November 16–17, 2004, p. 3.

3. Jessica T. Mathews, "Power Shift," *Foreign Affairs*, Vol. 76, No. 1; January/February, 1997, p. 51.

4. Ibid.

5. Kojima Akira, "Redefining the National Interest for a New Era: A New Paradigm for Diplomacy," *Gaiko Forum: Japanese Perspectives on Foreign Affairs*, Vol. 3, No. 1 (Spring, 2003), p. 7.

6. Quaid-e-Azam Muhammad Ali Jinnah's address to the Officers of the Staff College, Quetta June 14, 1948. Mr. Jinnah further said in his speech, "...the spirit (of the Constitution) is what really matters. I should like you to study the Constitution, which is in force in Pakistan, at present and understand its true constitutional and legal implications when you say that you will be faithful to the Constitution of the Dominion." http://www.mfa.gov.pk/Pages/Qua_Speeches/RESPONSIBILITIES_OF_THE_DEFENSE_FORCES.htm

7. Shuja Nawaz, *Crossed Swords: Pakistan, its Army, and the Wars Within* (New York: Oxford University Press, 2008), p. 411.

8. Christian Davenport, *State Repression and the Domestic Democratic Peace* (Cambridge: Cambridge University Press, 2007), p. 10.

9. Robert A. Dahl, *On Democracy* (New Haven & London: Yale University Press, 1998), p. 157.

10. Ibid.

11. Robert A. Dahl states that, "the prospects for stable democracy in a country are improved if its citizens and leaders strongly support democratic ideas, values, and practices. The most reliable support comes when these beliefs and predispositions are embedded in the country's culture and are transmitted, in large part, from one generation to the next. In other words, the country possesses a democratic political culture". Ibid.

12. Dr. Kaiser Bengali, "Making Sense of Pakistan and its Economy," December, 2007. A lecture at *Shirkat Gah Office*, Karachi. Posted February 10, 2008. http://www.teeth.com.pk/blog/2008/02/10/transcript-of-dr-kaiser-bengalis-lecture-making-sense-of-pakistan-and-its-economy

13. Jinnah's Presidential address to the Constituent Assembly of Pakistan at Karachi, August 11, 1947, http://pakistanspace.tripod.com/archives/47jin11.htm

14. Speech transcribed and translated from Urdu by the author. Aitzaz Ahsan's speech at Association of Physicians of Pakistani-descent of North America (APPNA), Washington, D.C. June 29, 2008, http://pkpolitics.com/2008/07/06/appna-convention-washington-dc/

15. Quaid-e-Azam, Muhammad Ali Jinnah died in 1948, while Prime Minister Liaquat Ali Khan was assassinated in 1951. For a detailed account of the influence of bureaucracy and its effects on the political process and the malfunction of political parties, see Syed Farooq Hasnat, "Bureaucracy, Political Process and Nation-Building: The Case of Pakistan, 1947–1977," in Professor S. A. H. Haqqi, ed., *Democracy, Pluralism and Nation-Building* (New Delhi: N. B. O. Publisher's Distributors, 1984), pp. 126–139.

16. In April 1953, Abdur Rashid Khan, a senior police officer of the North-West Frontier Province became its Chief Minister. A. M. Malik, Chief Secretary, became governor of East Pakistan in 1958.

17. K. K. Aziz, *Party Politics in Pakistan: 1947–1958* (Islamabad: National Commission on Historical and Cultural Research, 1976), p. 36.

18. Asaf Hussain, *Elite Politics in an Ideological State: the Case of Pakistan* (Kent: Dawson, 1979), p. 73.

19. Angas Maddison, *Class Structure and Economic Growth: India and Pakistan since the Moghuls* (New York: W. W. Norton & Cp., 1971), p. 136, quoted in Robert LaPorte, Jr., *Power and Privilege: Influence and Decision-Making in Pakistan* (Berkeley: University of California Press, 1975), p. 12.

20. Lawrence Ziring, *Pakistan: At the Crosscurrents of History* (Lahore: Vanguard, 2004), p. 146.

21. Robert A. Dahl and Bruce Stinebrickner, *Modern Political Analysis*, 6th ed. (Delhi: Pearson Education, 2003), pp. 103–125.

22. Ibid., p. 109.

23. *Dawn*, Editorial, March 23, 2004.

24. Hasan-Askari Rizvi, *Military, State and Society in Pakistan* (New York: St. Martin's Press, Inc., 2000), p. 200.

25. Ibid, p. 201.

26. The media and non-official circles accused General Akhtar Abdur Rahman, Chairman, Joint Chiefs of Staff Committee. Zia detested the idea of his fellow army generals being accused of any wrongdoings by a civilian political set-up.

27. Hasan-Askari Rizvi, op. cit., p. 202.

28. Hasan-Askari Rizvi, "Electoral Process in Pakistan," in *Pakistan: Unresolved Issues of State & Society*, Syed Farooq Hasnat and Ahmed Faruqui, eds. (Lahore: Vanguard Books, 2008), p. 18.

29. Mohammad Waseem, "Functioning of Democracy in Pakistan," in *Democracy in Muslim Societies: The Asian Experience*; ORF Studies in Contemporary Muslim Societies–IV, edited Zoya Hasan (New Delhi: Sage Publications India Pvt Ltd., 2007), p. 199.

30. Article 209 of the 1973 Constitution provides for the procedure to remove the judges of the Supreme and High Courts through the Supreme Judicial Council. The president has no authority to act on his own. "A judge could only be removed by the President on the report of the Supreme Judicial Council to the effect that he was incapable of performing the duties of his office or had been guilty of misconduct. Such a report could only be made after due inquiry and affording opportunity to the judge concerned to defend himself." Hamid Khan, *Constitutional and Political History of Pakistan* (New York: Oxford University Press, 2001, p. 501.

31. General Musharraf writes in his memoirs, "We have captured 689 and handed over 369 to the United States. We have earned bounties totaling millions of dollars." Pervez Musharraf, *In the Line of Fire: A Memoir* (New York: Free Press, 2006), p. 237. Lt. Gen. (retd.) Shahid Aziz, who served as the Chief of General Staff (CGS) from October 2001 to

December 2003, spoke to *The News,* a leading Pakistani newspaper, in which he disclosed that "We did not know for a long time that the Pakistani nationals were being handed over to the Americans by the ISI." He added, "It caused a lot of resentment in the top echelons of the Pakistan Army when they found this was happening. . . . Musharraf had got the ISI engaged to collaborate with the American CIA without the knowledge of the rest of Pakistan Army." Ansar Abbasi, "GHQ had strongly opposed handing over Pakistanis to US," *The News,* September 17, 2008.

   32. Ismail Khan and Carlotta Gall, "Pakistani Militants Hold Army Troops Hostage," *The New York Times,* September 4, 2007.

   33. Translated from Urdu by the author. Yousaf Raza Gillani, Chah-e-Yousaf Ki Sada (Reflections from Yousaf's Well) (Lahore: Nigarshat Publishers, 2006), p. 262. In equal terms, another leading Pakistani politician, who was the acting President of Pakistan Muslim League (N), and is a member of the National Parliament writes in his memoir, "Nothing has been achieved by 30 years of army rule. The ruler generals have not learnt the ways of neither governance nor professionalism or even understanding of the wishes of the people . . . Whoever questions the lack of intelligence of the generals is branded as a "traitor" and enemy of the country. Patriot in their eyes is only those who agree with them." Translated from Urdu by the author. Makhdoom Muhammad Javed Hashmi, Han! Mee Baghi Hu (Yes! I am a Rebel) (Lahore: Saghar Publishers, 2005), p. 155.

   34. Shuja Nawaz, *Crossed Swords: Pakistan, its Army, and the Wars Within,* op. cit., p. 411.

   35. Ron Suskind, a noted Washington, D.C. insider writes that President Bush and Vice President Cheney had made up their minds that the U.S. would prefer Musharraf over Benazir Bhutto. Suskind reveals that Musharraf had issued a warning to Benazir Bhutto, when she was preparing to go back to Pakistan for the national and provincial elections. He writes that once Musharraf during their telephonic conversation warned, "You (Benazir) should understand something. . . . your security is based on the state of our relationship." According to the writer, "She (Benazir) hangs up the phone feeling as though she might be sick." Ron Suskind, *The Way of the World: A Story of Truth and Hope in an Age of Extremism* (New York: HarperCollins, 2008), p. 268.

   36. *Press Release on BENAZIR BHUTTO'S ASSASSINATION,* http://extranet.gallup -international. com /uploads /internet/Press% 20Release% 20Surveys %20 after%20 Benazir %20Bhuttos% 20Death.pdf

   37. Bengal, which was later named East Pakistan, became the sovereign nation of Bangladesh, as a result of fierce and brutal civil war in 1971. The Indian armed intervention helped the Pakistani army to surrender, giving way for the secession of East Pakistan.

   38. Balochistan consisted of a number of princely states with Kalat being the largest and most dominant. The other states: Makran, Las Bela, and Kharan joined Pakistan at the time of its creation in 1947. The Khan of Kalat was hesitant to do so. After a year of tensions and negotiations, Kalat was made part of Baluchistan province in 1948. In 1958, the port of Gwadar, was purchased by Pakistan from Oman for 3,000,000 British pounds. Iftikhar H. Malik, *The History of Pakistan* (Westport, Connecticut: 2008), p. 133.

   39. *Pakistan: An Official Handbook, 1975–81* (Islamabad: Ministry of Information and Broadcasting, 1982), p. 26. The 1973 Constitution of Pakistan declares Urdu as the national language; It is the mother tongue of only 7 percent of the Pakistanis. Punjabi is most widely spoken not only in the province of Punjab, but also in such metropolitan cities of Sindh as Karachi. Moreover, the dialects of Punjabi are spoken in the thickly populated areas of NWFP province, where it is known as Hindco. It is estimated that 63 percent of the population speaks

Punjabi. Sindhi is spoken by only 12 percent of the residents of Sindh province. Pashtu, the mother tongue of the Pashtuns, Brohi, Balochi, and Pashtu, is spoken in Balochistan with a combine percentage of 16 percent.

40. Dennis A. Rondinelli, John R. Nellis, and G. Shabbir Cheema, *Decentralization in Developing Countries*, World Bank Staff Working Paper No. 58 (Washington, D.C.: The World Bank,1984), p. 1.

41. Ibid.

42. Katharine Adeney, *Federalism and Ethnic Conflict Regulation in India and Pakistan, op.* (New York: Palgrave Macmillan, 2007), p. 146.

43. Theodore P. Wright, Jr., "Center-Periphery Relations and Ethnic Conflict in Pakistan: Sindhis, Muhajirs, and Punjabis," *Comparative Politics*, Vol. 23, No. 3 (April, 1991), p. 308.

44. Ibid.

45. For more information on the new set-up see Syed Farooq Hasnat and Shehzadi Zamurrad Awan, "Gilgit-Baltistan: Striving for Political Maturity." *The News (on Sunday)*, August 29, 2010.

46. Mushtaq Ahmad, *Pakistan at the Crossroads* (Karachi: Royal Book Co., 1985), p. 42.

47. Ibid., p. 43.

48. Craig Baxter, "Constitution Making: The Development of Federalism in Pakistan," *Asian Survey*, Vol. 14, No. 12 (December, 1974), p. 1074.

49. The rights of the provinces are safeguarded through the establishment of *Council of Common Interests*, which being a constitutional body, overlooks the interests of the provinces.

50. See Oliver C. Cox, *Caste, Class, and Race: A Study in Social Dynamics* (New York: Monthly Review Press, 1959).

51. Based on practical expediency, certain voices were raised to further divide the provinces, so that numerical dominance of one province over the other could be removed. Theodore P. Wright, Jr., "Center-Periphery Relations and Ethnic Conflict in Pakistan: Sindhis, Muhajirs, and Punjabis," op. cit., p. 302.

52. Dr. Farooq Hassan, a noted jurist of Pakistan argues that the rule of military and a system of federation are contradictory to each other. "In (the) . . . political perspective the incumbencies of the military regimes in the country during periods of direct or indirect army-led rule have had a disastrous effect on the integrity of the country from the angle of the federal principle." Dr. Farooq Hassan, "Pakistan's Federal Structure and the Constitution of 1973," *The Muslim World*, Vol. 96, No. 2 (April, 2006), p. 276.

53. Katharine Adeney, op. cit., p. 141.

54. Craig Baxter, "Constitution Making: The Development of Federalism in Pakistan", op. cit., p. 1085.

CHAPTER 4

Balochistan: Tribes, Issues, and Discontentment

INTRODUCTION

Any uneasiness, disturbance, or uprising in the Balochistan province of Pakistan is considered a national security concern with regional and international implications. The province is the homeland of scores of tribes and sub-tribes who, for centuries, have settled their disputes more with violence and less with negotiation and have habitually resorted to taking up arms on trivial matters. The first part of this chapter will deal with matters and issues that have an impact upon the construction of socio-economic and political attitudes of present-day Balochistan. The second part of the chapter focuses on the current demands and attempts to resolve the grievances of the Baloch people.

This southwest province is strategically located and has borders with the important Middle Eastern countries of Iran and Afghanistan. It has a coastline of 750 kilometers (466 miles), which stretches from Hab near Karachi to the port of Gwadar, (built in part by the Chinese) near the Pakistan-Iran border, along the Arabian Sea. The westernmost part of Balochistan is not far from the strategic Strait of Hormuz. The port of Gwadar changed hands when in 1783 it was given to Oman by the ruler of Kalat State. The Pakistan government ultimately purchased it back in 1958. It is no wonder then that Oman has a sizable Baloch population, working in different occupations, including the Omani armed forces and as palace guards. The province is rich in minerals; the country's largest natural gas reserve is located in Sui, the homeland of the aggressive Bugti and Kalpar tribes.

Balochistan is an awkward part in the federation of Pakistan. Although the province constitutes 44 percent of the country's total land mass, according to the 1998 Pakistan census, its population is only 10 million, which represents about 4 percent of the country's residents, making the Baloch people the smallest ethnic minority in multiethnic Pakistan. The population is scattered, with a density of 18.9 per sq. kilometers (7.3 sq. miles), compared to Pakistan's population density of 166.3 per sq. kilometers (64.2 sq. miles). Balochistan is not all Baloch as its name suggests; this ethnic group, along with its nearest cousins, the Brahvis, are 54.76 percent of the total population of Balochistan. The rest of the population are Pashtuns (29.64 percent)[1], while small minorities are the Hazaras (Farsi-speakers), Sindhis, and Punjabis.[2] The settlers are known as Balochistanis, who by 2009 had become victims of target killings by Baloch clandestine terrorist groups with dubious agendas. Some Baloch tribes stand out as vocal, aggressive, and at times, defiant towards the central Pakistani authority in Islamabad.

Unlike the other four provinces, which Pakistan inherited from the British in 1947, Balochistan was given the status of a federating unit as late as 1970[3], with Quetta as its capital. The reason was that at the time of independence, Balochistan was divided into three sections. A large section was directly under British control and was known as 'British Balochistan.' The second section was under the jurisdiction of the Khan of Kalat, who exercised his authority on behalf of the British, and was paid an annual substantial sum for his services. The third section consisted of lease territories controlled by the British.

Twice in its recent past, Balochistan has become a cause of concern for regional and international interests. First, during the Soviet invasion of Afghanistan from 1979 until their exit in 1988, the area gained its strategic significance and then again, after the U.S. war against the Taliban from 2002 onwards. In 1980, a large influx of refugees took shelter in the provincial capital, Quetta and the Pashtun majority areas. Since Pakistan helped the *mujahideen* against the Afghan occupation, the Soviets in turn started to cultivate some elements of the Baloch tribes, inculcating a communist ideology as well as encouraging them to emphasize Baloch nationalism, even to an extent of demanding independence from Pakistan. The Soviet objectives, as was speculated at that time, were to obtain a port facility in the Arabian Sea and the Indian Ocean, so as to counter the U.S. presence in the Gulf. Selig S. Harrison examines this scenario, in the instance if the Soviets had decided to play its "Baloch card":

> Moscow would give the Baluch [*sic*] sophisticated weaponry, technical advisers, logistical support, and funds, but would seek to avoid the risks and costs of direct aggression. Alternatively, Moscow might seek to use the threat of a Baluch [*sic*] insurgency to pressure Pakistan or Iran, or both, into granting the use of Baluch [*sic*] ports for military purposes.[4]

Bogged down with the Afghan occupation, the Soviets refrained from interfering further in Pakistan, as their weak position would have made it "difficult to organize an insurgency and to legitimize an independent Baluch [*sic*] regime."[5]

When faced with external interests, the ramification of dealing with insurgencies complicates security concerns of the Pakistani government. The Pastners, in their study of south Balochistan, completed in 1977, comment that,

> The problems facing the Pakistani government in dealing with Baluch [*sic*] secessionist agitation have been exacerbated by the active role played by foreign powers in fomenting such movements, either because of animosity toward Pakistan and/or because specific Balouch [*sic*] territories flank a zone of growing influence. A case in point, Makran lies in a strategic position with its western border on Iran and its coastal access to the oil-rich Persian Gulf.
>
> The Kabul-based Pakhtunistan propaganda campaign is aimed at the Baluch [*sic*] as well as the Pathans, while Ulfat Nazim's World Baluch [*sic*] Organization, influenced by Marxist ideology, works out of Baghdad with Ba'athist backing and seeks to organize the thousands of Baluch [*sic*] migrant laborers in Dubai and Oman.[6]

Since 2002, it is speculated by many analysts in the United States that al-Qaeda and the Afghan Taliban leadership was and perhaps, still is hiding in Quetta, the capital of Balochistan and that the Pakistan establishment was "soft" on these terrorist/insurgent groups, which affected the U.S. and NATO war efforts in Afghanistan. The Pakistani government strongly denied this charge. All of these events together turned Balochistan into a high security-related province for Pakistan, as well as for the Afghan/U.S. security environment.

BALOCHISTAN AND THE FOUNDING FATHERS OF PAKISTAN

The founding fathers of Pakistan, like Muhammad Ali Jinnah and Prime Minister Liaquat Ali Khan, were aware of the backwardness of Balochistan in all spheres of life, and on a number of occasions showed their willingness to redress the sufferings of its people. Before the creation of Pakistan and immediately after independence, they had pressed for reforms in the region of Balochistan on a number of occasions in their policy statements. These leaders were sensitive to the fact that the *sardari* tribal system, as institutionalized by the British, had done a great harm to the ordinary people, stagnating their growth both economically and politically and forcing them to live in the "Dark Ages." Moreover, the lack of administrative and political structures was a handicap for any future developmental plans that needed to be addressed. The areas during the joint rule of the British and Khanate of Kalat fell behind economically and politically, in contrast to the territories, which were directly under British control.

In March 1929, well before the idea of Pakistan was even conceived, Muhammad Ali Jinnah presented his famous Fourteen Points, in a meeting of the council of the All India Muslim League. This was an alternative Muslim agenda for the forthcoming constitutional changes by the British rulers. Realizing that the people of Balochistan were far behind the rest of the British Indian Muslims, in Point 10 of the document, a demand was made from the British crown to upgrade the status of Balochistan "on same footing as in the other provinces."[7] Again in 1941, while making a statement to the Indian Legislative Assembly, regarding a cut motion moved by the Punjab member Syed Ghulam Bhik Nairang that no reforms had been introduced in Balochistan for 60 years and that it invites, "the attention of the government towards the urgency of introducing reforms in Balochistan," Jinnah repeatedly brought the attention of the Assembly to this important issue. He said that,

> I want to say . . . that the percentage of literacy in Baluchistan [*sic*] is the question that I put . . . For 1936–37 it is 1.6, pupils attending [the schools], whereas you find in every other part of India the lowest is 4.1 and even in Coorg it is 7.5. I have got here a Statement of Educational Progress in Baluchistan [*sic*] from 1932 to 1938–39, and let me tell you that it is as stationary as the Honourable [*sic*] Member was in his speech . . . What have you done with these lakhs that you have spent in Baluchistan? Please explain that to us.[8]

In July 1943, the Balochistan Muslim League held its third session in Quetta, where Jinnah, in his extensive address, made a comprehensive survey of the problems that confronted impoverished Balochistan and the causes of its backwardness. At that time, the creation of Pakistan was still doubtful, but Balochistan with a sparse and "enslaved" population was regarded an important area for the visionary leader like Jinnah. He was concerned in particular, about the extremely low literacy rate and the lack of the resolve on the part of *sardars* and *nawabs* to help their people. The concept of self-help was nonexistent, and there is little of it which can be found even in today's Balochistan. The examination of the "Balochistan problem" highlighted in 1943 by Muhammad Ali Jinnah is relevant, even in present times. He said further,

> Let me tell you my friends that Baluchistan [*sic*] is a historical place. It has got a wonderful history but you have (you will forgive me) lived the same life. You have not made progress with the world or even with India, you have still your own system, you have been indifferent to what was going on in the world. You cannot expect to build up greatly depending upon external help . . . I wanted to awake you from your fast sleep . . . You have begun to feel what self-reliance means, and what self-respect means . . . You must create healthy social conditions. You must raise your people educationally and economically and you must create honour [*sic*] and pride in your people that they may feel from within that it is a great thing to belong to this nation.[9]

While comparing Balochistan with the other provinces, Jinnah said that while other areas are more advanced, the Baloch people should show cooperation and discipline and shun away from jealousies and not quarrel over small matters. In the same speech, he dealt in detail with the defects of a feudal system that had existed in Balochistan. He advised the *sardars* and *nawabs* that they must "realize that India is moving fast, the world is moving faster than you can cope with it. You, therefore, have to consider the time in which you are living and you must, if you want to serve your people, if you want to serve your nation, you must adopt yourself to the times in which you are living and the time that is coming hereafter."[10]

The plight of the Baloch and Pashtun people of Balochistan remained a focus of All India Muslim League, under the leadership of Muhammad Ali Jinnah, who was worried about the dismal situation of literacy in the area and the lack of representation from Balochistan. He brought the issue time and again back to the notice of the British rulers, exerting pressure to introduce reforms in Balochistan. On November 30, 1945, Jinnah issued a statement challenging the statement of Col. W. R. Hay, agent to the Governor-General in Balochistan. Jinnah said that upon the request of the Muslim League, a resolution was passed in the Assembly, "undertaking to send a committee to Baluchistan [*sic*] to suggest reforms."[11] He stressed that the Muslim League had placed "enormous pressure" on the British colonial government since July, 1943 for reforms. He explained,

> When I was in Baluchistan [*sic*] I submitted a strong memorandum to the then AGG (Agent to the Governor-General) on various points and a debate was raised in the Assembly later. The case of Baluchistan [*sic*] was published and broadcast in a well considered pamphlet which was distributed to members of the Assembly in the beginning of 1944. I maintain that it is the presence of the Muslim League that has secured these few things namely acceptance of the principle of election to the Quetta Municipality, representation of Baluchistan [*sic*] in the central legislature and grant of more money for education.[12]

In the same statement, Jinnah rejected the nomination of a representative to the Council of State from Balochistan by British authorities. He said that the man nominated is only "a big Khan" with no qualifications for legislative work and what is required "is a representative of the people and not an ornamental person."[13]

Balochistan's underdevelopment, both in terms of the social sector and in the politico-administrative domain, was recognized by the Pakistan federal government in its earlier days. There was mayhem in the country because of communal riots between the Hindus/Sikhs and Muslims and millions of refugees had poured in from India. There was no infrastructure for the new government to conduct even minimum functions. The entire country needed reforms and Balochistan needed them more than the other provinces. This peculiarity of the Baloch backwardness should be examined within the overarching problems and constraints of the entire country.

When Jinnah, the new leader of Pakistan, visited Balochistan in February 1948, just six months after independence, he reminded the people of his extended "personal connection with Baluchistan [*sic*]." He emphasized that for a long time, he had been lending his voice to serving the rights of the Baloch people in the Indian legislature and elsewhere. Muhammad Ali Jinnah addressed these issues at Sibi Durbar in the presence of the representatives of the tribes and people of Balochistan. He highlighted the backwardness of the province by pointing out that although Balochistan was divided in several parts by the British, it was "bound together in shackles of backwardness."[14] He went on to say,

The administration handed over to us was on the one had [been] quite impervious to the desires and wishes of the people for moral and material progress, and on the other, impatient of criticism and oblivious of the necessity of political reforms of any sort. Consequently, the people of the Province remained in a static position educationally, socially, economically and politically. Nay, I would go so far as to say that the people had to content themselves for a long time with a state of political and administrative stagnation.[15]

At that occasion, Jinnah announced that Balochistan would be a Governor-General's province until such time the new Constitution of Pakistan came into being and then, it would acquire the full status of a province as part of a federating unit. He reminded the gathering that he would see that "all plans for the future political, economic, social and educational development of the Province will . . . (be) implemented."[16] However, Jinnah died just five months later and the burden of reforming Balochistan became the responsibility of Prime Minister Liaquat Ali Khan, who by the fall of 1950, had appointed a Reform Committee on Balochistan. He was assassinated in October 1951; however, the committee presented its report to the Constituent Assembly on November 17, 1951. The committee took notice of the difficulties of imposition of a democracy in Balochistan, as it would confront stiff resistance from a well-entrenched tribal system. Under the circumstances, it was suggested that "the traditional political order would not be disturbed but the structure of administration would be expanded."[17]

The political chaos that followed in the country and the subsequent Martial Laws were not able to allow for the required transformations in the province. Balochistan's backwardness can also be attributed to the lack of the determination of self-help, as mentioned before, and its culture of dependency (derived from the controlled *sardari* system). An easy way was found by the regional tribal leaders to blame either the federal government or the prosperous province of Punjab for all the miseries of the Balochi people, many of whom where inculcated in the centuries-old stagnant tribal system .

Sardars, Tribes, and Discontentment

Over the years, Pakistan has experienced insurgencies by groups with secular and jihadist agendas. Although these two groups have had different agendas, both challenge the writ of the state, whether for valid reasons or not. The Baloch uprisings occurred in 1948, 1958, and 1974. The ongoing conflict which started in 2004 was due primarily to the highhanded policies of General Pervez Musharraf. The insurgency was secular in nature; it had no similarity to the Taliban insurgency in northern Pakistan. The foundations of these revolts, for both administrative and political reasons, go back to the legacy of the British rule and the recognition and support of the institution of *sardars* by the British rulers, under Sir Robert Sandeman's "Forward Policy."[18] Firstly, the Sandeman strategy institutionalized the *sardari* system while leaving no place for ordinary tribesman to opt for alternatives. His life and death was at the mercy of the *sardars*, whose actions were usually brutal and arbitrary. Secondly, while the British started to give self-rule to its Indian subjects, who were directly under their authority, the tribal areas of Balochistan and the Khanate of Kalat remained in primitive conditions. Unlike the British-controlled areas, this region remained indifferent to the socio-economic and political movements that had started to emerge among the Muslims of British India. British Indian Muslims had moved ahead by forming associations and educational-political platforms for the purpose of reforms. And as witnessed during the Khilafat Movement (1919–1924), these Muslims had associated themselves with the larger Muslim community with its international ties.

This kind of political culture and broad-based perspective were totally alien to the tribesmen of Balochistan. An ordinary tribesman had no concept of the surroundings and activities beyond his immediate vicinity and sub-tribe. The *sardar* and his family had ample opportunity to be educated in the big cities and had the chance to make frequent visits to Europe, while for ordinary Baloch tribesmen even a visit to the provincial capital, Quetta, was a lifelong dream. When Pakistan inherited these areas of Balochistan, the misery of tribesmen was asymmetrical with other parts of the country. The tribal areas and the Khanate remained devoid of educational and health facilities, and other basic amenities. Even after gaining the status of a province for nearly thirty years, the influence of the British system remained. The system had "petrified tribal customs and strengthened tribal affiliation . . . (and) as a result, political allegiance and political party organization were unknown concepts in Balochistan. . . . Forms of political or religious mobilization were not only unknown phenomena . . . but a yet undiscovered strategy of struggle."[19]

Pakistan's leading English newspaper *Dawn*, wrote an editorial on this issue,

> The sardari system is a medieval abomination whose continuation in the 21st century has done incalculable harm to Balochistan. . . . Among other factors, the sardari system, revolving round the absolute powers of hereditary tribal chieftains—even the power of life and death over their subjects—has been a major cause of Balochistan's socio-economic backwardness.
>
> The horrors perpetrated by sardars on their own 'dissidents' is a story unto itself. Some sardars maintain private jails, and the punishment for disobedience can range from eviction from land to death. A foreign journal quotes a sardar as saying, "What is better than seeing your enemies driven before you and then taking their women to bed?"
>
> The reason why the sardars find themselves well entrenched in Baloch society is the neglect which Balochistan has suffered at the hands of successive federal governments. Sardari, along with feudalism in other parts of Pakistan, should have been abolished long ago. That this was not done has cost the province and the country dearly. Z. A. Bhutto abolished the sardari system following the insurgency in the wake of his dismissal of the provincial government, but it was later restored. That helped the sardars reassert their

power, which they guard jealously. Ironically, these slave-drivers claim to fight for such noble causes as justice and freedom, because Balochistan hardly has any middle class which could take up Baloch causes with sincerity.[20]

Whenever a *sardar* or the Khan of Kalat wanted to increase their allowances or desired to attract the attention of the federal government, they raised the alarm of Baloch misery and slogans of Baloch nationalism. But, at times, the federal government was equally responsible for being ignorant of Baloch sentiment. Problems arose when some of the Baloch elements carried themselves too far in demanding equal rights from the federal government. Some of them demanded complete independence, with little or no agenda or vision for the future, or even with a substantial support base. According to an assessment, it often happened that "a war-like atmosphere was created and there starts the wrangle, without clear goals."[21] Such situations created complications not only for Pakistan's national security, but had serious repercussions for neighboring Iran. Iran, with its own restless Baloch population, is highly sensitive to any similar moves by its Baloch minority. Tehran considers it as a threat to its national security.

The Baloch nationalists base their ethnic identity and nationalism on folklore, history, and the role of the Khan of Kalat, who under the guise of Baloch nationalism, was desperate to preserve his privileges originally granted by the British Raj. The objectives and agendas of the Baloch actions have been conflicting and even competing with each other. On the one hand, the Baloch leaders claim to belong to a unified Baloch "nation," while on the other hand, they are jealously divided among themselves. There is a long history of inter-tribal feuds leading to brutal murders, vendettas that have gone on for generations, and arson and looting. Baloch symbolic identity suffered a serious setback when in 1974, the first Baloch provincial government, as a result of the 1970 general elections, adopted Pakistan's national language, Urdu as a provincial language. At that time, it was revealed that the Baloch language does not have a script. The matter of the Baloch language as a symbol of nationalism is further confused by various dialects amongst the Baloch tribes, with Barahvi being a dialect of Dravidian background. Moreover, the Baloch population is more backward and illiterate than the Balochistani Pashtuns, who share a socio-economic and political landscape. Thereby, introduction of the Balochi language, even if otherwise possible, "would have been severely opposed by the Pakhtoons [*sic*], who would have demanded that their tongue should also be given official status."[22] Secondly, as the Baloch were a slight majority in the province, they would be unable to enforce their language on a number of sizeable minority ethnic groups.

Pakistan's weak political and federal structures made the Baloch susceptible to various anxieties from a deprivation-driven demand for legitimate/constitutional rights to ideologically motivated groups emerging with a leftist ideology and leaning towards the Soviet Union. Lengthy periods of dictatorial military rules with centralized governance kept the Baloch tribes away from the decision-making process and hindered their political maturation. *Sardars* have led ordinary Baloch, most of whom are illiterate and poor, to believe that the policies of the federal government and the province of Punjab are responsible for their misery—in spite of the fact that on numerous occasions these tribal *sardars* and *nawabs* (a title conferred for services rendered to the British Raj) had the chance to govern, but produced little change.

Table 4.1 shows that in last four decades, i.e., from 1972 until October 2009, a Punjabi was appointed only once to an important position of a governor and only

Table 4.1 Chief Ministers[1] and Governors[2] of Balochistan from May 1972 to October 2009

Chief Minister/Governor	Tenure	Ethnic Affinity
Ataullah Mengal	May 1, 1972 to February 13, 1973	Baloch
Governor's rule Akbar Bugti (Governor)	February 15, 1973 to January 3, 1974	Baloch
Jam Ghulam Qadir Khan	April 27, 1973 to December 31, 1974	Baloch
Governor's rule Ahmad Yar Khan (Governor)	January 3, 1974 to December 7, 1976	Barahvi / Baloch (Former Khan of Kalat)
Governor's rule Sardar Mohammad Khan Barozai (Governor)	December 7, 1976 to April 4, 1977	Pashtun
Martial Law Khuda Bakhsh Marri (Governor)	September 1977 to September 1978	Baloch
Martial Law Lt. Gen. Rahimuddin Khan (Governor)	September 1978 to March 1984	Pashtun
Martial Law Lt. Gen. Sardar F. S. Khan Lodi (Governor)	March 1984 to July 1984	Punjabi
Martial Law Lt. Gen. K. K. Afridi (Governor)	July 1984 to December 1985	Pashtun
Martial Law General (ret.) Musa Khan (Governor)	December 1985 to March 12, 1991	Hazara
Jam Ghulam Qadir Khan	April 6, 1985 to May 29, 1988	Baloch
Zafarullah Khan Jamali	June 24, 1988 to December 24, 1988	Baloch
Khuda Bux Marri (Caretaker)[3]	December 24, 1988 to February 5, 1989	Baloch
Akbar Bugti	February 5, 1989 to August 7, 1990	Baloch
Taj Muhammad Jamali	November 17, 1990 to May 20, 1993	Baloch
Zulfikar Ali Magsi	May 20, 1993 to July 19, 1993	Baloch

(Continued)

Table 4.1 (Continued)

Chief Minister/Governor	Tenure	Ethnic Affinity
Mohammad Nasir Mengal (Caretaker)	July 19, 1993 to October 20, 1993	Baloch
Zulfikar Ali Magsi	October 20, 1993 to November 9, 1996	Baloch
Zafarullah Khan Jamali (Caretaker)	November 9, 1996 to February 22, 1997	Baloch
Akhtar Mengal	February 22, 1997 to June 15, 1998	Baloch
Jan Mohammad Jamali	June 15, 1998 to October 12, 1999	Baloch
Martial Law Amir-ul-Mulk Mengal (Governor)	October 21, 1999 to November 30, 2002	Baloch
Jam Mohammad Yousaf	December 1, 2002 to November 19, 2007	Baloch
Mohammad Saleh Bhutani (Caretaker)	November 19, 2007 to April 8, 2008	Baloch
Aslam Raisani	April 9, 2008 to Present	Baloch

[1]The Chief Minister is the chief executive of the province, elected by the provincial assembly. The normal tenure in office is for five years unless he/she loses confidence of the majority in the assembly. The Chief Minister forms a cabinet, which acts as an advisory body. The Chief Minister and his cabinet must be members of the provincial assembly.

[2]According to the amended 1973 constitution, the governor of a province is appointed by the President of Pakistan, as representative of the federal government. Previously, this position was filled by the Prime Minister. The constitution regards this position as ceremonial, but as the country faced many Martial Laws and dissolution of the provincial assemblies, the powers of the governors enhanced—especially in the case of Governor Rule, where they had vast administrative powers.

[3]A caretaker Chief Minister is appointed as an interim arrangement—to look after the next elections. He is non partisan and does not take part directly or indirectly, in the next elections.

for about five months. In spite of the fact that Pashtuns form a sizable number of the population in the province, nearly all of the chief executives have been from the Baloch/Barahvi tribes, including the former Khan of Kalat. Notwithstanding the lengthy spells of Martial Laws or army-managed elected governments, the chief executives of Balochistan had the ample authority, resources, and skills to bring economic and social changes to their province, or at least to their respective constituencies, both in their official as well as personnel capacity, but none took advantage of their privileged positions. As a consequence, Balochistan lagged behind in all spheres of economic activity as well as in social change and attitudes. All of the politicians at high positions were *sardars* and *nawabs* implying that the real problem with Balochistan is the social structure, which does not allow for the political growth of the common tribesmen. While living in nearly the same conditions, other ethnic groups like Pashtuns and Hazaras are more educated and enterprising in securing government and private jobs. In drawing an analogy with the rulers of the princely states of British India, the same can also be said about the *sardars* and *nawabs* of Balochistan,

> By assuring protection to the princes against external aggression and internal subversion, the British had secured their undeviating loyalty to the empire, but had weakened their moral fiber. Used to luxury and servile flattery from an early age, the princes were, on the whole, and apart from honorable exceptions, a decadent class. Interested more in their palaces than in their people, they paid scant attention to social and political reforms or education in their territories were lower than in British India. . . . Civil liberties were virtually non-existent; the will of the ruler, rather than the rule of law, was supreme.[23]

At times, the political elite in Balochistan province adopted ideology and agendas provided by national political parties, but the leadership still largely come from "traditional ascribed elites."[24] A look at various results of the provincial assembly of Balochistan, from 1970 to 2008, reveal that political parties are constituted around the tribal chiefs, who in fact are a political party within themselves and "serve as engines of political vehicle."[25] None of the Balochistan-based political parties could muster a majority in the province, as they were confined to the areas of their respective party leaders who were none other than *sardars*. For example, in 1988, in elections in which all parties participated, out of the House of 45, the Balochistan National Alliance (BNA) led by Akhtar Mengal, and the Pakistan National Party (PNP) led by Nawab Aslam Raisaini, won four seats each, while the Balochistan National Alliance (BNA) led by Marri/Bugti *sardars*, won three seats. Five seats were won by independents, who were also *sardars*. On the contrary, in the Pashtun area, of the 11 seats only two were won by *sardars*, while the rest went to middle- and lower- middle-class Pashtuns.[26] Except for the Pashtun areas, the few seats that were taken by the national parties like Pakistan Peoples Party (PPP) and the Muslim League were also won by the Baloch *sardars*. In subsequent elections, either these parties were divided according to tribal composition or they boycotted the elections.[27] By the time the 1993 elections were held, Balochistan had turned into a "nonpolitical" province, where independent members and the coalition of small parties blurred chances of developing an effective electoral and political culture. This further eroded the rules, discipline, and political morality which is necessary for the development of political institutions.[28]

According to a Baloch nationalist writer, "(Baloch) nationalism is a double edge sword. On the one hand a lot is mentioned (by common people) about democracy, political freedom, social justice, national equality, national movement but the *sardars* and feudal are the ultimate gainers, as they were the ones leading these national movements."[29]

Whatever the reason for Baloch underdevelopment and frustration, the contributing bases for various types of uprisings in Balochistan were bad government, lack of sensitivity of the military dictators and the callous attitude of the elected civilian offices, both at the federal level and in the province of Balochistan. It is generally perceived that the federal government did not take Balochistan as seriously as it should, and this impression will not go away, unless visible and well-advertised socio-economic and political reforms are introduced. This discontentment, accompanied by chronic suspicions, only added to the intricacies of complicated domestic security issues of Pakistan.

According to a former Senator from Balochistan, who left his seat in protest on June 7, 2008, alleged that even after the formation of a democratic government in the country, military operations continued in Balochistan. Sanaullah Baloch, the Central Secretary for Information of the Balochistan National Party (Mengal), in his speech at the floor of the Senate condemned the murder of former governor and Chief Minister of Balochistan, Nawab Akbar Bugti,[30] and the detention of other political leaders. He further said, "Balochis [sic] were as patriotic to the country as Punjabis, Pukhtoons [sic], Sindhis and Seraikis. The reaction of Balochis [sic] against injustice is termed as mutiny."[31] In an April 2009 interview with Pakistan's widely read English newspaper, the former Senator spelled out a list of grievances of the Baloch inhabitants of the province,

> Unfortunately, our deaf regimes and policy makers are not used to logical arguments. They only understand the language of power, force, guns and canons. That is why several resistance movements in Pakistan have taken on an increasingly violent character. Unfortunately, this becomes the culture in states governed by dictatorial regimes.
>
> However, I don't think that the non-violent aspect of the Baloch struggle has been non-productive. Our political struggle, media campaigns, diplomacy, extensive inquiries on Baloch deprivation and its expression has widened our support beyond Balochistan and Pakistan.
>
> From 2002 to 2006, as an active member of the Senate, I did my best to highlight the Baloch people's plight. I was elected by the people to protect their rights, but we could not stop Islamabad's assault on Balochistan. We could not protect the innocent Baloch from disappearances, torture, displacement and we could not stop our resources' unabated exploitation. That is why we decided to quit the parliament. It is better to be among the people and tell them the truth as opposed to giving them false hope.
>
> Unfortunately, this has been the culture in Pakistan that all legitimate political movements against injustice have been labeled as foreign machinations and leaders of those movements have been called traitors and agents. Even the credibility of the lawyers' movement was questioned by the establishment. Human rights defenders have also been labeled foreign agents. These are old tactics that all despotic regimes use to undermine legitimate political movements.
>
> According to one study, rural poverty in Balochistan increased 15 percent between 1999 and 2005. The only "development" Balochistan has witnessed during Musharraf's rule is the 62 percent increase in police stations.
>
> Meaningful development can only occur if there is political empowerment, adequate healthcare, educational and employment opportunities and peace. At this moment, there is no spending in these sectors.[32]

What the Baloch leader failed to mention was the generations-old, defective socio-cultural composition of the Baloch society, in which the culture of self-help and an extended community feeling is lacking. To make matters worse, there is no urban culture In Balochistan, except in its capital Quetta which is a multi-ethnic city. The rest of the countryside does not even have villages as in other provinces of Pakistan, rather it has scattered settlements consisting of few houses. In such situation it becomes difficult to build roads, supply water, and provide other amenities to the scattered rural population.

Revolts and Insurgencies

Ever since Balochistan became part of Pakistan, it has faced two palace revolts and two insurgencies. The palace revolts were limited in nature and scope, led by the Khans of Kalat. The Khans had a long history of association with the British officers stationed in Balochistan area, as Kalat was a princely state under the British Raj. As was the custom with the British, wherever required they ruled by proxy, granting privileges to the tribal chiefs, in exchange for maintaining law and order and promoting British interests in their tribal jurisdiction. A number of treaties were signed between the rulers of Kalat and the British, in which the rulers were bound to follow British policies and to serve the interests of the British. It was, in fact, a "subordinate cooperation with the British" and with few isolated incidents, the Khans obliged the British crown faithfully.

At the time of the creation of Pakistan in August 1947, Ahmad Yar was the ruler of the state of Kalat. While all other princely states opted to join Pakistan, Ahmad Yar showed reluctance to do so. His objective was to extract as many privileges from the newly established state of Pakistan as possible, and to devise such a method where he could keep his privileged and pampered position intact. Khan's indecision prompted a Baloch like Muhammad Murad Awarani, secretary of Baloch Jama'at to say, "Kalat must accede to Pakistan and we draw attention of the Khan of Kalat that both on the grounds of geographic contiguity as well as the wishes of 3,000,000 Baluchis [sic], it should have acceded to the Pakistan Dominion."[33] "Both Pakistani and Baloch nationalists were to label him [the Khan] a greedy opportunist who betrayed both national causes to save his position and enlarge his wealth.[34] The Khan was accused of "trying to hunt with the hounds and run with the hare."[35] The last blow to Khan's ambitions, according to Wilcox, was dealt by the Indian government. He writes, "At a press conference on March 8, V. P. Menon (Secretary of the Ministry of the States) revealed: 'Kalat had approached the Government of India through an agent one or two months ago, but we refused to have anything to do with the State' ".[36]

In April 1948, the Khan of Kalat unconditionally acceded to Pakistan, but his brother Abdul Karim did not and crossed over to Afghanistan with some armed tribesmen. The Khan "issued a *firman* (order) denying any support whatsoever for this adventure,"[37] and branded Karim as a rebel. Karim returned after the Afghan government refused him any assistance and was arrested with his

12 soldiers on June 16, 1948 and with that, ended the palace revolt of 1948. Later, Karim and his followers were imprisoned. Ahmad Yar called a gathering of the *sardars* in Kalat in September 1949 and delivered a lengthy speech justifying the accession of his state with Pakistan, and "his love and regard"[38] for the new state. He went on to say,

> My brother had taken quite an unwise step. He turned against the Pakistan Govt. and fled to Afghanistan where some persons joined him and intended to do something. Acting statemenly [*sic*] I sent my uncle and teacher to him to tell him that in case he did not return he should consider himself to be no more from me. I am glad that he acted on my advice and returned here. But as he did not obey my instructions (instructions of an elder) he was sent to jail . . .
>
> In the meantime the Quaid-e-Azam died. It was our duty to serve him when he was alive. After his death it is our duty to serve Pakistan . . . Now that we have joined ourselves with Pakistan we should work for it. It we did not do so its bad effect will not only be confined to us alone but it will also effect [*sic*] Pakistan . . .[39]

According to Ayub Bakhsh Awan,[40] Abdul Karim's disagreement with his brother could not by any "stretch of imagination, be described as insurgency or insurrection."[41] It was he alone who acted without the backing of the Baloch population, as there was no reaction when he was arrested and put in jail along with approximately 100 servants.

Apart from other reasons, the former rulers of Kalat, Kharan, Makran, and Las Bela were lured to cede for financial benefits that they were offered by the newly established state of Pakistan. "Ahmad Yar of Kalat received an annual allowance of Rs. 4,250,000; Nawab Bai Khan Gichki of Makran Rs. 200,000; Mir Ghulam Qadir Khan of Las Bela Rs. 170,000; and Nawab Muhammad Habibullah Khan of Kharan Rs. 61,000. . . . the Khanate's state securities of Rs. 4,150,000, which had been blocked by the Government of Pakistan for some time after accession, were released and treated as the personal property of the Khan."[42] However, this sum was increased substantially in 1955, when these rulers ceded all of their authority to the province of "One Unit," West Pakistan.[43] While these Khans and *nawabs* filled their pockets to live luxurious lives, their fellow Balochs suffered in poverty, illiteracy, and misery.

The second palace revolt of 1958 was controversial and there is evidence that the Khan of Kalat, Ahmed Yar became an unwilling pawn in the greater game that was being played by the federal government in Karachi. Pakistani President Iskander Mirza was planning to impose Martial Law in the country and Khan, with his dicey reputation, became easy prey when Mirza accused the Khan of revolt and secession (in order to justify his Martial Law). Iskander Mirza, who had become exceeding unpopular, was convinced that there was a consensus among the political parties that he would be removed from office after the upcoming national elections in the beginning of 1959. The Khan of Kalat, Ahmad Yar, in his book, "*Inside Balouchistan* [*sic*]," writes,

The drama of my arrest was staged simply because President Sikandar Mirza wanted to put the country under Martial Law in order to keep himself in power by avoiding the General Election. Hence, Baluchistan [sic] was chosen as the starting point of the nefarious action which was designed to be applied to the whole of Pakistan later.... He wanted me to stand by him, and demanded from me Rs. 50 lacs to contest the elections, the amount being the bribe in lieu of his assurance given to me to withdraw Kalat from One Unit on the ground of popular agitation against it.[44]

However, A. B. Awan doubts the story of the Khan and suggests that he aspired to restore his state and threatened to instigate the people if they did not comply. He kept on repeating his outdated arguments based on the treaties that his forefathers had signed with the British Raj. As a reaction to the Khan's arrest, there were some disturbances in the Jhalawan area headed by Sardar Nauroz Khan Zarakzai, a supporter of the Khan, which went on for a year. Zarakzai, who was 90 years old, was arrested with his ten followers. His anger was "solely for his loyalty to his Khan and more accurately be described as his opposition to the government."[45]

Provincial Autonomy and Insurgency of the 1970s

Balochistan faced an intensive and prolonged insurgency in the 1970s during the tenure of Pakistan Peoples Party (PPP) under Zulfikar Ali Bhutto. Bhutto had promised provincial autonomy in the Constitution of 1973 which was adopted unanimously by the representatives of all four provinces of Pakistan.

In the 1970 national and provisional elections, Bhutto's party gained majority at the center and he was elected as Prime Minister, but lost in two provinces of Balochistan and NWFP. In these provinces, the National Awami Party (NAP) formed coalition provincial governments with Jamiat Ulema-e-Islam (JUI). Soon, differences developed between Bhutto and the NAP Balochistan leaders over a number of issues. The prime source of tensions remained with the personality of Bhutto, who wanted to acquire as much power as he could muster, negating the balance that was provided by the principles of federation in the 1973 Constitution.

Balochistan had become a province in 1970, and for the first time, two Baloch politicians, Ghaus Bakhsh Bizenjo and Ataullah Mengal, became Governor and the Chief Minister, respectively. Out of 21 provincial assembly seats, ANP won eight, JUI won three, and the rest of the seats were taken by either independents or smaller parties. According to these figures, the coalition had a clear majority, i.e., even without the help of independents or smaller groups. Although Bhutto had promised provincial autonomy, once he formed the central government, he desired to acquire more power for himself and his office. Differences arose between Bhutto and the NAP-JUI led coalition in Balochistan and he dismissed the provincial government in February 1973. There were charges and counter-charges by Bhutto and the Baloch leaders on a number of occurrences taking place in Balochistan. The federal government charged the province with overstepping its jurisdiction while "most opposition leaders rejected the Bhutto regime's accusations against the NAP leaders. They asserted that Bhutto himself had provoked an insurgency in Baluchistan[*sic*] and condemned his dismissal of the NAP-JUI government, as a design to bring the province under his control through undemocratic means."[46]

Bhutto found allies among the Baloch *sardars* and at the very start of the military operation in Balochistan, in April 1973, he appointed Nawab Akbar Bugti, *sardar* of Bugti tribe as Governor of the province. Then, he replaced him with another Baloch leader, the Khan of Kalat, Mir Ahmad Yar Khan, in October 1973, who remained in office until September 1977. However, the insurgency by the Marri and Mengal tribes continued for years costing heavy losses on both sides. Those Baloch nationalists who saw the revolt of these two tribes as an expression of Baloch nationalism found it difficult to explain the role of these two important Baloch personalities, as chief executives of the province, during the times when Baloch blood was being shed for whatever reason. It is pertinent to mention here that the Khan of Kalat described himself as Khan-e-Khana (Leader of all Baloch *sardars*). One explanation is that in severely competitive tribal rivalries and jealousies, one *sardar* tends to play against the other. A second explanation is that sending another tribe to the mountains and involving them in combat, lessens their numerical strength, thus strengthening the position of the opposing tribe. Lawrence Ziring summarizes this conflict between Bhutto and the Baloch tribes as follows,

> Balochistan was a region where tribalism reigned supreme, and where regional *sardars* commanded constituencies, in accordance with tribal practices. Historically, the writ of the *sardars* transcended central government law, and the PPP was determined to break the back of *sardar* power once and for all. Bhutto's policies were aimed at destabilizing traditional authority, but the tribals resisted the intrusion, forcing the PPP government to escalate the effort. Islamabad described the resistance as an insurgency, and what began as a minor display of force was transformed into a major military campaign.[47]

The opponents of Bhutto severely condemned him for using military force against the Mengal and Marri tribes while stating that political opponents should not be dubbed "secessionists." It was also pointed out in the press that in the Baloch tribal context, the "aspirations of the people" were "committed to their respective *sardars*."[48] Therefore, any harsh action against the *sardar* would ignite anger and bitterness among the tribesmen. The insurgency ended with the exit of Bhutto by Zia-ul-Haq's Martial Law in 1977.

The promised constitutional guarantees and powers for the provinces, for which Balochistan in particular has been agitating, can be summarized as follows:

a. *Division of powers between the center and the provinces*

> Although the framers of the 1973 Constitution promised to grant enough powers to the provinces, the real problem remained with the lack of the will of the central

government to implement the federal part of the Constitution, as according to its relevant Articles. Secondly, during the long spells of army rule, where the Constitution was suspended, the entire governmental and administrative structures were highly centralized. This is where Balochistan province lost its autonomy along with the other provinces. The matter of autonomy for the provinces had become a national issue, with consensus among all the political parties that promised autonomy has been provided to the provinces as required by the Constitution. But whenever it came to the practicality of the issue, the party in control of the federal government became hesitant to fulfill its promises, and delaying tactics were adopted to linger on the issue. As a result of the February 2008 elections, the Peoples Party has been in firm control at the federal level as well as in the Balochistan provincial assembly, but in spite of various pressures from the opposition and its coalition partners, it moved at a snail's pace to come up with a formula that could satisfy the residents of Balochistan. The Peoples Party of President Asif Ali Zardari, along with his allies in the parliament, had enough majority of two-thirds, in both Houses of the Parliament to amend the constitution. At least on this issue, there were enough votes for the long-awaited change, including that of the opposition parties. By the middle of 2009, the momentum grew into a forceful national consciousness which happened that in spite of the "elaborate provisions for safeguarding the interests of the provinces, in practice, most of these provisions have not been acted upon."[49]

b. *The Concurrent List*

The main demand of Balochistan has been the removal of the Concurrent List from the Constitution. The Constitution has divided the legislative powers by creating two lists. Schedule IV places 67 items in the Federal Legislative List, on which only the federal government has the jurisdiction to legislate. The Concurrent List consists of 47 items, on which both the federal and provincial governments can legislate. But in case of a conflict between the two, the federal law will prevail, thus providing more discretion and powers to the federal government. A great deal of public opinion in Balochistan believes that Concurrent List should be abolished which would be the advancement towards provincial autonomy.

On May 15, 2006, Pakistan's former Prime Ministers Benazir Bhutto and Nawaz Sharif, who were in exile as a result of Musharraf's military takeover, signed an agreement in London known as *Charter of Democracy* . . . According to Article 5 of the document, "The Concurrent List in the Constitution will be abolished." Other political parties, whether national or regional, also adhered to this principle.

c. *The National Finance Commission*

Article 160 of the Constitution of 1973 created the National Finance Commission (NFC), for the purpose of equitable distribution of financial resources between the federal and provincial governments, and among the provincial governments. Balochistan, being the least populated but poorest province, was denied its much needed revenues, as the criteria of distribution of revenue was based exclusively upon population.

The main objection of the smaller provinces, including Balochistan, was that the criteria of the distribution of national resources, on the basis of population was a disadvantage for the least-populated and least-developed province. Balochistan demanded a multiple criteria where poverty and underdevelopment also became part of the distributive formula. Balochistan, along with other provinces, also demanded the share of the Federal Division Pool (FDP) to be increased to more than 50 percent, instead of 45 percent. It became a major cause of friction between the Baloch population and the federal government.

Only three NFC awards were announced in 34 years.[50] The award of 2006 was imposed by a military dictator, General Musharraf, when a deadlock arose between the provinces and the federal government on the distribution of resources formula. During these long delays, interim arrangements were made for the transfer of resources, which became a source of desperation for the smaller provinces, especially Balochistan.

Finally, in December 2009, a landmark consensus was reached among the elected provincial governments and the federal government, on the one hand and within the provinces, on the other hand. Punjab, the largest province, which had benefitted the most from previous arrangements, conceded its stance and a multi-factor formula like backwardness, poverty, generation, and inverse population density was agreed upon. This consensus was considered a huge achievement in terms of inter-provincial harmony and a gesture of accommodation towards Balochistan.[51] In fact, Balochistan was "guaranteed a minimum award, with the centre pledging to make up for any shortfall."[52] The main feature of the seventh NFC award was that the provinces share from the divisible poll of the federal government increased from 47.5 percent to 56 percent in the fiscal year 2010–2011, which will increase to 57.5 percent in the subsequent years of the award. The credit for the award was given to the commencement of democracy in the country. In this regard, an editorial in the *Dawn* newspaper wrote, "The hammering out of a consensus among the centre and the provinces on the seventh National Finance Commission award is a major achievement and a positive event for those who believe that the future of a vibrant Pakistan lies in a democratic federation."[53]

ISSUES AND REASONS FOR ONGOING DISCONTENTMENT

Since 2004, the level of disappointment and resentment has increased in the Baloch areas of the province, accelerating in 2007, when the Musharraf regime tried to suppress the opposition by using brutal military force. His highhandedness and lack of sensitivity for the Baloch people alienated even those moderates who were open to dialogue and were ready to work in the prevailing political dispensation. But Musharraf carelessly dismissed any discontentment in the province. On March 26, 2005, when the province of Balochistan was inching towards increased agitation, he remarked, while addressing the members of his handpicked ruling party, "There is no military operation going on in the province nor is there any need for such an operation—there is no unrest in Balochistan as its people look forward to benefiting from the unprecedented development projects—it is only a handful of vested interests who are involved in recent acts of sabotage at a few places."[54] On the same occasion, he said that there is no reason for the armed attacks on government personnel, when Balochistan was undergoing a "large-scale development." His remarks came when on March 17, armed clashes had taken place between the Frontier Corps (a paramilitary force), and the Bugti tribesmen in Dera Bugti, a strategic gas-producing area.

On a number of occurrences the Pakistan leaders and foreign office have accused India of abetting unrest and rebellion in Balochistan. One such allegation came on February 3, 2010, by Pakistan's defense minister, Chaudhry Ahmad Mukhtar who charged India with interfering in Balochistan, and appealed to the international community to take notice of Indian involvement in Balochistan's[55] acts of sabotage and target killings. Previously, Prime Minister Syed Yousaf Raza Gillani, on the floor of the Pakistan parliament, stated, "I made it clear to the Indian prime minister that Pakistan had serious concerns over the Indian involvement and it was also mentioned by Indian PM Dr. Manmohan Singh in the joint declaration that was issued after the meeting,"[56] and that the evidence would be presented at some proper occasion. He continued, "We will decide when and at which forum we will present this evidence." Pervez Hoodbhoy, a university professor in Islamabad and a sympathizer to the Indian regional and international polices, was compelled to write that the Indian policy of interfering in Balochistan, by supporting some insurgent groups, so that it gets a "handle to exert pressure on Pakistan, ". . . is unacceptable."[57]

It is a historic reality that India, Afghanistan, and the Soviet Union have had an interest in stirring up the agitating groups of their choice, taking advantage of the tensions created by the federal authorities in Islamabad. In 1982–83 (during the height of Afghan-Soviet war), the Soviets helped create the Balochistan Liberation Army (BLA), supported by another Communist-indoctrinated group, the Baloch Student Organization (BSO). BLA went into hiding after the withdrawal of the Soviet troops from Afghanistan, but in 2002 it reappeared again. Most of the members of these two terrorist organizations received their education from Soviet institutions.[58] But it is also true that to address and solve the grievances of the Baloch people could reduce or eliminate the sore points of contentions, thus providing little or no opportunity for external countries to influence the Baloch tribes.

After the installation of the elected federal and provincial governments in March 2008, the federal government made a public apology to the Baloch people for past misdoings in the province. Talks were also offered to those individuals who had stayed away from the elections and were therefore not part of the parliament.

Shah Jahan Baloch, a Quetta-based educationalist, summarizes the reasons of discontentment in Balochistan as,

> The political instability, discontinuity of the democratic political process and lack of consensus on the critically unresolved issues relating to the relationship of province and federal governments had reached such a level where there is higher level of deficit of trust. . . . It is an undeniable fact that the people of Balochistan had been denied of their basic rights of development, education and to politically decide about their future because in all leading development programmes [sic] in the name of national policies the federal government had been the ultimate deciding factor and [the] provincial

governance system has mainly been used as implementing structure. As a consequence common people are still facing dual oppression from corrupt *Sardari* system redesigned during the colonial period and on the other side the public at large have not seen the results of the so-called democracy and elected governments at provincial level in shaping their real development. [The] Majority of the population is facing [the] lack of basic needs of life in this modern age and striving for water, shelter, food, health and education for the survival of their lives.[59]

The Baloch grievances can be categorize into five main areas, i.e., apart from the numerous administrative and socio-economic reasons as mentioned in the above quote.

Mega-projects, Gwadar Seaport, and the Saindak Copper and Gold Mines

In 1992, Prime Minister Nawaz Sharif, who had a knack for mega-projects, initiated a deep-seaport project at Gwadar which became operational in 2008. Earlier on March 20, 2007, the Chinese Minister of Communications, Li Shenglin had inaugurated the facility. Gwadar is the third port of Pakistan after Karachi and Port Qasim, and is more strategically located as it is 725 kilometers (450 miles) away from the Indian border. Pakistan needed this facility as it would be difficult for the Indian navy to blockade Gwadar, as happened at Karachi during the 1971 war, and which the Indians had threatened to do so again in 1999 during the Kargil conflict. The management of the port was given to a Singapore-based company, The Port of Singapore Authority (PSA) International. The deal is for 25 years, with a tax-free port status for the following 40 years.

Chinese engineers and government facilities have been targets of militant attacks in Gwadar where a number of Chinese have died and many more have been injured. It is suspected that these attacks are being carried by the agents of foreign powers who would not like to see China as a close ally of the Pakistani strategic interests in this Arabian Sea facility.

Balochistan also has known deposits of copper and gold at Saindak in the Chagai district. Both of these mega-projects are also being carried out with the assistance of the Chinese. These projects have been subject of focus, under one pretext or the other by the Baloch opposition blaming the federal government of usurping the rights of the Baloch people. Some nationalist Baloch leaders have conceived conspiracies behind these developmental projects while others see them as prospects for a better and developing Balochistan.

Gwadar Seaport

The local population initially welcomed the idea of Gwadar becoming a hub of economic activity with the prospect of developing into international city like Dubai, but later, General Musharraf's brutal suppression of the Balochi opposition raised many concerns by the Baloch people. According to an assessment, the usefulness of the Gwadar port will be primarily for the Baloch people,

> By making Gwadar the pivot of regional trade, Pakistan will also attract considerable investment into its most underdeveloped province, Baluchistan [*sic*]. These funds will allow for the construction of roads and rails linking the coastal region to the rest of Pakistan, Iran, and Afghanistan; will cultivate the region's vast and unexplored natural resources; and theoretically will allow for the socioeconomic uplift of the local Baluchis [*sic*] through various development projects.[60]

By 2005, China had contributed $198 million to Pakistan's $50 million, and involved 450 Chinese workers, to complete the first phase of the construction.[61] Although the multibillion dollar deep-sea harbor at Gwadar, constructed by Chinese companies, will provide tremendous job and financial benefits to the local residents in particular and to the Baloch in general, it was alleged by the nationalist Baloch leadership that these projects will also bring in a large number of people from other provinces which would undermine the Baloch majority in the area. It was also said that this influx would affect the culture of the Baloch society which is still not ready to accommodate "foreigners" amid their settlements. These complaints can be seen against the background of trust deficit between the federal government and Baloch tribal leaders. Another impression created was that it is federal government's plan to exploit this facility for their benefit, as "the Baloch are not stakeholders or beneficiaries, they strongly oppose it."[62]

In her testimony to the Senate Committee on Balochistan, Zobaida Jalal, a Baloch from near Gwadar and a member of National Assembly during the Musharraf regime, said that the development of Gwadar as an international port city will not affect the rights of the locals. She gave the example of Dubai where she said different ethnic communities are present with locals being in a minority. She went on to say that the rights of the minorities can be protected through various laws and that, "Land in Gwadar, which had no value, is selling for millions of rupees, benefiting the local Baloch population economically,"[63] As a part of the solution, the opposition Baloch leaders repeatedly demanded that the port "should be placed under the control of the provincial government. The provincial cabinet should have a major say in this and other regional projects."[64]

On November 24, 2009, Senator Raza Rabbani, Chairman of the Aghaz-e-Huqooq-Balochistan (AHB) (Beginning of the Rights of Balochistan), presented a package to redress the problems of Balochistan to the joint session of the Pakistani Parliament. The announcement was made on behalf of the Prime Minister and his government. Article 23 of this document dealt with the Gwadar issue, as follows:

> (i) All new mega projects to be initiated with the consent and approval of the provincial government. The share of the province in its profits/benefits to be assured in the contact/ agreement, (ii) The concept of public-private ownership in such projects to be followed

where ever possible, (iii) In Gwadar, there shall be a free economic zone and political activities in the said zone may be regulated by an appropriate law to be framed in consultation with all the stakeholders, (iv) In Gwadar, all or as far as possible, appointments in BS-1 to 16, should be from the local population, (v) In Gwadar, the local youth should be provided technical training and absorbed in GPA, GDA and Special Economic Zone, (vi) Preference should be given to the qualified local contractors while awarding contracts related to the port, (vii) Compensation and reallocation of all those fishermen, who are being displaced due to the Gwadar Port must be finalised [sic] immediately, (ix) The two jetties agreed to be constructed for the fishermen on the eastern and western bays be constructed, (x) A fisheries training centre [sic] as required to be established under the 9th Five Year Plan for Balochistan be constructed, (xi) A portion of the revenue collected by the Gwadar Port Authority be allocated for the development of the province, (xii) The chief minister shall be the ex-officio chairman of the Gwadar Development Authority and there shall be seven members from the province on the Board of Directors, (xiii) The provincial government of Balochistan will nominate a person duly qualified to be the Chairman of the Gwadar Development Authority.

From the document, it becomes clear that the demands of those opposing the manner in which Gwadar port was being conducted were taken into account. The control of the port was handed over to the provincial government and it was given authority to nominate the Chair of the Gwadar Development Authority. On December 30, 2009 Chief Minister of Balochistan, Nawab Aslam Raisani was appointed as Chair, Gwadar Port Authority. In this manner, the federal government fulfilled its promise of handing over the port to the provincial government, as mentioned in the Balochistan package of November 2009.

Saindak and Reko Diq Copper-Gold Mines

Copper was discovered at Saindak by the government of the Pakistan-owned company, Saindak Metals Ltd (SML). The deposits were originally discovered in 1970s with the help of a Chinese engineering company, but the project could not be carried out because of the lack of capital. However, in the late 1990s, the project was leased to a Chinese company, Metallurgical Construction Corporation (MCC) for ten years beginning in September 2002.[65] According to a Balochistan-based economist, "Under the lease agreement, MCC was to run the project on an annual rent of $500,000 plus a 50% share of copper sales to the Pakistani government."[66] As no monitoring mechanism exists, it is difficult to estimate the amount of benefits that Pakistan derives from the mines vis-à-vis the Chinese.

Apart from Saindak, in 1993 copper was also discovered in Reko Diq near the Chagai Hills by world's largest business company, BHP Billiton. They had taken a risk by entering into a joint venture with the government of Pakistan by investing $7 million in the project.[67] BHP Billiton was later joined by an Australian-based company, Tethyan Copper Company Limited in this venture.

Muslim Lakhani, Chief Representative of Tethayn in Pakistan, said that while previously Balochistan had been ignored, now the ongoing project will provide job opportunities for the Baloch people. He went on to say,

> The Balochis need to get more than what they are getting, not only in terms of money but also in terms of simply someone listening to their grievances. Twenty-five percent of the net profit of this project belongs to Balochistan—in fact, in this case, they are protecting their interest. When you are fair, people will support you. You don't just need government support, you need people support.[68]

Article 28 of Aghaz-e-Huqooq-Balochistan (AHB), which deals with the Sandak project says that "The federal government from its 30% shares in the project will immediately give 20% to the province. On completion of the project and when the foreign company withdraws, the project shall be owned exclusively by the province." However, in December 2009, the Balochistan provincial government terminated the contract with Tethayn alleging irregularities. The project is now managed by the Balochistan government's Department of Mines and Mineral Development. The provincial government has also acquired the services of Pakistan's nuclear scientist, Dr. Samar Mubarakmand, who is now chair of the board of governors. This was accomplished with a promise that the new arrangement "will create thousands of high paying jobs and would give a massive boost to the local economy."[69]

Article 33 of the AHB addresses the reservations expressed about the minerals as the following:

> 33. Profit Sharing In Existing Agreements:
> It is proposed that existing agreements on projects such as SANDAK, REKODIC and others where agreements have already been negotiated, the federal government may reconsider the agreements concerning the sharing of income, profits or royalty between the federal government and the provincial government.
> By taking the above mentioned measures, the Balochistan package started a process where the natural resources were to be owned and managed by the provincial government.

Exploitation of Natural Gas Reserves

Baloch nationalist leaders came up with forceful arguments charging that the federal government does not pay Balochistan reasonable royalties for national resources, especially for natural gas. Although according to the Constitution, Article 161 (i), "the net proceeds of the Federal duty of excise on natural gas levied at well head and collected by the federal government, and the royalty collected by the Federal Government, shall not form part of the Federal Consolidated Fund and shall be paid to the Province in which the well head of natural gas is situated." During Musharraf's regime, his ally Jam Mohammad Yousuf, the Chief Minister of Balochistan, substantiated the opposition's charges by complaining that his province was not getting its due share in gas royalties and gas development surcharges, and as a result, the "provincial government was forced to get overdraft and loans from banks to complete ongoing development projects and meet non-development expenditures."[70]

AHB addresses the question of the gas royalty and related issues of the Sui Gas Fields (the largest in Pakistan) as well as arrears, which the federal government owes to the province of Balochistan. Articles 22, 24, 26, 27, 29, and 34 of the document, read as follows:

> Article 22. Rationalisation of the Royalty Formula: (i) Rationalization of the royalty formula and the Gas Development Surcharge have been done, (ii) The concept of public-private ownership in the areas of a district granted for exploration should be followed. Where contracts are awarded, the said district should be given 15% of revenue to be received by the provincial government, (iii) Due representation should be given to the province on the boards of the PPL; OGDC and Sui Southern Gas, (iv) Distribution companies should be obligated under contract/law to provide on priority basis gas to the district where it is explored, (v) In case of a successful find the federal government shall spend an amount equivalent to 10% of the net profits on development projects in the area. The ascertainment of profits shall be open to scrutiny by independent/third party auditors, (vi) The federal government has released the accrued Production Bonus to the districts producing oil and gas. This policy will be strictly implemented.
>
> Article 24: (i) There should be a special development package for the area (Sui). (ii) The armed forces should be systematically withdrawn from the area.
>
> Article 26: Gas Development Surcharge: The federal government agrees to pay the arrears of Gas Development Surcharge from 1954 to 1991. This is a total amount of Rs 120 billion payable in 12 years.
>
> Article 27: Ownership in oil and gas companies: In organisations such as PPL, OGDCL and Sui Southern, the province will be able to purchase up to 20% of the right shares when offered in the open market.
>
> Article 29: Uniform Price of Gas: There shall be a uniform price of gas throughout the country for the purpose of calculation of GDS.

Building of Cantonments

As Balochistan is inhabited by fierce and aggressive tribes who sought their disputes through the use of arms, there are frequent clashes between various tribes which are beyond the capacity of police to manage. The tribes also resort to arms and killings when in disagreement with the federal government. Musharraf's policies also gave rise to attacks on government property. The military regime in Islamabad believed that force was the only solution to these uprisings, and in 2004 it decided to build three military cantonments in Sui (a Bugti stronghold), in Kohlu (mostly inhabited by the defiant Marri tribe), and at Gwadar Port, where the Chinese were the target of the dissidents. Whatever the reason, the building of cantonments for paramilitary forces became a point of resentment for the Baloch people. Instead of bringing peace, there was a wave of sabotage upon government installments, especially gas pipelines and transmission towers. The Baloch nationalists saw the construction of the cantonments as an attempt by the government to suppress their "legitimate demands" by using additional military force, notwithstanding the internal division of the tribes, which made matters still worse. For example, the Bijarani tribe (a clan of the Marris) has always disputed the claim of the Marris to the potential natural resources in the Kohlu area. In 1997, they attacked and tried to capture the town of Kohlu for that purpose. Another recent example can be given of the "Pat Feader" region of Naseerabad district, where in January 2010, two factions of tribesmen clashed using heavy weapons, resulting in a number of causalities. The paramilitary Frontier Corps (F.C.) had to be deployed to stop the tribal bloodshed.[71] Strong feelings still exist among the general population of Balochistan province that some type of military operation is still being conducted against the nationalists. However, the governor of Balochistan, Nawab Zulfikar Magsi, has insisted that there was no military operation in any part of the province.[72]

The AHB document, in its Clause 15, tried to remove the objection of military cantonments by committing that, "Construction of new Cantonments in Sui and Kohlu be stopped for the time being. Army will be withdrawn from Sui after handing over the duties to F.C. F.C. will also take over the already constructed Cantonment at Sui." It was reported that the question of not building new cantonments in the province had the consent of the military chief, Ashfaq Pervez Kiyani.[73]

The Kidnapping and Disappearance of the Baloch People

During Musharraf's Martial Law, a number of people were reported to be "missing" in Pakistan, especially in Balochistan province.[74] Many in Balochistan believe that these people have been kidnapped by intelligence agencies, under the pretext of committing acts of terrorism and anti-state activities. Baloch nationalist parties believe that most of these people are innocent and are members of Baloch nationalist parties or groups. AHB in Article 12 address these questions as follows,

> The names of missing persons be identified and following actions be taken immediately, after verification, in any case, if they are found to be in custody. (i) Those persons against whom there are no charges be released. (ii) Those persons against whom there are charges be brought before a court of competent jurisdiction within seven days for trial (effective from the date of promulgation of commission). (iii) Such persons be allowed legal consul of their choice, the government should assist them in this regard in accordance with law. (iv) Family members of such persons be informed accordingly and allowed visiting rights.

In spite of the pledge made in the AHB document to deal equitably with the matter of missing persons, the controversy regarding the number of the missing and their whereabouts remained a source of great concern for their relatives and friends. By the end of 2009, according to government figures, there were 6,000 to 8,000 missing persons from Balochistan during the Musharraf era. According to Prime Minister Gillani, in December of that same year, there were 992 missing persons, of which 262 were eventually released from government custody. He assured the Parliament that the government wiould do its utmost to locate and release more political workers and legal cases against the others would be withdrawn. The dispute, however, remained regarding those who were arrested for charges of terrorist activities. A thin line existed, during the military rule of Musharraf, between those who were his opponents and those who were actually accused of sabotage, murders, and other terrorist activities like the bombing of railway tracks, power lines, etc.

Murder of Akbar Bugti

On August 26, 2006, former Governor and Chief Minister of Balochistan, 82-year-old Baloch leader Nawab Akbar Khan Bugti was killed by security forces in a military operation, along with his 37 armed guards. Akbar Bugti was also the head of Jamhori Watan Party (JWP), a Balochistan-based political party and chief of his tribe. Bugti has been involved in a dispute with General Musharraf for a "proper share" from gas reserves at Sui, his homeplace.

When Bugti started applying pressure tactics for settlement of the Sui gas royalty, Musharraf, warned him in March 2005 with grave consequences. He said, in a *Geo* television interview, "Don't push us. It is not the 1970. We will not climb mountains behind you. You will not even know what and from where something has come and hit you." This was an obvious threat to eliminate the Baloch leader. In an interview to a Karachi-based weekly, *Newsline* of June 2005, Bugti responded: "The general (Musharraf) has promised to hit us in such a way that we will not know what hit us. In one sense, it is quick death that he is promising us. He could do this to me, and to a few other Baloch leaders, but not to the entire Baloch nation."[75]

Bugti's death was regarded as an extra-judicial murder by the people of Balochistan and elsewhere. Soon riots erupted in which many people lost their lives and scores of others were injured. His death undoubtedly exacerbated the already fragile security situation in the province. The security landscape of Balochistan drastically changed. Simmering resentment and complaints against the federal government soon turned into a low-intensity insurgency in some pockets of the Baloch areas. Bugti's killing provided the already active dissidents with a raison d'état to raise arms against the Pakistan army and paramilitary forces. Target killings of non-Balochs or settlers became a daily routine, which triggered a reaction from the Pakistani security agencies. Punjabi, Sindhi, and Pashtun businesses were specially targeted. Even teachers, and others doing menial work were not spared from the violence. It was feared that soon Balochistan would lose much needed expertise to cater for the needs of the province. AHB, like other Baloch-related issues, mentions the murder in Clause 14, which reads, "A fact finding Commission headed by a retired Judge of the Supreme/High Court be constituted to determine the circumstances leading to the death of Nawab Akbar Bugti Shaheed (Martyr)."

Reflecting on the Balochistan security situation, former Lieutenant General Abdul Qadir Baloch, a member of the opposition party Muslim League (Nawaz), and a former governor of Balochistan, pointed out that the "murder" of Akbar Bugti acted as "a fuel on the fire." He stated that there was no justification to remove him in this manner, and that before the tribal leader's death, Balochistan was not in a state of rebellion, "it was the use of violence for which compelled the Baloch youth to become radical." During the later state of affairs, the Baloch leader opined that in the target killings and sabotage, India may have a role.[76] Expressing similar views, an editorial in an Urdu national newspaper, Jang wrote that it was, "the murder of Akbar Bugti that worsened the security situation of the Balochistan province."[77]

MISCELLANEOUS DEMANDS

Apart from the previously discussed main concerns of Baloch political leaders, the following list of Baloch as a well as Pakistan specific issues is worth noting. (See Table 4.2.) Some of the Baloch demands are common to that of Pakistan, while others are unique to the Balochistan situation. Some Baloch nationalists have deliberately mixed the two to instigate the illiterate and semi-literate population of tribal Balochistan. In order to address at least one major issue of unemployment, the government offered 5,000 jobs in the first phase, with a promise of providing more opportunities for the future as promised by the AHB package. It was reported that there was an enthusiastic response from Baloch youth as 38,000 applied for various job positions.[78] The federal government, as part of reconciliation, also took further steps towards the dissident Baloch leadership.

Table 4.2 Miscellaneous Grievances and Problems of Balochistan

Grievances/Problems	Classification
Lack of political representation	Pakistan-related
Under-representation in the army/civil service	Balochistan-related
Domination by the establishment	Pakistan-related
Low literacy rate	Balochistan/Pakistan-related
Poverty	Balochistan/Pakistan-related
Socio-economic disparity	Pakistan-related
Menace of the Sardari system	Balochistan-related

It withdrew 89 police cases against the leaders and cadres of various nationalist parties, including that of the president of the Baloch Republican Party (BRP), an extremist outfit responsible for various violent acts in the province.

The AHB took notice of the socio-economic problems of the province with a promise of addressing them at the earliest possible date. Baloch leaders repeatedly complained that many promises were made in the past in order to remove the grievances of Balochistan, but nothing much has happened since then. In order to make sure that this time matters are taken seriously, an attempt has been made by the federal parliament to evolve a follow-up mechanism, as follows:

E. Monitoring Mechanism

36. Parliamentary Committee on National Security: It is proposed that the federal government, provincial government and other departments/agencies involved in the implementation of the proposals shall brief the Parliamentary Committee on National Security on the status of implementation on a monthly basis.

37. Parliament: The federal government and the provincial government shall every three months lay a report before both Houses of Parliament, separately, on the state of implementation of the proposals. The two Houses shall separately allocate appropriate time for discussion on the said report.

38. The Standing Committee on Establishment of the Senate of Pakistan: The Standing Committee on Establishment of the Senate shall present a report every three months on Item No. 25. The Senate chairman, after the report has been laid in the Senate, transmits the same to the speaker, National Assembly of Pakistan, for information of that House.

39. Certification: The federal minister for inter-provincial coordination shall at the end of each financial year certify to both the Houses of Parliament separately, the amount of monies spent for the implementation of these proposals.

POLICY POSITION OF POLITICAL PARTIES AND GROUPS

Table 4.3 represents the various agendas and policy positions of modern interest groups with the purpose of exerting maximum pressure on the federal government. However, a number of nationalist leaders are fixated upon the perception that the affairs of Balochistan are micro-managed by the Islamabad-based establishment, meaning the army and the intelligence agencies. The pressure of these Baloch leaders "gains more strength" because of past events, which together create a "bond and a nucleus." That compensates for being a small minority in the federation of Pakistan.

The random killings of non-Baloch settlers by secessionist terrorist groups like the Balochistan Liberation Army (BLA) has deprived the province of the expertise which is essential for the socio-economic development of the area. According to a fact-finding report by Human Rights Commission of Pakistan (HRCP), an independent and non partisan body,

It is evident that the common people in the province fear not only the state apparatus, such as the intelligence and security agencies, but also the non-state actors, the militant

Table 4.3 Various Baloch Political Parties and Groups*

Parties/Groups	Leader/s	Ideology	Agenda	Tactics
Pakistan Peoples Party	Haji Lashkari Raisani	Constitutionalist	Parliamentary Democracy	Political Participation
National Awami Party (until 1978) Balochistan National Party (BNP-Mengal)	(i) Ataullah Mengal (ii) Akhtar Mengal	Constitutionalist/ Revisionist	Autonomy/ Revision of Constitution	Political Participation/ Pressure Tactics (Boycotted 2008 Elections)
Balochistan National Party (Awami)	Senator Israr Ullah Zehri	Constitutionalist	Parliamentary Democracy	Political Participation
National Party (NP)	Mir Hasal Khan Bizanjo	Constitutionalist	Parliamentary Democracy	Political Participation
Jamhori Watan Party (JWP)	Akbar Khan Bugti (Founder) Talal Akbar Bugti	Constitutionalist	Parliamentary Democracy	Political Participation/ Pressure Tactics (Boycotted 2008 Elections)
Jamhori Watan Party (JWP)-Aali Group	Mir Aali Bugti	Constitutionalist	Parliamentary Democracy	Political Participation
Baloch Qaumi Movement	Mir Zafarullah Khan Jamali	Constitutionalist	Parliamentary Democracy	Political Participation
Baloch National Front (Alliance of 8 Nationalist Parties) (BNF)[1]	Ghulam Mohammed Baloch of the Baloch National Movement was Secretary General (killed in April 2009)	Secessionists	Independence	Pressure Tactics/ Agitation
a. Baloch Republican Party b. Balochistan Liberation Army (BLA) Military Wing	a. Nawab Sardar Brahamdagh Khan Bugti b. Mir Balach Marri (killed in November 2007)	Secessionists	Independence	a. Guerilla Warfare/ Murders of Non-Blochs b. Guerilla Warfare/ Murders of Non-Blochs (Declared Terrorist Organization by Pakistan in October 2006. Similar Action by UK and U.S.)
Baloch Liberation United Front (BLUF)	Spokesperson: Mir Shayhaq Baloch? (information is sketchy)	Secessionists/ Anarchists	Anarchy	Target Killings

(Continued)

Table 4.3   (Continued)

Parties/Groups	Leader/s	Ideology	Agenda	Tactics
Baloch Students Organization (Azad)	Bashir Ziab Baloch	Secessionists/ Communists	Independence	In Forefront During 1973–1977 Insurgency; BLA Supporters

All political parties and groups ask for more provincial autonomy and equitable distribution of natural resources. Further, they demand control of mega-projects in Balochistan.

[1]The group comprises of:

- Baloch Students Organization (Azad)
- Baloch Bar Association
- Baloch Women Panel
- Baloch Baloch Watan Movemnet
- Baloch Unity Conference
- Baloch Human Rights Council
- Baloch Watan Movement
- Baloch Republican Party

Baloch organizations [*sic*], as well. Several Baloch young men frankly admitted to HRCP that Baloch militants were involved in targeting and killing non-Baloch people including teachers, but some Baloch representatives of teachers' associations were in a state of denial. They presented a conspiracy theory and said that intelligence agencies were involved in target killings of non-Baloch people, which seemed absurd.[79]

It is probable that with the introduction of Balochistan package and the introduction of reforms for a more workable federal system, as promised by the NFC Award and the necessary changes in the Constitution, Balochistan would settle down to a more serious business of socio-economic development, which is urgently needed for their impoverished people. However, there remains plenty of apprehensions about the seriousness of the federal government to implement the reforms, in letter and in spirit. According to a newspaper report on the National Assembly proceedings, retired Lieutenant General Abdul Qadir Baloch questioned the seriousness and effectiveness of the AHB. Part of his speech (with newspaper comments), on the floor of the House as reported in the news media, is as follows,

> Nobody dared play or sing the national anthem in Baloch dominated areas and even claimed that in a recent event, the chief minister and six of his ministers attended a function in Khuzdar, but only after driving to the venue in their official vehicles sans the national flag. But the most dangerous bit he saved for [the[last and it becomes all the more alarming because the man making this claim is both a retired army general and someone who was himself in-charge of the province during the de facto military rule of General Musharraf.
>
>   The general charged, and quoted the incumbent CM in support of his argument, that people were still being picked up clandestinely and in broad daylight by "agencies" and that there was a "parallel government in Balochistan." Who is this government, he

bitterly asked. He should know, and I'm sure he does, because he had remained part of that same apparatus at one time. Maybe it's time the general did his moral bit and spilled some vital beans in the larger national interest. Like seasoned politicians, he also wanted the house to shun everything else and hold an intense two-day debate on Balochistan issue. Who could argue with that, but telling the truths that he is privy to, would be a much better start to understanding and helping resolve the "Balochistan conundrum."[80]

CONCLUSION

Balochistan's backwardness in education and social sectors were recognized by Muslim leaders even before the creation of Pakistan. After independence, Balochistan, time and time again, had to find out a way for the support of institutions in the Baloch areas and later in the province. There are two aspects to the problems which Balochistan faced. The first aspect is the overall backwardness of Pakistan, and the lack of proper planning to address deficiencies, accompanied by rampant corruption by bureaucrats and military generals. Included in this exploiter group are politicians as well. The second aspect relates to exclusiveness of the Balochistan situation, where the resources were not fully utilized nor given enough attention by the federal government to support the socio-economic conditions of the people. The present low indicators for development in Balochistan were inherited from the time of the creation of Pakistan; however, the situation has become worse over time. According to government of Pakistan's Economic Survey of 2007–2008, Balochistan, with a 42 percent literacy rate was far behind that other provinces. The conditions in the Baloch areas are even worse.

Balochistan, which had remained calm in the post-national and provincial elections of February 18, 2008, provided hope that the Musharraf's dictatorial regime's callous attitude towards the Baloch population would be addressed and that a chronic sense of depravation and frustration is nearing an acceptable solution. But this did not happen as the government was too slow to act and was busy in consolidating its strength in all parts of Pakistan, even where it needed to pause and compromise. In the beginning of 2009, much was said and written about the volatile situation in parts of the Balochistan province, but few steps were taken by the federal and provincial governments, even to understand the real issues. The killings of three Baloch nationalist leaders in April 2009 only added fuel to the fire, triggering protest marches and strikes in the far-flung areas of the province. Protest meetings in sympathy with the slain were also held in Lahore, Islamabad, and Karachi. These political activists had been members of a committee locating persons who went missing during the Musharraf rule.

The highlight of the current Baloch situation was Interior Advisor Rehman Malik's explanations of the killings and other happenings in Balochistan at a closed-door Senate session on April 23, 2009, which was rejected by Baloch senators. A well-known and respected Baloch Senator, Hasil Bizenjo of the National

Party, remarked after the session that the government had not addressed the real issues of Balochistan and that Malik's accusation of foreign involvement required more evidence.

Troubles in Balochistan took place at a time when Pakistan was threatened by further intrusion of the Taliban into the settled areas of the North-West Frontier Province (NWFP). Against this unsettling background, attending to the problems in Balochistan was urgently necessary. This requires, first of all, recognizing that a large segment of the Baloch population feels wronged, and that a common source of the frustration is the belief that the province receives little attention from the government and a smaller share of resources than are due. This perception has a mixture of truth and exaggeration, but a real frustration cannot be denied. As it is commonly said, at times perceptions are more effective and lethal than realities. It is also important to recognize who actually rules Balochistan— neither the government nor bureaucrats imported from other provinces, but a team of Baloch tribal *sardars* and representatives of the people.

In 2010 the Zardari government made several half-hearted attempts to address the convulsions in Pakistan's largest and most strategic province. The government tried to repair the damage inflicted by Musharraf regime's murder of a Baloch tribal chief, Akbar Bugti and his other "anti-Baloch" policies. President Zardari has publicly apologized to the people of the province for past unjust practices and promised to constitute a commission to take stock of the demands of the Balochi people. On his first visit to Quetta, he announced a development package of Rs 46.6 billion for the province and has promised more to come. Zardari remarked, "My government won't hesitate to make constitutional amendments in the light of legislators' recommendations to solve problems of the province." But little has come from these promises from the President. At least, the urgency of the redress has beenmuch slower that the speed of events, violent and otherwise, taking place on daily basis in Balochistan.

There is no doubt that Balochistan has been a top priority of the government, notwithstanding the challenges of confronting militants in the Federally Administrated Tribal Areas (FATA) and Swat. The following steps could help improve the dismal situation in Balochistan and bring its people into the national mainstream, both in socioeconomic and political terms:

Balochistan needs "freedom" from some of its anti-development *sardars*. The people of the province should be involved in massive developmental projects. In the past, these *sardars* and *nawabs* usurped Baloch resources, leaving the people poor, illiterate, and frustrated.

A consensus exists among various analysts of ethnicity that since "ethnicity is a complex social, political and psychological problem, economic backwardness, demographic complexity or cultural suppression upgrade the enigma of ethnonationalism." In the case of Balochistan, a "non-participatory political system increased the problem of ethno-nationalism in the Baloch populated areas of the province." To redress the problem, provincial autonomy in fiscal matters in particular, as well as administrative reforms are necessary. However, Balochistan also needs reforms in education and other social sectors which will weaken the hold of the "anti-development" *sardars* and *nawabs*, thus providing space and opportunity for people to make decisions for themselves.

NOTES

1. Because of their sizeable presence in Balochistan, the Pashtuns hoped for a balance between the two ethnic groups. It is in this context that when a Baloch governor was appointed in 2009, the Pashtun tribal *jirga* chair, Amanullah Achakzai appealed to President Asif Ali Zardari to reconsider his choice and appoint a Pashtun as a governor, as the Chief Minister was a Baloch. *Dawn*, April 7, 2009.

2. The Hazara are a tiny minority residing in southeastern Quetta. According to a 1975 estimate, their population ranges from 50,000 to 60,000. They speak Farsi and migrated from Afghanistan about eight centuries ago. The most prominent Hazara was General Mohammad Musa, who was Commander-in-Chief of the Pakistan Army and later Governor of West Pakistan from 1967–1969. He also became governor of Balochistan from December, 1985 to March 12, 1991. For details of the Hazaras, see Dr. Mohammad Owtadolajam, *A Sociological Study of the Hazara Tribe in Balochistan (An Analysis of Socio-cultural Change)*, (Quetta: Hazaragi Academy; [Tanzeem Nasle Nau Hazara Mughal], 2006). The Sindhis are farmers who settled in the arable lands in the east, while most of the longtime Punjabi settlers are in Quetta city.

3. During the British rule, Balochistan consisted of four princely states: Kalat, Makran, Kharan, and Las Bela. A treaty was signed between the Khan of Kalat and the British agent to the Governor-General in Baluchistan, Sir Robert Sandeman, in 1876, according to which territory under the Khan's jurisdiction was brought under British control which included Kharan, Makran, and Las Bela. By 1887, a large part of present-day Balochistan came under the British authority.

4. Selig S. Harrison, "Baluch Nationalism and Superpower Rivalry," *International Security*, Winter 1980/81 (Vol. 5, No. 3), p. 153.

5. Ibid., p. 163.

6. Stephen and Carroll McC. Pastner, "Adaptations to State-Level Politics by the Southern Baluch," in Lawrence Ziring, Ralph Braibanti, and W. Howard Wriggins, eds. *Pakistan: The Long View* (Durham, N.C.: Duke University Press, 1977), p. 136.

7. The Fourteen Points of Muhammad Ali Jinnah are regarded as "safeguards for Muslims of India," Waheed Ahmad, ed., *Quaid-i-Azam Mohammad Ali Jinnah: The Nation's Voice towards Consolidation–Speeches and Statements, March 1935–March 1940* (Karachi: Quaid-i-Azam Academy, 1992), pp. 528–529.

8. Waheed Ahmad, "General Budget Demands: Reforms in Baluchistan," *Quaid-i-Azam Mohammad Ali Jinnah Speeches: Indian Legislative Assembly, 1935–1947* (Karachi: Quaid-i-Azam Academy, 1991), pp. 501–503.

9. " 'Enormous Spadework'–ML has established dominant ML Ministries wherever we are in Majority," Waheed Ahmad, ed., *Quaid-i-Azam Mohammad Ali Jinnah, The Nation's Voice, Vol. III–Unity, Faith and Discipline, May 1942–October 1944* (Karachi: Quaid-i-Azam Academy, 1970), pp. 235–236.

10. Ibid., p. 237.

11. "ML pressure secured principle of election to Quetta Municipality, Balouchistan representation in central legislature and grant for education," Waheed Ahmad, ed. *Quaid-i-Azam Mohammad Ali Jinnah–The Nation's Voice, Vol. IV: Towards the Popular Verdict–Annotated Speeches, Statements and Interviews, November 1944–April 1946* (Karachi: Quaid-i-Azam Academy, 2000), p. 340.

12. Ibid., p. 341.

13. Ibid., p. 342.

14. "Speech by M. A. Jinnah at Sibi Durbar" *Sibi*, February 12, 1948, in Z. H. Zaidi, editor in chief, *Jinnah papers–Pakistan: Struggling for Survival, 1 January–30 September 1948*; First Series, Volume VII, First edition (Islamabad: Culture Division, Government of Pakistan, 2002), p. 102.

15. Ibid.

16. Ibid., p. 105.

17. Wayne Ayres Wilcox, *Pakistan: The Consolidation of a Nation*; 3rd ed. (New York: Columbia University Press, 1966), p. 148.

18. Stephen and Carroll McC. Pastner, "Adaptations to State-Level Politics by the Southern Baluch," op. cit., p. 120.

19. Martin Axmann, *Back to the Future; the Khanate of Kalat and the Genesis of Baloch Nationalism, 1915–1955* (New York: Oxford University Press, 2008), p. 78.

20. "Up against sardari system," *Dawn* (editorial), August 26, 2006. Sylvia A. Matheson narrates the views of Nawab Akbar Bugti, a Bughtai *sardar*, when she met him for an interview, in these words, " 'Of course,' said the Nawab, 'you must remember that I killed my first man when I was twelve!' . . . Well, the man annoyed me. I've rather a hasty temper you know, but under tribal law of course it wasn't a capital offence, and in any case as the eldest son of the Chieftain I was perfectly entitled to do as I pleased in my territory. We enjoy absolute sovereignty over our people and they accept this as part of their tradition." Sylvia A. Matheson, *The Tigers of Baluchistan*; with a new introduction by Paul Titus (New York: Oxford University Press, 1997), pp. 1, 3.

21. Dr. Shah Muhammad Marri, *Baloch Quam: Qadeem Ahad se Asr Hazar Tak* (*Baloch Nation: From Ancient Era to Present Times*) (Lahore: Takhliqat, 2000), p. 319. Translated from Urdu by the author.

22. Janmahmad, *Essays on Baloch National Struggle in Pakistan* (Quetta: Gosha-e-Adab, 1989), p. 292.

23. Chaudhri Muhammad Ali, op. cit, pp. 218.

24. Stephen and Carroll McC. Pastner, "Adaptations to State-Level Politics by the Southern Baluch," op. cit., p. 138.

25. Safdar Sial, *Election 2008: Political Disintegration in Balochistan*, January 24, 2008; Pak Institute of Peace Studies, http://san-pips.com/index.php?action=san&id=42.

26. Professor Aziz Muhammad Bugti, *Balochistan: Sayasi Culture aur Qabale Nizam, Urdu* (*Balochistan: Political Culture and Tribal System*) (Lahore: Function House, 1995), p. 105.

27. For a detailed account of provincial elections, see Dr. Inam ul Haq and Professor Anwar Ruman, *Balochistan Aazadi ke Bade (1947–1997)*; Urdu (*Balochistan after Independence: 1947–1997*) (Quetta: Mushawara Talime Tahqaq, 1997), pp. 118–144.Professor Aziz Muhammad Bugti, *Balochistan: Sayasi Culture aur Qabale Nizam*, Urdu (*Balochistan: Political Culture and Tribal System)* (Lahore: Function House, 1995), p. 105

28. Professor Aziz Muhammad Bugti, op. cit., p. 105.

29. Dr. Shah Muhammad Marri, op. cit., pp. 318. Translated from Urdu by the author.

30. *The Nation*, May 31, 2009.

31. Ibid.

32. The Baloch leader denied allegations that Baloch leaders had a fair chance to bring changes in the province, but they failed to do so. He explained that the Baloch leaders were not given a chance to serve their people and that the existing tribal system is not responsible for the underdevelopment of the Baloch people. He said that more political and economic empowerment can bring constructed changes in the Baloch society. *Dawn*, April 23, 2009. In an article, the former Senator reminded the ruling Pakistan Peoples Party (PPP) of the promises made to the Baloch people. He pointed out these promises: a) completely ending the military operation and halting the construction of military and paramilitary cantonments, b) withdrawing security forces, c) repatriating and rehabilitating displaced persons, d) cancelling civil/military land allotments, e) demilitarizing the area, f) ensuring equal wellhead prices for Balochistan's gas, and h) abandoning torture camps and establishing a 'truth and reconciliation commission' for the trial of those involved in killing veteran Baloch leaders Nawab Akbar Bugti and Balach Marri, and other human rights violations. "Baloch demands still unmet," *Dawn*, February 19, 2009.

33. *Dawn*, November 14, 1947, quoted in Ibid., p. 78.

34. Martin Axmann, op. cit., p. 298. Ahmad Yar received an annual allowance of Rs. 281,000 from the British, which was raised to Rs. 650,000 by the Pakistan government.

35. Wayne Ayres Wilcox, op. cit., p. 80.

36. Wayne Ayres Wilcox, op. cit., p. 80. The author quotes *Dawn*, March 29, 1948 for this report.

37. Ibid., p. 81.

38. Ibid., p. 236.

39. Ibid., p. 237.

40. Known better as A. B. Awan, he held two important positions in the federal service of Pakistan. He was Director of Intelligence as well as Secretary, Ministry of Home Affairs.

41. A. B. Awan, *Baluchistan: Historical and Political Processes* (London: New Century Publishers, 1985), p. 212.

42. Martin Axmann, op. cit., pp. 262.

43. Ibid., p. 241. With the establishment of "One Unit" in West Pakistan, the Balochistan states ceded all of their powers, authority, and sovereignty to the government of Pakistan, on January 1, 1955. Baluchistan [*sic*] States Union Merger Agreement, Article II read: The members of the Council of Rulers shall be entitled to receive annually from the Government of Pakistan for their privy purse free of all taxes the amount given below:

His Highness, the Khan–i–Azam of Kalat	Rs. 6,50,000 (Rupees, six lacs and fifty thousand)
The Nawab of Makran	Rs. 2,25,000 (Rupees, two lacs and twenty-five thousand)
The Jam Sahib of Las Bela	Rs. 2,00,000 (Rupees, two lacs)
The Nawab of Kharan	Rs. 70,000 (Rupees, seventy thousand)

44. Mir Ahmad Yar Khan, *Inside Balouchistan: A Political Autobiography of His Highness Baiglar Baigi Khan-e-Azam XIII* (Karachi: Royal Book Company, 1975), pp. 174, 191.

45. A. B. Awan, *Baluchistan: Historical and Political Processes,* op. cit., p. 228.

46. Anwar H. Syed, *The Discourse and Politics of Zulfikar Ali Bhutto* (London: The Macmillan Press Ltd, 1992), p. 185.

47. Lawrence Ziring, *Pakistan in the Twentieth Century: A Political History* (Karachi: Oxford University Press, 1997), p. 391.

48. Burney, *Outlook*, June 16, 1973, quoted in Ibid.

49. Hamid Khan, *Constitutional and Political History of Pakistan* (Karachi: Oxford University Press, 2001), p. 889.

50. The first NFC Award was announced in 1974, the second in 1979, the third in 1985, the fourth in 1990, the fifth in 1996, and the sixth in 2000.The NFC Awards of 1979, 1984, and 2000 ended in a deadlock as the provinces could not agree on a unanimous formula of resource distribution.

51. The seventh NFC Award raised the share of the provinces from 47.5 to 56 percent with the assurance that it would be raised to 60 percent in due course. The thorny issue of multiple indicators was resolved as follows: (a) Population: 82%; (b) Poverty/Backwardness: 10.3%; (c) Revenue Collection/Generation: 5.0%; (d) Inverse Population Density: 2.7% (Urban-Rural). According to the mutually agreed-upon formula, Punjab will receive 51.74% of the resources, while Sindh, NWFP, and Balochistan will receive, 24.55%, 14.62%, and 9.09%, respectively.

52. *Dawn* (editorial), December 13, 2009. The editorial went on to comment: "The consensus on the seventh NFC award is a sign that, political differences aside, not only do the provinces and the centre want to make democracy work, they in fact can do so when given the time and space to make difficult decisions."

53. Ibid.

54. *Pakistan Times*, March 26, 2005, http://pakistantimes.net/2005/03/26/top1.htm

55. http://www.zeenews.com/news601367.html. Earlier, in October, 2009, Interior Minister Rehman Malik said that he has "solid evidence of India's interference in Balochistan." He went on to say, "I invite their (India) interior minister or anyone else (to come to Pakistan) and I will put on record all the material about India's interference in Balochistan. I'll prove it to the world." http://www.hindustantimes.com/News-Feed/pakistan/Pak-has-evidence-about-India-s-involvement-in-Balochistan-Rehman-Malik/Article1-467673.aspx

56. *The News*, December 10, 2009, http://www.thenews.com.pk/arc_default.asp

57. Pervez Hoodbhoy, *The Hindu*, November 27, 2009, http://beta.thehindu.com/opinion/ lead/article56002.ece

58. Lt. General Abdul Qayyum, "Balochistan's Commotion: What is the Truth?," *Nawa-e-Waqt* (Urdu Newspaper), May 1, 2009.

59. Shah Jahan Baloch, "Balochistan needs political response," *The Frontier Post*, May 5, 2009.

60. Ziad Haider, Baluchis, Beijing, and Pakistan's Gwadar Port, *Georgetown Journal of International Affairs*, Volume 6, Number 1 (Winter/Spring 2005), p. 97.

61. *The News*, April 14, 2001.

62. "Pakistan: The Worsening Conflict in Balochistan," *Asia Report N° 119,* September 14, 2006, International Crisis Group, p. 14, http://www.crisisgroup.org/library/documents/asia/ south_asia/119_pakistan_the_worsening_conflict_in_balochistan.pdf

63. *Report of the Parliamentary Committee on Balochistan*, Senate of Pakistan, Report 7; November, 2005, Islamabad, p. 44.

64. Interviews, Gwadar and Quetta, December–March, 2006, *"Pakistan: The Worsening Conflict in Balochistan,"* op. cit., p. 15.

65. Syed Fazl-e-Haider, "China digs Pakistan into a hole," *Asia Times on line*, October 5, 2006, http://www.atimes.com/atimes/South_Asia/HJ05Df01.html

66. Ibid.

67. Saniyya Gauhar, "MINING Pakistan: a copper state?" *Pak Tribune*, November 28, 2006, http://www.paktribune.com/pforums/posts.php?t=2836&start=1

68. Ibid.

69. Ashraf Javed, "Reko Diq Project: Contract termination may tarnish Pak image," *The Nation*, January 13, 2010. Ashraf Javed, a columnist for Pakistan's leading Lahore-based English daily paper expresses apprehensions about the Balochistan government's action. He writes that in such huge projects, international investment is required and secondly, it needs high-level local experts, (which will not be easy to find). He further says: "the termination of the contract with world's leading gold and copper mining firm could mar Pakistan's image as an investment destination, and the multinational corporations would not invest in a country where deals were cancelled after finalization [*sic*] of the contract."

70. *Dawn*, June 12, 2006, http://www.dawn.com/2006/06/12/nat21.htm

71. *Dawn*, January 23, 2010.

72. *Jang* (Urdu), June 28, 2009. The governor admitted that the deployment of the Frontier Corps is not the answer and political dialogue is the desirable option for peace in the area.

73. *The News*, November 24, 2009.

74. People were missing from other parts of Pakistan as well. It is common knowledge in Pakistan that most of these missing persons were handed over to the American government by Musharraf regime for remuneration. No charges were brought against these missing persons nor was due process followed. However, a number of such persons were later recovered from various agencies of the Pakistan government.

75. Amir Mir, "High time to take up Bugti murder case," *The News*, August 27, 2009.

76. *Nawa-e-Waqt*, February 24, 2010. The general expressed his views on a TV talk show, *Waqt*, hosted by Salman Ghani.

77. *Jang* (editorial), June 12, 2009.

78. *Dawn*, January 18, 2010.

79. "Pushed to the wall," Report of the HRCP fact-finding mission to Balochistan, (October 5–11, 2009) (Lahore: Human Rights Commission of Pakistan, 2010), p. 18. According to the same report, in 2009 there were a total of 141 target killings, of which 118 ordinary residents were killed, while 83 were injured. On the other hand, 158 security personnel were killed and 7 injured in incidents of target killing in the Balochistan province. According the report, "The government's failure to arrest and prosecute the perpetrators of violence is another reason that discouraged non-Baloch teachers to continue working in Balochistan." p. 20.

80. *The News*, February 25, 2010.

CHAPTER 5

Pakistan under Siege: Extremism, Militancy, and the Emergence of Terror Groups

INTRODUCTION

For many Pakistanis, and for the rest of the world, the increasing militancy in various parts of Pakistan with multiple manifestations came as a puzzling quandary. The induction of extremism and militancy has three different expressions in Pakistan. The first expression came in the form of widespread sectarian killings, which peaked in the mid-1980s, while the second was the Afghan invasion of the Soviets and its implications, and the third expression was the fallout of the post-2000 events when the U.S. military attacked Afghanistan, subjecting the country to massive bombing raids in which thousands were killed and injured. A large number of Taliban disappeared into the local tribes, while its leadership, along with its followers sought refuge in the tribal belt of neighboring Pakistan. The overspill of the Afghan military situation began to have serious ramifications upon the tribal areas of Pakistan, which later stretched to other parts of Pakistan. Various military campaigns by U.S. and Pakistan military forces in the tribal areas, not only gave rise to armed resistance, but also uprooted the traditional and delicate socio-cultural system in the centuries-old tribal system. This provided a space for the militant groups to take charge of the area in all fields of activity. Eventually, these types of militancy and extremism merged to an extent that it became difficult to distinguish between the two different forms of radicalism.

The violence-laden sectarian extremism became visible and gained strength, mainly due to the policies of Zia-ul-Haq, who encouraged a certain interpretation of Islam. In the 1990s in particular, a drastic progression of sectarian killings took place in the most populous province of the Punjab, with occurrences in other parts of the country as well. These disparaging developments, accompanied by the lack of political institutions and the erosion of political parties, further complicated the already fragile societal balance. Traditional Pakistani society has not been inclined towards religious extremism, nor has there been a sustained historic pattern of violence as a means of achieving religious or political objectives. Repeated extended military rules have shaken the cohesion of the society, and there was hardly a mechanism left for crisis management which is essential for the stability of any social order. Such an apparatus becomes necessary to buffer the negativity of the extremes, thus providing equilibrium and a relative tranquility within a society.

Until the beginning of 1980s, Pakistani society was reasonably tolerant. In 1968, a huge mass movement against the dictatorial rule of Ayub Khan went on for months, in nearly all of the big cities and towns of Pakistan. There was hardly an instance of sabotage or any other type of violence from the agitators. In fact, this extended mass revolt, in search of the rule of law and justice, demanded freedom and democracy and a freely elected Parliament. Another mass movement against the rigging of the 1977 general elections followed the same fairly violence-free pattern.

Decades of military rule have created a way of life where real Pakistani values were undermined, which ultimately eroded for the worse. Oppression, intolerance, and disregard for law were practiced by the ruling elite as an accepted model. Taking advantage of the Afghan situation in the 1980s, General Zia-ul-Haq further inculcated a culture of violence with his deceitful rule. While the Afghan resistance went on, his inept military administration silently adjusted to the culture of violence and militancy within Pakistani society. Regional secular parties were created to protect the narrow objectives of the junta, which as a result undermined nationally acknowledged political entities. These narrowly focused military-sponsored political groups were based upon hatred and suspicion which became instrumental in disturbing the peace and tranquil balance of Pakistani society.

Pakistan's decision to take part in the Afghan resistance against the Soviets in the 1980s had tremendous negative impact upon Pakistani society. The fallout of the events of post-1979, when the Soviets occupied Pakistan, had intense and long-lasting effects on Pakistani society which continues to haunt Pakistan even today. The country became a hub of arms flow to Afghanistan and in return, 3.5 million refugees sought shelter in the Pakistani cities and countryside; most of them resided in NWFP and Balochistan because of their ethnic and linguistic affinity. A large number of unemployed and dislocated Afghan youth had little choice but to join the ever-growing religious schools, funded mostly by the United States and Saudi Arabia, followed by the Gulf states. Not to be left behind were the local traders, with Deobandi and Ahle-Hadees sectarian leanings.

After the Soviets left Afghanistan in 1988, the military took upon itself the assignment of playing a "role" in the war-torn country. The establishment's interests were based upon the egoistic and self-defeating multifaceted conviction that they could play a role in the making and maintenance of a regime of their liking in Afghanistan. Their close ties with the Taliban encouraged the militant Islamist organizations in Pakistan to go ahead unabated with their extremist agenda. The Pakistani governments callously allowed the march towards the "Talibanization" of Pakistani society, inducting culture of hate and bigotry, which ultimately ruined the centuries-old traditions and values of harmony between divergent sectarian sects.

In Pakistan, a strong connection between rising religious bigotry/terrorism and poverty and role of dictatorial rule based upon a well-defined hierarchical pyramid formed a formidable monster, which is difficult to understand and to control. A well-known columnist sums up the dynamics of extremism in the country in the following paragraphs,

> Under the governmental and administrative extremism, various extremist movements, organizations and tendencies came into being, which continue in the present circumstances, as well. It should be admitted that extremism, which General Musharraf is apprehensive about, is encouraged and promoted by the clandestine agencies operating under the military governments. It includes the linguist and ethnic extremism in the urban areas of Sindh and the nation wide spread of sectarian fanaticism. These have been directed by the hidden but influential personals.
>
> Today, the effects of extremism are visible, where one extremism is confronting another, to the unease of General Musharraf. It should be understood that non-democratic and unconstitutional system of government and extremist linguist and sectarian organizations are natural allies of each other. One cannot function without the other. The military governments need the support of extremist organizations after they remove the democratic government and people's representatives, as these organizations cannot operate under a democratic setup. As a basic rule such organizations are initially dependent on the military governments but later they become close and equal allies of each other. When genuine organizations supported by the people are sidelined, a competitive struggle takes place between the military regime and the extremists, to fill the vacuum.[1]

Madrasas

Many researchers and analysts blame the faulty education system whether *madrasa*-related or otherwise to the rise of "radical Islam." Even in the middle of 2009, and in spite of the promises made by the newly elected Pakistani government to exercise a strict control over the *madrasas* and their activities, it is estimated that even in city like Karachi, the *madrasas* have continued with the goal of spreading bigotry. In 2009, there were 2.7 million children who attended 20,000 *madrasas* in Pakistan.[2] In an investigative report, Zubeida Mustafa, a well-known journalist writes,

> The entire tenor of the curricula ensures that students are subjected to a massive dose of indoctrination. If you look at the textbooks minus the title page it is difficult to differentiate one from the other. Be it an Islamic book or books of English, Urdu or Pakistan Studies, each begins with chapters which are entirely religious in content or have a strong religious undertone. At one time even a biology book contained an *ayat* on *jihad*.[3]

This is, in spite of the fact that the Madrasas Reform Committee, constituted in 2009 to reform the functioning of these institutions, has not started its work even after a lapse of more than a year (as of this publication).[4] According to Zubeida Mustafa, ". . . the psyche of a large number of youth enrolled in government schools is no better than what *madressah* [*sic*] education produces. It is, in fact, more dangerous because few people seem to be aware of the curriculum of hatred taught in our schools."[5] The solution to the problem which the present political elite fail to understand is that minor changes in the syllabus can bring about a huge change in the curriculum of these schools. All that is needed to be done is to teach a "softer version of Islam as it used to be before the hardliners took over."[6]

Ever since the events of 9/11, *madrasa* education has been looked upon with suspicion, as there is a lack of government oversight regarding the type of instruction being provided. During the Soviet occupation of Afghanistan, these *madrasas* were encouraged by the state of Pakistan, as well as by U.S. intelligence agencies since these institutions became a recruiting ground for the "foot soldiers" of the Afghan "international *jihad*." The real pressure on Pakistan, regarding the control and monitoring of the *madrasas,* came after the July, 7, 2008 London bombings. The suicide bombers, who were British citizens and the product of British society in terms of education and work, were traced to these institutions in Pakistan. It was established that they had received training and indoctrination in militancy from militant groups in Pakistan. There was tremendous pressure from the United States and the European community on the Musharraf government to crack down on these centers of militancy, especially those who were involved in inculcating a militant indoctrination among its students and to reform and monitor some 11,491 institutions with 1.7 million students.[7] However, unofficial figures estimate that the enrolled students range from 12,000 to 15,000.

A proclamation in June 2002 was made with the title, "Voluntary Registration and Regulation Ordinance," but it was rejected by the majority of the *madrasa* managements, under the plea that they would not accept any government interference. The ordinance, as the name suggests, asked for the voluntary registration of the *madrasas*. It also established provincial *madrasa* boards and imposed a ban on the enrolment of foreign students, with official permission.[8] According to well-researched findings on the *madrasas* situation as it stood in 2009,

> To fulfill the declared objectives of madrasa reform, a five year project was formulated by the Ministry of Education at the cost of approximately $100 million. The plan was to

provide facilities to 8,000 madrasas in terms of teachers' salaries, textbooks, stationary [*sic*], libraries and computers. Again, the federation of the madrasa organizations, Ittehad Tanzeemat-e-Madaris-e-Diniya, refused to oblige despite a series of meetings between its representatives and the officials of the Ministry of Education and Ministry of Religious Affairs. The government announced several deadlines for the madrasas' registration but the response from the madrasas was of continued defiance. It was only when the second ordinance was amended to remove the requirement of reporting the income and expenditure statements to the government that the madrasas agreed to register.

Before the promulgation of the ordinance of 2005, about 6,000 madrasas were registered under the Registration of Literary, Scientific and Charitable Societies Act, 1860. From 2005 to 2007, 8,072 more madrasas were registered. The total number of registered madrasas at the end of 2007, according to the former religious affairs minister, was 14,072. It is apparent, therefore, that despite their contestations, a large number of madrasas in Pakistan are now registered with the government, although their registration could not be attained under the newly-issued ordinances. The curricula of the madrasas are regulated by their respective boards, and have not undergone any significant changes in their core content since inception in the 19th century. Some modern subjects such as English, history, math, etc., have been introduced in several madrasas, especially at the elementary level, and some large madrasas have started some specialized courses on Islamic economics and finance. However, in an overwhelming majority of cases the higher level madrasas remain committed to their traditional curriculum.[9]

Because of other pressing problems in Pakistan like power shortages, high inflation, a rising poverty level, and a fierce insurgency with and acts of terrorism, further *madrasa* reforms and their implementation is no longer a priority. There was hardly a new approach or policy introduced to the Pakistani Parliament throughout 2009 and 2010.

The institution of *madrasas*, as it exists today is complicated, and does not provide clear answers. "On the one hand, this institution is sunk in its general deplorable and pathetic conditions and, furthermore, faces the problem of sectarianism. On the other hand, it has become a place of resistance against the American occupation of Afghanistan and America's increasing control of Pakistan."[10] The option of taking over the *madrasas* by the government has many pitfalls and at times, the situation looks impractical and difficult. General Musharraf made attempts to regulate these institutions but failed. The Zardari government of the Pakistan Peoples Party did the same and met a similar fate,

> The process of takeover is not simple ... because out of some 20,000 *madressahs [sic]* which are now said to exist in Pakistan, most do not even have more than a room attached to the *masjid*, so what would the government take over? A mud-walled structure? And what would it do to these *madressahs [sic]*? Add them on its already dead weight of thousands of state-run schools? Obviously, something needs to be done, but is that something?[11]

In recent years, analysts dealing with the question of militancy and its source in Pakistan have started looking beyond the *madrasas* to find a solution to this grave crisis faced by the state and society of Pakistan. There is a strong view held that "*madrasahs* [*sic*] Education System doesn't automatically lead to the spread of violence and militancy in the society. The proponents of this approach however admit that the introduction, by some seminaries, of military training and the breeding of a particular violent political ideology led to spreading militancy in Pakistan religious institutions".[12] These centuries-old institutions became militant when they were used by the state as a deliberate policy to encourage resentment and to build up a hate hysteria against the Soviet occupation of Afghanistan and later, the Kashmir issue. In fact, the *madrasas* were used by the interested establishement to fulfill their foreign policy agenda. It is another matter that some of these *madrasas* later became breeding grounds for sectarian and ideological hatred and bigotry while targeting the state of Pakistan and the members of opposing Islamic sects, like *Shias* and *Baralvies*.

Over the years, the government of Pakistan has been negligent towards the education sector creating significant gaps to be filled by private schools and in this case, the *madrasas*. With the virtual collapse of the public school system, there has been an expansion of schools into the private sector, with an enormous fee structure which is beyond the capacity of a vast majority of families. In this case, the best choice for the parents is to send their children to the *madrasas*, as they believe that it will provide education which is of better quality when compared to the poor public school system. To make matters worse, in the 2010 annual budget, the federal government announced a 73 percent reduction of the higher education sector budget. This drastic reduction will have a negative bearing even upon the ongoing projects of various public universities. Pointing out the consequences of this drastic reduction for education, the president of the Pakistan Economy Watch (PEW) said that "the poor have been deprived of basic right to education by slashing the budgetary allocation, which amounts to encouraging those who consider education a profitable business." He went on to say further, "Many private educational institutions have raised fees from 15 to 30 percent after the budget that is unfortunate. Reduced allocation for education is a wrong political decision. As a result, number of children who have no access to schooling will swell from 30 million."[13]

A recent study by the Brookings Institution assesses a possible link between militancy and the public educational sector. The report based its findings on surveys, interviews with ordinary Pakistanis, as well as "interviews of prominent Pakistanis based inside and outside the country."[14] It states at the outset,

> The Pakistani education sector, like much of the country's public infrastructure, has been in decline during the last few decades. Despite recent progress, current school attainment and literacy levels remain extremely low. Poor school performance across Pakistan would therefore seem an obvious area of inquiry as a risk factor for conflict.[15]

The highlight of the report is a negation of the previously held view that *madrasas* are mainly responsible for militancy, "Religious seminaries that are not militant should be treated with respect and not conflated with militant seminaries."[16]

This well-researched Brookings report spells out nine "key findings," on the state of education in Pakistan which are detailed as follows:

Finding 1: Demand for education within Pakistan far exceeds the government's ability to provide it.

Finding 2: Contrary to popular belief, *madrasas* have not risen to fill the gap in public education supply and have not been one of the primary causes of the recent rise in militancy.

Finding 3: Beyond *madrasas*, the education supply gap in and of itself likely increases the risk of conflict in low-income countries, including in Pakistan, highlighting the importance of expanding educational access.

Finding 4: A nuanced analysis of the mechanisms whereby education may exacerbate conflict risk suggests that in addition to access, education quality and content may be just as important for promoting stability.

Finding 5: Poor education-sector governance creates huge discrepancies in the public education system, inflaming citizens' grievances against the government.

Finding 6: Poor learning outcomes hinder the development of the core skills, including those related to good citizenship, that are needed to help mitigate extremism.

Finding 7: The curriculum and teaching in government schools help create intolerant worldviews among students.

Finding 8: Schools do little to prepare students for the labor market, frustrating young achievers and increasing the pool of possible militant recruits.

Finding 9: Education provision is highly inequitable, exacerbating grievances by those left out of the system.

Apart from the quality of education, a low literacy rate by itself becomes a reason for militant organizations to recruit frustrated and ignorant youth. For some time, Pakistan has had one of the lowest literacy states in the world. According to UNESCO figures, the literacy rate stands at 55 percent and Pakistan is ranked as one of the lowest (160th) literate countries in the world community.[17] Tariq M. Ashraf illustrates that 40 percent of DJE (Dissent Jehadi Elements) who are involved in terrorist activities are poor and that 79 percent of them have a high school or below education.[18] Table 5.1 provides interesting statistics on the terrorist youth, involved in sectarian killings.

Table 5.1 Statistical Profile of Sectarian Terrorists

1	Age	Average age 20—30; 14% less than 20
2	Education	36% high school & below; 19% illiterate; 30% from *madrasas*
3	Weapons Training	5% in Pakistan; 95% abroad
4	Motivation	93% by speeches/literature

Source: Syed Tauqir Shah, "Madrassah Reform: Politics, Policy or Polemics," November, 30, 2004; CSA, Lahore, http://www.policy.hu/shah/report/Presentation-Madaris%20CSA.pdf

Socio-Economic Factors

There is a widespread belief that weak socio-economic institutions, especially increasing poverty in Pakistan, should also to be analyzed as a possible cause of increasing militant tendencies. But the data speaks otherwise, as according to a study, poverty decreased between 2001/2002 and 2005/2006 in Paksitant while there was a significant surge in incidences of terrorism. Furthermore, "militant recruitment from some particularly poor regions, namely rural Sindh and much of Balochistan, appears to be fairly low. There is thus little evidence to support the contention that poverty, in and of itself, fuels extremism."[19] However, poverty is a contributing factor for increased extremism in the country, for example in the areas of south Punjab. According to an analysis, "Studies on the socio-economic profiles of militants would suggest, however, that poverty is a contributing factor pushing people towards militancy, provided an enabling environment already exists. The lack of employment opportunities for the educated, as well as deficiencies in the public school system also appears amongst the factors that drive militancy."[20]

Even as a contributing factor, the socio-economic conditions of Pakistani society cannot be undermined. In fact, apart from the ideological and malfunction of the political and constitutional institutions, a lack of functional socio-economic structures remain a significant driving force behind the increasingly militant mindset in the country. Socio-economic issues such as the wide and ever-increasing gap between the rich and poor, the failure of the state to provide adequate educational facilities, the lack of health amenities, social injustice, unemployment, and serious concerns of human security, including a deteriorating law and order situation, also have significant bearing upon the social fabric of the country.

It is an established fact, recognized by both analysts and policymakers, that in order to contain militancy as well as insurgency, it is important to win the battle for the hearts and minds of the Pakistani people. The management of these socio-economic issues becomes important, as they not only provide a level of contentment to the general population at the grassroots' level, but also create a bond of trust between the people and the government. As already discussed in previous chapters, poor governmental policies are held to be responsible for the prevailing conditions in Pakistan. Bad policies, denial of justice, and the lack of opportunity have created relative deprivation and frustrations in Pakistani society.

As a result of the widening resource gap and increasing despair accompanied by poor governmental policies, extremism and violent tendencies were provided plenty of impetus among the underprivileged to grow. In this context, poverty by itself became a major socio-economic medium in Pakistani society. In Pakistan, nearly two-thirds of the population and 80 percent of the country's poor people live in rural areas. Most of them do not have access to the adequate basic needs of life.[21] Poverty, in this case, takes away from other basic necessities like food, shelter, health, education, and even justice. This "poverty of opportunity" results in hopelessness, despair, and depression in society which in most cases, eventually becomes violent as the ultimate option for the survival of the weakest. To make matters worse, inflation increased from 7.7 percent in 2007 to 20.8 percent in 2008, and to 14.2 percent in 2009.[22] It is to be noted that the FATA areas remain the most backward region in Pakistan, with 60 percent of the people living below the poverty line. According to the White Paper (2010) issued by the provincial government of the Khyber-Pakhtunkhwa Finance Department, this border area remains the poorest in Pakistan, with an overall incidence of poverty at 44 percent as compared to 23.9 percent for Pakistan overall.[23] A recent study conducted by Lahore University of Management Science (LUMS) reveals that the incidence of poverty in South Punjab is 50.1 percent.[24] About 36 percent of the rural population in South Punjab is poor which makes it the second highest percentage, when compared to other provinces of Pakistan.[25]

The above-mentioned areas have become the main centers for the recruitment and training of militant groups. The widening resource and income gap also encourages locals to join the anti-government elements. For example, Balochistan has been the ignored region in terms of resource distribution and economic development for decades. This weakness was used as a primary agenda and propaganda tool by the anti-government groups to gain support and legitimacy. It resulted in a series of uprisings and encouraged insurgent movements in the region. A similar trend, although with its own features, has been witnessed in the areas of FATA and Southern Punjab.

These observations reflect that poverty and illiteracy are the main contributing reasons for militancy. An increasing trend of poverty and illiteracy reduces the probability of employment opportunities. Thus, unemployment becomes another key issue for Pakistan. The estimated rate of unemployment in 2008 was 12.6 percent, which rose to 14 percent in 2009.[26] Pakistan also suffers from both underemployment and cyclical unemployment which makes the situation even worse. During the past few years, the problem of power shortages has severely affected daily earners and factory workers. Because of the lack of planning and foresight of the government, a large percentage of youth is unemployed. Unemployment enhances the general feeling of despair and sense of alienation from the system, and thus encourages resentment against the established rule and societal norms. In this psychological tug-of-war, those affected find militancy a tempting alternative to bring about a change in society.

At the same time, years of disappointment with the prevailing government, has made these militants reject everything modern along with a Western solution to their dismal plight. In this stressful environment, militant organizations find it convenient to attract a considerable number of frustrated recruits. This environment also creates a relationship of dependency between the recruits and the

Table 5.2 Youth Unemployment in Pakistan, 2001–2007

Year	Sex	Youth labor force	Youth unemployed	Youth unemploy- ment rate (%)	Adult labor force	Youth population
2001	M/F	–	1,357	–	–	–
2002	M/F	11,996	1,381	13.41	28,211	27,631
2003	M/F	–	1,609	–	–	–
2004	M/F	13,071	1,528	11.69	29,981	29,991
2005	M/F	–	1,557	–	–	–
2006	M/F	14,447	1,249	8.645	32,555	31,460
2007	M/F	14,139	1,057	7.475	33,415	31,957

Source: UN Statistical Division, http://unstats.un.org/unsd/default.htm

organization as it provides food, shelter, and a generous amount of money. In this way, the new members are compelled to fulfill the aims and objectives of these organizations. Recruits are trained and brain-washed in order to accomplish their tasks for the organization. U.S. Secretary of State Hillary Clinton was correct in stating that, "We cannot stop terrorism or defeat the ideologies of violent extremism when hundreds of millions of young people see a future with no jobs, no hope, and no way ever to catch up to the developed world."[27]

Table 5.2 illustrates that, in the embryonic stage of militancy, youth employment was on a higher scale.

Yet another factor that promotes despair and frustration is corruption. In recent years, corruption has become a serious concern for Pakistan, as it has started to have its effect on the functioning of the society, thus undermining basic institutional structures. For many in Pakistan, corruption has been institutionalized. The Chair of Transparency International Pakistan, Syed Adil Gillani said that terrorism was the direct result of poverty, which had resulted due to corruption. Moreover, due to bad governmental policy, government not only loses the trust of the people, but also its credibility abroad. Economic threats, food and electricity shortages, inflation, and poverty are the result of massive corruption in the public sector.[28]

The National Corruption Perception Survey 2009 by Transparency International illustrates that in general, corruption increased from Rs. 45 billion in 2002 to Rs. 195 billion in 2009.[29] It is significant to note that the institution of police is ranked at the top, among the most corrupt sectors in Pakistan. In any society, law enforcement agencies are considered to be the main instruments to counter militant measures. This adverse situation provides a stage for militant groups to perform illegal acts, thus creating anarchy and disorder in the society. Rule of law also provides strength to the system as it makes it more accountable and transparent to the people. The report of International Crisis Group, *Pakistan's Tribal Areas: Appeasing the Militant* published in 2006 reveals that the only way to deal with the challenges of militancy in FATA is to ensure rule of law and the availability of political and civil rights.[30] It is imperative to note that along with FATA, areas like Balochistan and southern Punjab, where there has been a vacuum for rule of law for decades, are the core centers of militant movements. The lack of systemic approach towards capacity and institutional-building further acts as a catalyst to set the stage for militant trends in Pakistan.

Militant Culture and Sectarian Violence

A vast majority of the Pakistani population are followers of one of the four schools of Islamic interpretation: Bralivi or Sufi order, Ahle Hadith, Deobandi, and Shias. The first three are grouped together as Sunnis, but Brailvis are closer to Shias in their beliefs and rituals than to the other two Sunni sects of Islam. The Barelvis believe in Sufism and its practices, including the application of music (Qawwali) to provide spiritual inspiration to its followers and other practices which are more moderate when compared to other Sunni schools of thought. The Deobandi school regards music as un-Islamic and displays of pictures as a *shirk* (partner to God) and therefore forbidden; they have many other practices which are rigid and have a narrow interpretation of religious texts.[31] Although these variant religious interpretations have a vast intellectual gap between them, different sects had generally lived and practiced their exclusive rituals peacefully side-by-side. "Thus, for the first 25 years of Pakistan's existence, religious extremism was rare, sectarian strife was limited and the two religious parties that predated partition (creation of Pakistan)—Jamiat Ulema-i-Islam (JUI) and Jamiat-i-Islami (JI)—played, at best, a marginal political role."[32]

According to an estimate, 80 percent of the Pakistani Sunni population are believers of Sufi traditions, while only 10 percent are Deobandis, mostly located in the Pashtun-populated parts of Pakistan. Due to the designed policies of former General Zia-ul-Haq and contrary to the population representation of the country, some 64 percent of the total seminaries are run by Deobandis, 25 percent by the Barelvis, six percent by the Ahle Hadith, and three percent by various Shiite organizations.[33]

However, in the 1980s a clear division started to emerge, "when both rabid ideology and jihad were introduced to the area. Zia-ul-Haq (1977–1988) patronized and encouraged the opening up of religious seminaries that, unlike the more traditional madrassas [*sic*], usually attached with Sufi shrines, subscribed to *Salafi* ideology."[34] Zia-ul-Haq promulgated a number of laws which he ascribed to Islam, but in fact were closer to the Deobandi and Ahle Hadith interpretation of religious laws and practices. He also encouraged the radical clerics to disperse such financial resources as the *zakaat* (alms-giving) and *usher* (harvest tax), which led to their social importance and helped to gain political influence. The single most vital factor which inculcated the culture of extremism and bigotry among Pakistani youth was the school curriculum. In their formative stage of life, children are bound to be influenced by what they are taught. Even during the ten-year democratic rule of Prime Ministers Nawaz Sharif and Benazir Bhutto (1988–1999), which was focused on their own political survival, these practices continued unabated. Such issues as the growing religious intolerance and the roots of sectarian violence were either ignored or undermined and were not considered as important enough to be seriously addressed by these two leaders. Because of the stalling, infighting, and practices to undermine the rule of each other, little attention was paid to the fact that Pakistani society was shifting towards extremism with disastrous results. The sectarian violence that had grown in the 1980s reached its peak during the decade of 1990s. This was in spite of the fact that both Nawaz Sharif and Benazir Bhutto and their political parties adhered to mainstream Islamic interpretation and were believers in the liberal interpretation of Islam as opposed to the more conservative Deobandi and Ahle Hadith schools of thought.

These tendencies gained in content and practice in the post-1979 Soviet invasion of Afghanistan. A major portion of U.S. and European funding for the "international *jihad*," a term coined by U.S. intelligence agencies, was disbursed to the militant religious outfits both in Afghanistan and Pakistan. The ten years of Zia's rule strengthened the religious extremists to an extent that they had become "a state within the state," with serious threats to the security of Pakistan, as witnessed in subsequent events.

It was a lack of vision and outlook together with dubious policies that allowed such trends in the society to go unnoticed by these leaders. Prime Minister Benazir Bhutto went to the extent of nominating a radical cleric, Fazlur Rahman as Chair of the National Assembly's Standing Committee on Foreign Affairs. He used this position to establish contacts in the Middle East and to build up a network to receive financial aid from the ruling elite of those countries as well as from the Pakistani expatriates. He had the dubious reputation of being corrupt and his opponents labeled him as "Maulana Diesel," because of his alleged unethical and corrupt involvement in diesel permits during the Peoples Party government. Nawaz Sharif, on his part, appointed a well-known radical, Lieutenant General Javed Nasir with connections with the fundamentalists, as Director General of the Inter-Services Intelligence Agency (ISI).

By this time, the Afghanistan connection had become a pivotal focus of the ruling elite of Pakistan and as a consequence, even when General Musharraf with an apparent liberal outlook and agenda took over in 1999, nothing changed and Pakistani society further drifted towards fanaticism, bigotry, extremism, and militancy. It is not only the militant groups that flourished, there was a more dangerous trend of radicalism in the younger generation who otherwise had nothing to do with the extremist organizations. Deprived of educational and other facilities, a large number of children were forced to remain home or quit school because of financial constraints. Left with no option, these children were compelled to join *madrasas*, a large number of them unregistered, with no government-approved prescribed curriculum. Every such institution followed the teaching methods taught according to their own interpretation of Islam. As most of the *madrasas* belonged to the well-organized and pampered Deobandi doctrine, children became fodder and easy prey in the hands of the terrorists who used them as suicide bombers. They were trained to kill fellow Muslims belonging to different schools of thought and their prey were the Shias, followed by the Bravelies. The main recruits of the Afghan *jihad* came from *madrasas* of the Deobandis and Ahle Hadith,[35] where they received support and protection by fellow Salafi-influenced Taliban and al-Qaeda leaders.

Another factor which helped to spread sectarian extremism in Pakistani society was the failure of the majority Sufi order to confront and opposes these interpretations of Islamic code, which were counter to their centuries-old teachings. They remained segregated in their shrines, docile and uninterested in whatever went around them. They failed to realize that the dogma that was being spread in the society was against the traditions and teachings of the Sufi saints, who were responsible for the introduction and spread of Islam in South Asia.

According to data collected and assessed by Vali Nasr, sectarian-related attacks between 1990 and 1997 were rampant and deadly; "assassinations, machine-gun attacks on mosques and explosions have claimed 581 lives and over 1,600 injured between 1990 and 1997 (100 between January, and July 1997, and 70 in the first 10 days of August 1997)."[36] In the initial stages of the sectarian blitz, a Shia militant group with the name of Sipha Muhammad came into being retaliating against the Deobandis, but soon this group disbanded.[37]

According to another estimate between 1987 and 2002, 1,016 Pakistanis were murdered in sectarian-related incidents and more than 2,000 were injured.[38] The sectarian militants had the support and protection of the Taliban regime (1996–2001).

The resistance against the Soviets was initiated by the United States to inflict a deadly blow upon the Soviet Union's fragile economy and its viability to continue with a broken socio-political system which could not withstand the test of new global requirements. The United States, which initiated and financed the international *jihad* found a willing partner in Pakistan's military dictator, Zia-ul-Haq while the Saudis provided the required financial assistance. In order to provide the jihadies (motivated foot soldiers) for Afghanistan, Zia-ul-Haq encouraged the establishment of militant religious institutions and transformed the existing Deobandis- and Ahle Hadith-run *madrasas* into virtually military training camps. To motivate the young recruits, it became necessary to introduce literature which called for jihad and hatred against the non-believers, at that time meaning the Soviets. But the military dictator did not stop here; he even changed the curriculum of state-run schools, introducing lessons of militancy, bigotry, and hatred. Extremist Pakistan was certainly harmful for the well-being and harmony of the people, but it nevertheless served the immediate U.S. interests in Afghanistan. Not to be undermined was the influx of more than 3 million Afghan refugees into Pakistan, which caused a societal imbalance. Unlike Iran, which also hosted a million refugees, the Pakistani authorities gave a free hand to the refugees.

Murder and attacks on the mosques[39] of those who resisted this alien creed became a common occurrence. Taking advantage of rampant poverty, unemployment, and poor government, youth were literally taken from their mothers' laps, brainwashed, and indoctrined and then were dispatched unprepared to the war zones, where either they disappeared or only their bodies returned home. All of this was done in the name of *jihad* and Islam. The Taliban had declared their civil war against the fellow Muslim Northern Alliance as a holy war by issuing a *fatwa* in this regard. Inculcated by the Talibanized *Mullas* of Pakistan, this poison of hate devastrated families all around Pakistan. Love and compassion gave way to the new language of extremism and terrorism. The language of firearms became a fashion of the time and Pakistani society gradually lost its sanity and above all, its balance. Society had finally succumbed to the alien culture and habits. Different networks established by the Talibanized Pakistanis established close contacts with the Taliban of Afghanistan and with al-Qaeda, as well.

The concept of *jihad* varies in the Islamic context. Firstly, it is taken as a defensive war imposed upon a state. Secondly, the government of the day is responsible for the protection of its citizens. But Zia's *jihad* was given a new description where it became offensive and could be carried out by groups having their own preferences and targets. In this case, the state was just a manager of the activities. When the war ended in Afghanistan and the Soviets left, the *jihad* culture and the militant groups, some of them sectarian, had no direction. But one thing was for sure and that was the fact that this extremist and bigoted culture had taken root in the Pakistani society. Sectarian groups, armed to the teeth with U.S. and Saudi money, with just a 20-percent following, started to take control of the mosques all around Pakistan. During the Taliban rule, the members of sectarian groups, with their connections with the Taliban leadership took refuge in Afghanistan— many of them being the proclaimed offenders.

The most adverse fallout of interference in the Afghan affair distorted traditional Pakistani society, hitting at its ideological roots, notwithstanding the gun and drug culture. Pakistani society was constructed on the premises of love and peace. The Sufis and poets like Shah Abdul Latif Bhatai, Khwaja Ghulam Farid, Waris Shah, Khushal Khan Khattak, Bullay Shah, and many others preached messages of love, kindness, compassion, tolerance, and forgiveness. Under the influence of these saints, a large majority of Pakistani society knew no other norms but of Islamic kindness until the Talibanization of the society started with the rigid and bigoted Deobandis and Ahle Hadith as they started to edge out the majority Barelvis or followers of Sufis from most of the mosques and other religious institutions. Every aspect of modernization (should not be taken as

Westernization) was vigorously opposed by the "new" militant groups, arresting the process of progress and innovation in the country. Zia-ul-Haq encouraged this transformation, while the successive governments looked the other way. These so-called religious cults, sectarian and otherwise, introduced hate, murder, and bigotry into the minds and hearts of Pakistani youth. The sectarian murders were wrongly attributed in the Western press as a Sunni/Shia conflict; it was, in fact, the Deobandi/Ahle Hadith onslaught against this Muslim minority. Women were looked down upon by these extremists and their rights were grossly violated. For example, Deobandi-Shia violence erupted in Hangu and Tank near the Afghan border, during the month of Muharram[40] in 2006 and intra-Sunni conflict marred the Khyber Agency, where Deobandi Mufti Shakir and Bralevi Pir Saif confronted each other throughout the year.

The Lahore terror attack of July 1, 2010 upon the shrine of a Sufi saint, popularly known as Data Ganj Baksh, was blamed on Sipah-e-Sahaba (SSP) by the Barelvi religious leaders. More than 50 devotes died and many more were injured. Hazrat Data Ganj Bakhsh Ali Hajveri, a Sufi scholar traveled from Ghazni in Afghanistan in the eleventh century to Lahore, to preach the message of Islam through love and compassion, according to the teachings of the Sufis. In the past, there have been similar attacks on the Sufi shrines and processions (the March 2009 attack on the shrine of Rehman Baba, a seventeenth-century Sufi poet of the Pashto language; the March 2010 attack on the procession celebrating the birthday of Prophet Muhammad in D. I. Khan, a district in NWFP; the June 2010 bombing of the shrine of Mian Umar Baba).[41] Earlier, on April 12, 2006, a Barelvi Conference to celebrate the birthday of Prophet Mohammad in Karachi was hit by a suicide bomber, killing at least 70 people. It also killed all prominent leaders of the Sunni Tehrik. Reflecting on the Lahore blast, Pakistan's leading newspaper wrote in its editorial that,

> The Data Darbar complex that has, for centuries, stood at the heart of Lahore has never known anything like it. The suicide bombers who struck Thursday night stole at least 40 lives. They also stole the sense of calm that is the hallmark of Sufi shrines and which hang everywhere at Punjab's biggest shrine as thousands of devotees gathered for traditional Thursday night ceremonies intended to pay tribute to a man who played a crucial role in the spread of Islam in the region. It is not easy to say what chain of violence the dastardly suicide attacks are linked to. They could be the latest in the sequence of blasts at Sufi shrines that have taken place across Khyber-Pakhtoonkhwa [sic] since 2008.[42]

There was a sharp reaction by the Barelvis and the shocked followers demanded to be armed so that they could confront "the persistent onslaught by the Taliban militants, not only in Punjab but also in Khyber-Pakhtunkhwa and Sindh provinces."[43] The chief of Sunni Tehrik[44], Sarwat Ejaz Qadri, blamed the two banned terrorist groups Sipah-e-Sahaba (SSP) and Lashkar-e-Jhangvi for the attacks on the Sufi saints. He warned these two groups of possible retaliation. According to a commentator,

There have always been differences between different religious sects, but what happened at the Data Darbar has been generally received with shock and horror. And, its repercussions are going to be far more serious than earlier assaults on the shrines of Sufis like Rahman Baba. Popular feeling is that the country is hit by a wave of sectarian clashes, except that this time it is the Sunnis pitted against the Sunnis and not Shias.[45]

The Punjab government came under tremendous pressure to close the central office of the SSP and arrest its members in Jhang district. The police also removed the flags of the banned terrorist group, which raised the questions as to why the banned organization was allowed to function and its flags displaced in the first place. The clueless government functionaries had no answers for their unexplainable acts.

Broadly, the militant groups active (or previously active) in Pakistan can be classified in the Table 5.3.

Outbursts of Violence and Terror Attacks

The accelerating violence and terror attacks, in which suicidal attacks were introduced for the first time in Pakistan, started in 2007. This new dimension of extremism and terrorism had two sides. Both are ugly and brutal, as demonstrated by the massive Islamabad Marriott Hotel attack in October 2008 in which more than 50 innocent people lost their lives and many more were injured. It also destroyed a symbol of the Pakistani establishment and an icon of "Western culture." The other side of the war was being fought in the mountains of the tribal belt near Afghanistan, stretching some 27,220 square kilometers (10,507 square miles), and where more than 3 percent of the Pakistani population live. Attacks from gunship helicopters, fighter planes, and tanks have also killed and injured scores of innocent Pakistanis, among them women and children. Unfortunately, these killings have been dismissed as "collateral" damage. Many Pakistanis object to this term arguing that the killed are not considered humans or fellow Pakistanis. Thousands have also been made homeless, forced to take refuge in non-combat areas.

For years, the neglect of Islamabad establishment and their vague and confusing policies towards the conflict in Afghanistan and its ties with the tribal areas of Pakistan have culminated in the most treacherous conflict, with no end in sight. Many warned that if not understood and managed accurately, this conflict can engulf the whole of Pakistan, turning it into killing fields, where no city, town, and no sanctuary will be safe. This is exactly what has happened. The unchecked simmering tensions have matured as a full-fledged war; you can call it by any name: the American war, the Pakistani war, etc. The most frightening aspect of the fighting was that it could have taken the shape of an ethnic conflict, as well, with disastrous consequences.

To a large extent, whatever went on in Pakistan in the violent post-2007 years, it has as its basis Pakistan policies adopted during the Afghan *jihad*. Not to be

Table 5.3 Militant Groups and Their Composition

Militant Groups	Date of Origin	Agenda	Sphere of Influence	Leadership	Comments
Tehrik-i-Taliban Pakistan (TTP)	December 2007–Present	Dislodge U.S. and NATO forces in Afghanistan; Attacks on Pakistan military as well as the civilian population	FATA; Links with SSP & LeJ	Baitullah Mehsud (Dec. 2007–Aug. 2009) Hakimullah Mehsud (Aug. 2009–Present)	Although the TTP was banned as a terrorist outfit on August 25, 2008, (freezing its accounts and assets) it still exists in the North-West Frontier regions, especially in the FATA Agencies.
Sipah-e-Sahaba Pakistan (SSP)	1985 (Banned in 2002)	Sectarian; targeting Shias and Bravelies. To declare Pakistan a Deobandi Republic	Punjab: Links with TTP and Al Qaeda	Haq Nawaz Jhangvi, Zia-ur-Rehman Farooqi, Eesar-ul-Haq Qasmi, and Azam Tariq formed the SSP. Jhangvi, its leader was assassinated in 1990 and was replaced by Azam Tariq, who was murdered in October, 2003. He was succeeded by Ali Sher Hyderi (fourth head of SSP), who also met the same fate in August 2009.	The terror outfit now operates under its new name, Ahle Sunnat Wal Jamaat.

(Continued)

Table 5.3 (Continued)

Militant Groups	Date of Origin	Agenda	Sphere of Influence	Leadership	Comments
Lashkar-e-Jhangvi (LeJ)	1996 (Banned in 2002)	Named after the slain SSP leader Haq Nawaz Jhangvi; same agenda as SSP but more violent and bigoted.	Punjab; Karachi Links with TTP and al-Qaeda.	Akram Lahori and Riaz Basra; Basra was killed in May 2002.	It was formed as breakaway extremist group. Many terrorist attacks are ascribed to this group. Being a Punjab-based group, the provincial government has not taken necessary measures to curtail its activities.
Sipah-e-Muhammad Pakistan (SMP)	1993–2001	Shia group created to counter Deobandi terror organizations like Sipha-e-Sahaba & Lashkar-e-Jhangvi.	Suspected links with the Iranian government.	Ghulam Raza Naqvi, imprisoned for murder charges.	It was declared a terrorist organization on August 14, 2001; now disbanded.
Jaish-e-Mohammad (JeM)	2000–2001	Kashmir-related *jihadi* group.	Responsible for series of attacks in Indian-held Kashmir.	Masood Azhar	Created after a split from Harkut-ul-Mujahideen; operating under a new name of Jamaat-ul-Furqaan.
Lashkar-e-Taiba (LeT)	Early 1990s–2001	Kashmir-related *jihadi* group	Responsible for series of attacks in Indian-held Kashmir.	Hafiz Muhammad Saeed	Banned in 2002; operates under a new name, Jamaat-ud-Dawa (JUD).
Tehrik Nifaz-i-Shariat Muhammadi (TNSM)	1992	Links with TTP in 2007.	Agenda to implement Islamic law in the area.	Sufi Muhammad	Swat- and Malakand-based; banned in 2002

overlooked is the fact that Pakistan became a staging ground for the war of resistance in Afghanistan. Militants from all around the world, in particular the Middle East, were granted Pakistani visas, and traveled on to Afghanistan to participate in the fighting. They were sponsored, encouraged, and facilitated by the U.S. as well as Pakistani intelligence agencies. These "fighters" had close contacts with the militant *madrasas*, as they took advantage of the weak Pakistani administration and the support of the militancy by the establishment. These ties were maintained even after the war ended in Afghanistan and a civil war and further chaos started there.

The Afghan *jihad* expanded itself into a regional *jihad* as these militant groups were also utilized in Kashmir, although it did more damage to the genuine freedom struggle there, as all activities in the area were placed together as terrorist activities. Even with the "about-turn" shift of General Musharraf in 2001, the double-faced policy continued. But the terrorist and extremist groups had become too powerful and daring to succumb to any government pressure. In 2007, the Red Mosque (Lal Masjid) incident provided ample proof that these groups were, in effect, not easy to control. Once the government approached the groups with a heavy hand, they retaliated with bomb blasts, most of them suicidal. By that time, various militant groups, sectarian as well as FATA-based and Afghan-focused, had joined hands against the state of Pakistan. More than 500 military personnel were killed in suicide attacks in the 13 months following the Red Mosque incident, in comparison to 79 deaths, between 2006 and July 2007. Around 60 percent of the militant's targets were security personnel.

The number of terrorist attacks has since multiplied many times since 2007. The average death toll increased from 83 deaths per month in 2008 to 90 deaths in 2009. The terrorist groups also expanded their area of activities during this period; Khyber-Pakhtoonkhaw (KP)[46] province remained the main focus of such suicidal attacks. From 2002 to 2008, 41 percent of the attacks took place in KP, followed by 21 percent in the Punjab, expanding to the Azad Kashmir region, Southern Punjab, and Sindh province. The targets of the terrorists were not only the law enforcement agencies, like the army, air force, and police, but also government installations, educational institutions, including schools, and Sufi mosques and shrines.

The Tehrik-i-Taliban Pakistan (TTP) is not a monolithic group, but consists of loose militias of tribesmen from North and South Waziristan. Eventually, the TTP was able to spread its influence into other parts of the FATA and places like Swat Valley. In Swat, another militant group emerged with the name of Tehreek-e-Nafaz-e-Shariat-e-Mohammadi (TNSM), which took control of the area by late October 2007. Swat, which used to be a peaceful tourist resort, soon turned into a battleground between uneducated, extremist religious leaders and Pakistani security agencies. In 2009, a peace treaty was concluded between the government of NWFP and the militant leaders, in which the demands of TNSM were accepted by imposing Nizam-e-Adil (or religious jurisprudence) in Swat and neighboring Malakand Division. However, the peace treaty could not sustain itself, due to the unending demands of the militants. In early May 2009, it was decided by the federal government to take charge of the deteriorating situation and the Pakistan army was given the task of crushing the militants, which they eventually did. Although, the TNSM was not a part of the TTP, it is estimated that they received assistance from them whenever required. The common agenda of both organizations was to undermine the state of Pakistan, with a difference that TNSM was confined to a particular area, while the TTP had a much wider scope of operation, with countrywide links to sectarian groups.

The TTP, led by uneducated tribal gang leaders, with the erroneous interpretation of the Islamic laws, concentrated on undermining the writ of the Pakistani state by conducting attacks on the security forces in the FATA and in some districts of the NWFP province. Later, when the army undertook military operations against the militants in South Waziristan, the TTP coordinating with various extremist groups, especially the sectarian outfits in the Punjab and Sindh, conducted suicidal attacks, killing scores of not only government functionaries, but also innocent civilians, including women and children.

The presence of U.S. military might inside Pakistan territory, through drone attacks, has become a recipe for further complications. By all evidence, in these actions, women and children were repeatedly killed while the "real" targets escaped unharmed. The U.S. insensitivity to Pakistan's sovereignty has further complicated the already complex alignment between the tribes of FATA and the establishment in Islamabad. The tribes suspect that Islamabad is cooperating with the United States while the Zardari government is struggling to prove that they alone have jurisdiction over Pakistani territory. The war has become a three-dimensional conflict, with involvement of the Pakistani establishment, the tribes of FATA, and the U.S. military. The U.S. military, by crossing over the Pakistani border, gives the impression that Pakistan is part of the war theatre in Afghanistan and that the Pakistani government and its people are just pawns in this "great game."

CONCLUSION

It can be argued that the issue of militancy in Pakistan society is more complex than it was first thought to be. It becomes a challenge for the analysts and policy planners to reveal the real reasons for the "sudden" ascent of militant tendencies in Pakistan. In the background of the armed militancy exists an overall culture and tradition of intolerance, which was nurtured by the extensive military rule in the country and which affects all levels of state institutions (including the military and bureaucracy) and is not confined only to non-state actors. On the other hand, when it comes to a violent resentment, it is not restricted to the "Islamic militants" or sectarian fanatics alone; it is a part of more comprehensive phenomena.

To uncover the truth of the situation in Pakistan, a narrow approach, which is intended for political and security purposes, must be broadened in general. We have to look far beyond the closed walls of the *madrasas* and their curriculum. The problem lies in the extended society, the manner in which the state is being governed, and the types of relief a citizen is denied, through normal economic, legal, and administrative/political methods. This is accompanied by the feeling of deprivation among a large majority of the people. Sponsored and encouraged by the corrupt military and civilian regimes, it has become an accepted norm to look for shortcuts, strive for illegal benefits, and become wealthy overnight, no matter what it takes. This practice has severely compromised merit and the term *mediocre* has replaced those of *excellence* and *professionalism* in all levels of society. These trends promote militancy, as citizens have no customary channels to redress. An understanding of this phenomenon could help us locate the level and kinds of frustration that is prevalent in Pakistani society.

On a broader spectrum, it has become fashionable to trace all acts of violent behavior to Islamic community. There is so much rhetoric in this regard that all other possible reasons for the rise of militancy in Pakistan have been set aside. The international media follows the activities of the militant groups with something akin to excitement and links them only with Muslim ideology, no matter where they are located. It is as if the origin and manifestation of extremism and terrorism is only confined to Islam, or at least to people who believe in the religion and call themselves Muslims. The elements of dissent and revolt are branded as acts of extremism which is evil and must be crushed, with whatever means the ruling junta has at its disposal. In this way, the extremism or militarism of the state received its authenticity from the international community.

In the present war against terror, Muslim societies in general have been elusive in providing an explanation. Regarding the rise of militancy, various apologetic arguments are presented by the analysts of these societies in general and of Pakistan in particular. Some of the leaders of the Muslim countries, for the sake of convenience, do not make a fair distinction between different Islamic groups. In Pakistan and elsewhere, there are those that remain a part of the political process, with well-defined political agendas, while others rely purely on sabotage, killings, hate, and bigotry. The latter groups does not believe in a peaceful participation in country's political process, are obscure, and can be categorized as extremist or even terrorist orgnanization.

There is also a third category of extremist religious groups, which are sectarian in nature, confining their murders to the community. This deliberate mixing of groups by political analysts has created more problems than presenting a solid solution against terrorist groups and their acts. By alienating main stream political parties and narrowing their support base, the dictatorial regimes provided more ground to the extremists. But this is how a dictatorship works.

The dynamics of the global terror campaign is having a significant impact on global politics as well as strategies. What if these groups get hold of a "dirty bomb"? The consequences of this possibility are frightening and beyond imagination. U.S. Republican Congressman from Colorado, Tom Tancredo had said that in case of a terrorist nuclear attack on the United States, Mecca should be bombed. Responding to this threat, a Syrian political analyst, Ahmed al-Haj Ali held that, "American mentality imagines that a religion is attacking another religion, and here lies the danger." Associate Press (AP) writer Diana Elias warns that such sentiment "comes from our Americans' general misunderstanding of Islam, American jingoism, the constant suggestions of religious crusade by American leaders, or deep fear-filled wounds of a young country which has little recent memory of enemies coming to our home turf, this line of extremist response should be addressed."

The changed perspective of conflicts requires that nations like Pakistan with a huge defense budget and a top-heavy army should reconsider their security options. As examples of other war theaters show, these new conflicts can be fought successfully without the shining insignias of the elite class. Genuine requisites to protect a nation include the strength of people through their strong civil institutions as well as the require involvement by the people in the decision-making process.

In Pakistan, there is a strong link between rising religious bigotry/terrorism and poverty and the role of dictatorial rule based upon a well-defined hierarchical pyramid. In conclusion, we can say that despair and frustration arising from the extended military rule is directly linked to an unjust socio-economic order and foreign policy issues in which strong feelings exist among the Islamists, secularists and nationalists alike, that the national interests are being compromised.

NOTES

1. Ata-ur-Rehman, "One radicalism leads to another," *Nawa-e-Waqt*, November 13, 2006, Urdu column, author's translation.
2. Zubeida Mustafa, "Education and Bigotry," *Dawn*, July 14, 2010.
3. Ibid.
4. Ibid.
5. Ibid.
6. Zubeida Mustafa, "Militancy and Education," *Dawn*, July 7, 2010.
7. Government of *Pakistan, Pakistan Education Statistics, 2004–2005* (Islamabad, 2006).
8. "To fulfill the declared objectives of *madrasa* reform, a five year project was formulated by the Ministry of Education at the cost of approximately $100 million." Mumtaz Ahmad, "Madrasa Reforms and Perspectives: Islamic Tertiary Education in Pakistan," Islamic *Education in Bangladesh and Pakistan: Trends in Tertiary Institutions*, NBR Project Report, The National Bureau of Asian Research, April, 2009, p. 4. http://www.nbr.org/publications/specialreport/pdf/Preview/PR09_IslamEd.pdf
9. Ibid., p. 5.

10. Dr Muzaffar Iqbal, "Madressah takeover," *Dawn*, June 5, 2009.

11. Ibid.

12. Umer Farooq, "Pakistani Madrasahs . . . Heated Debate Rages," *The Journal of Turkish Weekly*, August 7, 2005, http://www.turkishweekly.net/news/16985/pakistani-madrasahs -8230-heated-debate-rages.html

13. "Pakistan Higher education spending cut by 73 per cent," *The Nation*, June 13, 2010.

14. In the introduction of the report, which spells out the framework of the investigation, it is mentioned that its scope is to see the educational system of Pakistan comprehensively, rather confine it only to the *madrasas*, in order to look for answers for the reason of growing militancy in the country. Rebecca Winthrop and Corinne Graff, "Beyond Madrassas: Assessing the Links between Education and Militancy in Pakistan," Center for Universal Education at Brookings (Washington, D.C.), Working Paper 2 (June, 2010), p. 3.

15. Ibid., p. 1.

16. Ibid., p. 50.

17. *The Nation*, July 29, 2010.

18. Tariq M. Ashraf, op. cit.

19. Safiya Aftab, "Poverty and Militancy," *Pips Journal of Conflict and Peace Studies*, Vol. 1, Issue 1 (Oct.–Dec., 2008), p. 76.

20. Ibid.

21. Arshad Ali, "Militancy and Socio-economic problems: A case study of Pakistan," http://www.issi.org.pk/photos/MILITANCY_AND_SOCIOECONOMIC.pdf

22. http://www.theodora.com/wfbcurrent/pakistan/pakistan_economy.html

23. http://www.nwfpfinance.gov.pk/White_paper_%202010-11.pdf

24. The districts in the South include Rahim Yar Khan, Bhawalpur, Bhawalnagar, Multan, Lodhran, Vehari, and Khenwal.

25. Imran Sharif Chaudary, "Poverty alleviation in southern Punjab (Pakistan): An empirical evidence from the project area of Asian development bank," *International Research Journal of Finance and Economics*, 2009. http://www.eurojournals.com/irjfe_23_02.pdf

26. https://www.cia.gov/library/publications/the-world-factbook/fields/2129.html

27. *The Nation*, January 7, 2010.

28. *Daily Times*, November 18, 2009.

29. http://www.transparency.org

30. "Pakistan's Tribal Areas: Appeasing the Militants," *Asia Report N° 125*, December 11, 2006; International Crisis Group, December 11, 2006.

31. The Barelvis believe that the Prophet is a superhuman and is present all the time, while the Deobandis argue that the Prophet is a mortal man. The other main difference between these two sects is that Barelvis, like Shias, revere the family of the prophet, known as Ahl al-Bayt, and grant the family a special status in their prayer sermons and otherwise.

32. Alex Alexiev, "The Pakistan Time Bomb," *Commentary*, p. 47.

33. "Barelvi Islam," *Globalsecurity.org*, http://www.globalsecurity.org/military/intro/islam -barelvi.htm

34. Ayesha Siddiqa, "Terror's Training Ground," *Newsline*, September 9, 2009, http:// www.newslinemagazine.com/2009/09/terror%E2%80%99s-training-ground/

35. Historically speaking, the Deobandi establishment staunchly opposed the Pakistan movement and its leader Muhammad Ali Jinnah. Their argument was that the leadership of Muslim League, the political party that propounded the idea of a new state, was secular and therefore, lacked the legitimacy to lead the Muslims of British India.

36. S. V. R. Nasr, "Islam, the State and the Rise of Sectarian Militancy in Pakistan," in Christophe Jaffrelot, ed., *Pakistan: Nationalism without a Nation?*, (New Delhi: Manohar Publishers & Distributors, 2002), p. 85. Figures compiled by Nasr.

37. C. Christine Fair, Neil Malhotra, and Jacob N. Shapiro, *The Roots of Militancy: Explaining Support for Political Violence in Pakistan,* December28, 2009, p. 8, http://cerp.org .pk/files/wp/wp_4b5a213c21b30.pdf

38. Muhammad Amir Rana, translated by Saba Ansari, *A to Z of Jehadi Organizations in Pakistan* (Lahore: Mashal, 2009), p. 140.

39. Shia mosque is popularly known as Imambarghah.

40. The first ten days of this Islamic month are revered as a mark of respect for the martyrdom of the grandson of the Prophet, Imam Hussain.

41. *The News*, expressing apprehension about the deteriorating terror situation in Pakistan commented, "Beyond this general antipathy or helplessness, there is the looming danger of terrorism taking on a more visible sectarian face in the coming days. This is not to suggest that the anti-imperialist face of terrorism emanating from Afghanistan and Fata is distinct from its sectarian sibling. The two are intricately connected. The empowerment of the High Church Deobandi-Ahle Hadith School, in the words of Khaled Ahmed, and its weaponisation [*sic*] in the Afghan proxy Jihad has had sectarian side-effects in the past and for obvious reasons. Why should this time be different?," http://www.jang.com.pk/thenews/jul2010-weekly/nos-11-07 -2010/spr.htm#1

42. The News, http://www.jang.com.pk/thenews/jul2010-weekly/nos-11-07-2010/ spr.htm

43. *Shaiq Hussain,* "Sect of problems," http://www.jang.com.pk/thenews/jul2010-weekly/ nos-11-07-2010/spr.htm#1

44. Sunni Tehrik was founded in 1990, as a Barelvi organization to confront the offense of Deobandi and Jamiat Ahle Hadith.

45. Shaiq Hussain, op. cit.

46. The name of North-West Frontier Province (NWFP) was changed to Khyber-Pakhtoonkhaw (KP) in April 2010, as a result of a constitutional amendment.

CHAPTER 6

War for South Waziristan

INTRODUCTION

The ongoing conflict between the state of armed forces and the extremists/ insurgents in the FATA area in general and Waziristan in particular, is the most serious security threat that Pakistan has encountered since the creation of Bangladesh in 1971. For Pakistan, this war started after the invasion of Afghanistan by the U.S.-led coalition in 2001. After the fall of Taliban regime, many of its operatives crossed the border into Pakistan and entered the "safe havens" of the frontier zone between Pakistan and Afghanistan in Waziristan due to its strategic proximity. They started "hit-and-run" attacks on the coalitional forces in order to provide assistance to the remnants of al-Qaeda and the Taliban, who had retreated to their villages and mountains so as to avoid the more powerful forces of the United States and its allies. In response, the U.S. government put pressure on the Musharraf regime to contain militants in the rugged mountains of Waziristan by launching a military operation.

To start a military operation was difficult choice for Pakistan, especially for the army, which since 1979, had established close contacts with the tribes to encourage them to help the Afghan struggle against the Soviet occupation. Now, in changing circumstances, to turn against them for whatever reason was not an easy proposition. The tribesmen considered the ongoing Taliban struggle against the U.S. presence in Afghanistan as a war of liberation and justified this conflict as confronting the "U.S. war against Islam." From 2002 until 2008, under U.S. pressure, Pakistan carried out military operations half-heartedly, most of the time relying more on para-military forces like the Frontier Constabulary with poor results. These inconclusive operations were followed by hasty peace deals which hardly stood the test of time. The biggest drawback in this entire matter was that these military maneuvers were not really regarded as an upcoming insurgency, but were regarded as achieving a reasonable level of peace and control over the area. There was no desire to establish state rule for reasons that were understandably enshrined in the historic dealings with the FATA.

The lack of well-planned strategy and counter-insurgency measures went in favor of the Tehrik-i-Taliban Pakistan (TTP). The TTP managed to gain sympathy among the locals, thus strengthening their base. After every military operation, they gained time, regrouped and recruited new entrants, enhancing their strength which later on became a serious challenge for the Pakistani military. The military made the tactical mistake of releasing POWs and weapons, and even handed over the territory that had come under their command back to the militants as part of various peace deals. These actions only encouraged the militants and they saw them as a weakness of the Pakistan government and army. The TTP started to take more daring steps to challenge the rule of the state in FATA and their terrorist activities across the country while at times directly targeting the army facilities, like GHQ at Rawalpindi and the ISI buildings. Other law enforcement agencies such as the police also became their prime target in mainland Pakistan. These actions put the Pakistan government and the military establishment on the defensive. In other words, Pakistani military strategy was more of a reaction to U.S. demands rather than one that served the national interests of Pakistan. The indecisiveness prolonged the conflict as well as damaged the prestige of the military. It also caused many human casualties, damage to property, and the displacement of the thousands. Most harmful of all, it caused great financial strain on the Pakistani economy with huge monetary losses of $35 billion since the start of the conflict in 2001. Hundreds of FATA residents in general and those of South Waziristan in particular, lost their lives due to widespread, ruthless, and random terrorist attacks which killed innocent women and children in large numbers. Many soldiers and government functionaries also lost their lives in the war for Waziristan.

Presently, the importance of Waziristan, both North and South, is judged by the presence of the remnants of al-Qaeda and the level and potency of the TTP leadership. The aggressiveness of the Mehsud tribe and its alliance with various neighboring tribes and other militant groups from mainland Pakistan for training purposes, makes the area the most volatile for Pakistani security and also for the war theater in neighboring Afghanistan. The combination of these two situations complicates the military options of Pakistan as well as poses a serious challenge for the strategic interests of Pakistan. Before Baitullah Mehsud was killed on August 5, 2009, in a U.S. drone attack, he had led many campaigns against the Pakistani security forces. At that time, he was in involved in fierce fighting with the Pakistani Army. In particular, South Waziristan has been the center of terrorist activities, which were planned and targeted against security agencies within Pakistan, later extending to ruthless attacks against the civilian Pakistani population.

South Waziristan, with Wana as its summer headquarters, bordering Afghanistan to the west and the Balochistan Zhob district to the south, is one of the seven tribal agencies of northwest Pakistan's FATA region. As a whole and for Waziristan in particular, the FATA presents a unique setting in terms of its strategic geographic location, rugged landscape, and the volatile nature of its tribes. The region is located along the border with Afghanistan, surrounded by Afghanistan to the northwest, Khyber-Pakhtunkhwa province to the east, and Balochistan to the south, with a small southern part that borders the Punjab.

Living up to its tradition of being an area of resistance, both North and South Waziristan became a center of activity for the supply line of *mujahideen* fighters when Afghanistan was occupied by the Soviet forces. It also served as a launching pad for the Afghan resistance and became a main source of supplies for the fighters in Afghanistan. South Waziristan has a long history of resistance and fighting. Rahimullah Yusufzai, a well-known journalist and resident of Khyber-Pakhtunkhwa Province, draws an analogy between the past and the current conflict. According to the analyst, "The roots of Islamic militancy (in FATA) lie in the regional and international patronage of religious extremists during the anti-soviet jihad, during the (Afghan) civil war and Taliban rule which radicalized the area."[1] The consequence of these related developments was that militants and ideologues like the Taliban gained in stature and started to dominate the socio-economic and political affairs of the area. As a fallback, residents were influenced by the agenda of the militants, which rationalized its actions on Islamic ideologies which were much different from those of mainstream Islam. It is a well-established fact that finances play an important role in the strengthening of such propaganda as "...donations were showered on the Jamiat Ulema-e-Islam, a Pakistan organization ideologically associated with the Taliban movement, which then established a network of Islamic schools and had funds to operate them."[2]

According to a report by a Peshawar-based research institute,

Both North and South Waziristan are of strategic importance because of geography and location close to the Afghan districts of Khost, Paktika and Paktia. Historically the Daurs, Wazirs and Mahsuds who live in Waziristan have played defining role in Afghan dynastic struggles in the past. For example it was with the tacit support of the British, that Nadir Khan returned from France and raised a tribal warring party of Wazirs and Mahsuds from Waziristan to snatch the Afghan throne from King Amanullah. Nadir Khan became the Afghan king in 1929, mainly due to the effort of the tribes from Waziristan. Since Nadir Khan did not have money to pay the warriors, he allowed the Wazirs to loot Kabul for five days. This experience provided the Wazirs the opportunity to earn money from raiding Afghanistan and in 1933 they again attacked Matun in Khost. Britain finally used air power demolishing the houses of the attacking tribesmen to stop the incursion. Even Hitler in 1938, wanted to foment trouble in Waziristan by using his link with the ex-Mufti of Jerusalem, Amin Hussaini. The later *[sic]* sent a Syrian relative to create rebellion in Waziristan and to work for the restoration of the former king Amanullah. Britain had to use force and bribe *[sic]* to obtain the surrender of the Syrian, who was better known as the "Shami Pir" or Syrian Pir in Waziristan.[3]

Contrary to general belief, the Taliban of Waziristan are different from the Taliban of Afghanistan. While the Afghan Taliban has a definite agenda against the foreign presence, the Pakistani Taliban is engaged in "agenda-less" conflict with the Pakistani army, and is restricted to a confined territory. In the past, these tribes had a fairly good understanding and history of goodwill with the Pakistani armed forces. Historically, the tribes of the FATA region in general and Waziristan in particular served as a buffer between Pakistan and Afghanistan, thus relieving the Pakistan army of its security concerns about hostile Afghanistan, especially until the establishment of the Taliban government in 1996.

Although some of the members of the Wazir tribe, along with Mahsud tribe, have flourishing businesses, especially with transportation in mainland Pakistan, they consider Afghanistan as their backyard. These tribes have moved into Afghan territory at will in the past and feel no hesitation in going there now especially since they consider it their religious duty to fight a holy war for the removal of foreigners from an Islamic land. It was for this reason that the former governor and a vocal British tribal administrator, Sir Olaf Caroe, wrote, "Kabul will always need the good will of Pakistan to keep Wazir ebullience within bounds."[4]

It will not be fair to generalize the hostility of all the tribes towards the government of Pakistan, or to state that that they are sympathizers of the Taliban or al-Qaeda. There are few tribesmen who even understand the complicated and confused ideology or agenda of foreigners, like Osama bin Laden. It is the U.S. drone attacks and killings of the relatives and friends of these men that generates hostility towards the Pakistani and U.S. forces. Another factor to be noted is the reluctant refuge given to the Afghan fugitives by common tribesmen, who under circumstantial pressures are forced to "go along with the tide" and are eventually are caught in the crossfire, literally and figuratively. Yet another group of tribesmen, who are not only evasive but hostile to the militants, are the Shia tribes of Para Chinar region. Due to their religious differences with al-Qaeda and the Taliban, they "are helpful to Pakistani forces in actions against the militants. According to one source, at least five major operations in this area have been conducted on the basis of information provided by the Shia tribes."[5] The other non-Shia tribes that oppose the Taliban and al-Qaeda and provide assistance to the Pakistani troops are the Zali Khel, Kari Khel, Yar Gul Khel, and the Naziri Khel sub-tribes of the entrenched Waziri tribe of North and South Waziristan. Other tribes like Masood Zai and the Ahmad Zai also present a challenge to the monopolization of the extremist insurgents. These tribes also have settled in Bajaur Agency, and the Bannu and Dera Ismail Khan settled areas.[6] On a number of occasions, the "inter-tribal conflict (followed) a massive army operation against the Taleban [*sic*] in South Waziristan."[7] In one such incident at a garrison town of Jandola in South Waziristan, 22 members of the pro-government Bhittani tribe were kidnapped and then killed by Baitullah Mehsud's militants.[8] Several such incidents have been ongoing features of the war for South Waziristan. In order to understand the causes and effects of Waziristan insurgency, it is important to understand this area in a situational and historical context.

BACKGROUND

The seven agencies or administrative subdivisions of FATA are Bajaur, Mohmand, Khyber, Orakzai, Kurram, and Waziristan. Wazirstan is divided into two parts, North Waziristan and South Waziristan, while South Waziristan is the largest agency in the FATA region and the Wazirs and Mahsuds tribes of Pashtun origin who live here are more numerous in number than other tribes of Waziristan.[9] Most of the Waziristan population lives in dismal conditions, where according to the government of Pakistan census of 1998, "approximately 83.8 percent of households in North Waziristan are constructed from unbaked bricks or earth and only 59.8 percent of all homes have electricity. Over 79 percent of the homes in South Waziristan are made of unbaked bricks or earth and only 58.7 percent of all households have electricity."[10] The reason why South Waziristan is the least-developed agency in FATA can be judged by the fact that less than half of its population uses kerosene oil for lighting and meal preparation. As a result of isolating Waziristan along with other agencies of FATA, the area has remained impoverished with a poor literary rate (17 percent, out of which female literacy is a fictional 3 percent) and near non-existent health services.[11] Due to the lack of adequate infrastructure, like good roads and railways, 30 percent of South Waziristan is totally inaccessible. This poverty makes the residents of South Waziristan more susceptible to join the ranks of the militants and even to become suicide bombers. The lack of literacy and jobs, further complicates the matter, as militants with financial resources and outreach can relate to their needs more than the government of Pakistan, which has proved to be negligent towards the development of the area. This is the main reason why even those Waziristani people who are not in favor of the terrorist activities are not critical of the Taliban either.

Traditionally, Waziristan occupied a special status in the state of Pakistan; it was autonomous, and cherished for its services towards the defense of Pakistan on numerous occasions. Before the turmoil in Afghanistan, the tribes of Waziristan acted as supportive partners to the government and helped the armed forces when called upon. That is why Warzirstan was kept largely autonomous, with minimum interference from the federal government; the arrangement worked perfectly well for the interests and security of the state, with little or no disorder in the region. After independence in 1947, the tribal areas were accorded a special status by the founder of Pakistan, Muhammad Ali Jinnah, which is embodied in the Pakistani Constitution. Jinnah, as a gesture of goodwill and trust, ordered the withdrawal of all military forces from the tribal belt, particularly from Waziristan, as the key tribes consisting of Wazirs and Mahsuds had contributed heroically to the Kashmir struggle.

On April 17, 1948, the founding father Quaid-e-Azam, Jinnah spoke to a grand tribal *jirga* of FATA tribesmen at Government House in Peshawar, promising not to interfere in their affairs, induct the tribesmen into the Pakistan government and society, and to announce that Pakistani troops were to be withdrawn from Waziristan. He went on to say,

> I am glad to note that you have pledged your loyalty to Pakistan, and that you will help Pakistan with all your resources and ability. I appreciate this solemn declaration made by you today. I am fully aware of the part that you have already played in the establishment of Pakistan, and I am thankful to you for all the sympathy and support you gave me in my struggle and fight for the establishment of Pakistan. Keeping in view your loyalty, help, assurances and declarations we ordered, as you know, the withdrawal of troops from Waziristan as a concrete and definite gesture on our part—that we treat you with absolute confidence and trust you as our Muslim brethren across the border. I am glad that there is full realization on your part that now the position is basically different. It is no longer a foreign Government as it was, but it is now a Muslim government and Muslim rule that holds the reigns of this great independent sovereign State of Pakistan.
>
> . . . Pakistan has no desire to unduly interfere with your internal freedom. On the contrary; Pakistan wants to help you and make you, as far as it lies in our power, self-reliant and self-sufficient and help in your educational, social and economic uplift *[sic]*, and not be left as you are dependent on annual doles, as has been the practice hitherto which meant that at the end of the year you were no better off than beggars asking for allowances, if possible a little more. We want to put you on your legs*[sic]* as self-respecting citizens who have the opportunities of fully developing and producing what is best in you and your land. You know that the Frontier Province is a deficit province, but that does not trouble us so much. Pakistan will not hesitate to go out of its way to give every possible help—financial and otherwise—to build up the economic and social life of our tribal brethren across the border.
>
> I agree with you that education is absolutely essential, and I am glad that you appreciate the value of it. It will certainly be my constant solicitude and indeed that of my Government to try to help you to educate your children and with your co-operation and help we may very soon succeed in making a great progress in this direction.
>
> You have also expressed your desire that the benefit, such as your allowances and *khassadari [sic]*, that you have had in the past and are receiving, should continue. Neither my Government nor I have any desire to modify the existing arrangements except, in consultation with you, so long as you remain loyal and faithful to Pakistan.

The Pakistani Constitution of 1973 gives a special status to the tribal areas under Sections 246 and 247. These sections define the area and state that the "jurisdiction of the Supreme Court and Higher Courts of Pakistan, the institutions guaranteeing fundamental rights to the Citizens of Pakistan, will not be extended to the tribal areas. The Constitution further provides that the President of Pakistan will legislate and make decisions about the area."[12]

Ever since the above-discussed promise of Jinnah, these tribal agencies are controlled by a combination of Frontier Crimes Regulations (FCR) and tribal traditions which have been practiced for centuries and by generations. According to these laws and traditions, political parties could not operate as Pakistan's Political Parties Act was not extended to the tribal areas. As a consequence, political parties could not field candidates in the general elections. It was in 1997 that, for the first time, this system of election (universal right to vote) was introduced into the tribal territories. Earlier, about 37,719 tribal *Maliks* (tribal leaders)[13] were the only voters allowed to elect their representatives. The problem with a restricted right to vote was that it had deprived the overwhelming majority of tribal people from electing their representatives. It was also susceptible to corruption, "Those few thousand Maliks openly sold their votes, thus the one with more money could reach the representative bodies."[14]

According to traditional practices, the federal government of Pakistan supervises the tribal agencies, including that of South Waziristan through its representative known as a political agent.[15] The *Malik*, as the elder of a tribe, is a hereditary intermediary between the tribe and the political agent or agency administration. In normal circumstances, before the arrival of the militants in the region, criminal cases were resolved through centuries-old understanding known as *Rewaj*, while administrative/political disputes were dealt by *jirga* (council of tribal elders). These arrangements were accepted by the British colonial rulers and later successive Pakistani governments, at least before 2001. While the government avoided interference in the affairs of the tribal areas, it was expected that the tribesmen avoid controversial matters in the settled areas.

Religion and culture play an important role in the lives of the people of South Waziristan and the FATA region. But the kind of rigid Islamic interpretation and bigotry witnessed during recent years, including suicidal attacks with a religious connotation is a new phenomenon. This was introduced by the foreign non-Pashtun elements of al-Qaeda, and adopted by Pakistani militants for strategic convenience. The Pashtun honor code *Pushtunwali*, which predates Islam, is comprised of a non-written code of ethics combined with the traditional lifestyle and religion, and functions a guiding principle of Pashtun society. According to researcher Thomas H. Johnson,

> to understand the Pashtuns, and in many respects the Taliban, it is important to understand their tribal code known as Pashtunwali, which translates as "the way of the Pashtuns." The Pashtuns live in a tribal culture and the Taliban are intimately aware of this fact and play on its implications. For example, the Taliban will regularly appeal to people's sense of 'Pashtunism' in their narratives."[16]

In research conducted by the U.S. Naval Postgraduate School at Monterey,[17] this tribal code is described in detail with explanations,

(a) *Nang (honor)*. Under this code a tribesman is obliged to employ every means possible to shield and protect his honor and the honor of his family. The honor of a Pashtun rests on a host of apparently small nuances which, if infringed, demand a restoration of honor even at the cost of one's life.

(b) *Badal (revenge)*. This concept most often refers to "revenge killings." When a family member is killed or the honor of a woman in one's family is involved, a "revenge killing" is necessary to restore family honor. This killing can be immediate or occur generations later if the family whose honor has been violated is in a weak position at the time of infraction. The Taliban use the concept of *badal* to recruit new fighters into by alienating the population from the Coalition forces because of the civilian deaths from Coalition bombings and "hard knock operations."[18]

(c) *Melmastia (hospitality)*. This concept gives new meaning to the Motel Six slogan "We'll leave the light on for you." *Melmastia* means offering hospitality to all visitors without hope of remuneration or favor and also enjoins the obligation of protection. Any Pashtun who can gain access to the house of another Pashtun, can ideally claim asylum in the house, regardless of the previous relationship between the two parties. The Taliban use this to their advantage and thus have a built-in auxiliary for insurgency efforts with food and shelter wherever they travel within the Pashtun belt.

(d) *Nanawatay (forgiveness)*. This means to go in and seek forgiveness from the victim to whom a wrong has been done. It is used when the vanquished party is prepared to go to the house of his enemy to beg forgiveness and make peace with him. This is the only alternative to *Badal*. Overlooking this factor by foreign forces has enabled Taliban to exhort aggrieved persons to join the insurgency to restore their honor or avenge the death of family members.

(e) *Hamsaya (neighbor)*. This literally means "one who shares the same shadow." This can be compared to early clientele states or later vassal states during medieval times. It is a broad concept of servitude for protection from stronger tribes, including military service in exchange for land (*mlatar*). This concept explains how tribes quickly follow whoever is the strongest and how the Taliban consolidated power so quickly in the 1990s. The Pashtun tribes have generally remained embroiled in clan and tribal rivalries. However, they rally against outsiders if threatened. They are politically very savvy and use alliances and counter-alliances to their advantage, using this ability in the present war against terror. "The rules of this war are a far cry from the easy slogans of 'you're either with us or against us.' Indeed, Pashtun history is filled with heroes who played both sides for the benefit of tribe, family, and honor."[19]

The religious and tribal mix is complicated and overlaps. Kristin Mendoza, writing for a Harvard Law School research project, explains the formation and dynamics of the Afghan Pashtun society, which applies equally to the Pashtuns of FATA,

> While Islam connects virtually the entire Afghan population, the society is divided along ethnic and tribal lines. The largest ethnic group, the Pashtuns, is also a tribal group. Tribes are formulated through patrilineal descent, and the notional ancestor of all Pashtuns is Qays, who, it is said, received Islam directly from the Prophet Muhammad.

Effectively, Pashtuns deny having any pre-Islamic past or experience of conversion. Being Muslim is thus inextricable from their tribal heritage. In this way, what is Islamic and what is tribal overlap. Defense of tribal forms, for instance, can easily escalate into a defense of the faith, as demonstrated in the first.

Anglo-Afghan War and the *jihad* (struggle) against the Soviets, where tribes fought alongside one another against a non-Muslim entity. However, it is clear that conflicts do exist between tribal codes, for instance, and Islamic law. These conflicts are what bring the mulla into his authoritative role, clarifying "what the Book says," referring to the Quranic [sic] text, but also to its legal interpretation as embodied in *fiqh* (Islamic jurisprudence).[20]

There has always been general realization that the British granted administrative system needed amendments, as it could not handle the emerging socioeconomic challenges, nor was it suitable for the demands of political developments in other parts of the country. Even the illusionary concept of stability through this system could not be guaranteed on permanent premises,[21] because the induction of locals in the political process is the only way which the government can ensure the stability of the system. It was at late as August 2009 that a package of reforms was introduced in the area. According to the President's spokesman, "President Asif Ali Zardari tonight announced major legal and political reforms in the tribal areas to extricate them from a century of bondage and subservience and usher them into the mainstream of national life, describing it as a gift to the nation and the tribal people on the nation's 62nd Independence Day."[22] These laws were expected to bring a change for the better, but the events in the area took over the priorities of the government. A status quo has been maintained, with less chance of any noticeable inroads in the future as these reforms are still not implemented in true letter and spirit.

Radicalization of Waziristan

As previously stated, the militants in South Waziristan are comprised of those tribesmen who were involved in the Afghan *jihad* in 1980s. Later, this attitude of militarism was reinforced, although for different reasons by the invasion of U.S. and NATO forces in Afghanistan after the events of 9/11. In the past, the Waziri tribe in particular has habitually resisted any foreign forces which appeared with the intension of occupation, or subjugation. Extremely jealous of their identity, they felt any interference was a threat to their customs and traditional values. Such attitudes in modern history can be traced back to the British *Raj* in India, when British forces tried to intervene in the area, including Afghanistan in the latter half of the nineteenth century to contain a possible Russian invasion in India through FATA. The failure of British Afghan policy forced a change of attitude in 1901, when the Frontier Crimes Regulation (FCR) for the FATA was enforced. While the British maintained their presence through forts, the internal matters of the tribes were left to themselves, as they were used to self rule. Under this system, the chiefs of the tribes (*Khans/Maliks*) would be rewarded with monetary or valuable goods for their cooperation; lack of cooperation or resistance would bring about a military (intervention).[23] In spite of the British concessions and appeasement, they "continued to face resistance by the Pashtuns, the ethnic identity which was at the center of contention during the wars. Most of this resistance transpired in what is now the Northwest Frontier region of Pakistan (NWFP)."[24]

As previously mentioned, even after independence, the new Pakistani administration continued the policy of non-interference and minimum control over the area. As a result of this policy, although FATA tribes were fairly independent in their affairs, the region remained in the background of mainstream Pakistani politics and economy. Nevertheless, the FATA tribes and especially the tribes of Waziristan, helped the Pakistani army in time of need. For example, in 1948 when Pakistan needed proxy warriors, these tribes were in the forefront of the Kashmiri conflict, and their services are even recognized today. The negative aspect of this policy of maintaining and depending on irregular tribal militia was that ultimately these tribes became strong and independent of the state. As observed in the present conflict, they were eventually able to effectively challenge and engage in conflict with the Pakistan army and the government.

Another factor which radicalized the area emerged in recent years when the tribes were encouraged to become irregular warriors, known as *Lashkaris* after the Afghan crisis in 1979, who, as Western analysts suspect, also took part in the Kashmiri uprising from 1989 onwards. These proxy warriors were well-equipped during General Zia's era and the United States paid billion of dollars under the Reagan administration for the development of these tribes against the Soviet occupation of Afghanistan. Political parties like Jamat-e-Islami (JI) and Jamiat-e-Ulema-e-Islam (JUI) became the main backers and financiers of various Islamic groups, with their roots in Waziristan. These parties and their influence grew unchecked with the passage of time. Religious politicians like Maulana Sami-ul-Haq, operated hundred of religious seminaries to recruit and mobilize young boys for *jihad* against the Soviet Union in Afghanistan. Many of the children of 3.5 million Afghan refugees were trained in these seminaries. It can be said that the Afghan *jihad* radicalized the Muslim community around the world, especially Arabs and Central Asians who actively participated. Generous donations from Wahabi and Deobandi groups came from these countries and from other parts of the world as well. On its part, Pakistani intelligence agencies made great efforts to recruit such elements, along with the help of the U.S. Central Intelligence Agency (CIA). This, in turn, affected the social fabric of Pakistan and the ideological basis of Waziristan in particular.

After the dismantling of the Taliban regime by the U.S military, many al-Qaeda and Taliban fugitives entered tribal areas of Pakistan and became welcome guests of the local tribes. The leadership remained hidden in Afghanistan and re-emerged with the resurgence of the Taliban in 2006.[25] By the end of 2008, it was estimated that they controlled more than 70 percent of Afghanistan. Initially, the Pakistan-based Taliban gathered in South Waziristan, but later spread to other agencies of FATA. They were successful in establishing close relations with the locals on the basis of ideology, marriage, and money. For example, the successor of Osama bin Laden, Ayman al-Zawahiri married into the Mamond tribe of Bajaur Agency.[26] In the meantime, the centuries-old *Malik* and political agent system gave way to militant *mullas* and the traditional contact between the government of Pakistan and the ordinary tribesmen was severed, making them a vulnerable pawn in the hands of the extremists. Professor Marvin G. Weinbaum, a well-known scholar on the issue, while giving testimony to the U.S. Armed Services Committee, confirmed a widely held view that one of the main reasons for the radicalization of the tribal areas in general and South Waziristan in particular is a change in the power structure. This change allowed the militants to hold ground in the tribal areas of Pakistan. He explains dynamics of this transformation as part of,

> the dismantling of a system of political control through the gradual destruction of legitimate political structures. Previously, the *malik*—the secular leader of the village or tribe—was the local political authority. He was elected by a *jirga* in the village and through an Islamabad-appointed political agent received government funds and handled relations with the state. The *mullah*—the local religious authority—was clearly subordinate, and in most cases completely apolitical. However, from the regime of General Zia-ul-Haq onward, the state started to fund the *mullahs* directly, giving them financial independence. Over the years the *mullahs* took on an enhanced political role in the tribal community and gradually became more powerful than the *malik*. With new resources and status, the local religious figures were able to emerge as key political brokers and, very often, promoters of militancy. Empowering the *mullahs* made these border areas more hospitable to radicalized local tribesmen. With the *malik* significantly weakened it became harder if not impossible for disgruntled citizens to protest the presence of the Afghan fighters and foreigners.
>
> Radical Islamic *mullahs* in the tribal belt and NWFP were valued for recruiting the Afghan *mujahideen* during the jihad. Economic and social deprivation of young Afghan refugees made their camps in Pakistan fertile ground for recruiting Afghan insurgents and imposing the doctrines of the Islamists. The Islamabad government, financed by the US and Saudi Arabia, poured money and arms into the border regions, further empowering the *mullahs* and their young militant followers. Opposition to the changes was difficult since the Afghan anti-Soviet insurgency and Taliban movement carried religious sanction, and had the backing of the Zia regime. Pakistan's support for the Taliban regime in the 1990s resulted in the further usurpation by Islamist militants of traditional tribal leadership.[27]

One of the major steps of insurgency is to weaken the backbone of the state by targeting law enforcement agencies and gaining sympathy among the locals. The Taliban in South Waziristan did the same. The Taliban had targeted the tribal administrative system time and again with an agenda of creating a vacuum by weakening the state authority which they hoped to fill. The erosion of state administrative structures, "created space for the Taliban, who initially charmed people by offering parallel security and justice systems, establishing their own courts in almost all parts of FATA and in some areas in the settled districts of the NWFP."[28]

Waziristan remained one of the most affected areas in FATA, because of its shared border with Afghanistan. Although fierce and warlike in their own right, the tribes of South Waziristan were exposed, for the first time, to the radical doctrine of an organized *jihadi* mind-set. The "presence of Arab fighters coupled with Saudi funding paved the way for induction of Wahabi ideology into key madrassas; the region previously followed moderate school of thought and jurisprudence."[29] And, as a consequence, the moderate religious groups were soon overtaken by the extremists who started an onslaught of atrocities and ruthless killings upon the defenseless Muslims in the name of religion. With the Afghanistan Soviet crisis over, the Taliban started to attract the imagination of the people of Waziristan, whom they supported during the civil war in 1990s and later, after the invasion of allied forces in 2001.

According to a well-informed Pakistani journalist, financial benefits were largely responsible for al-Qaeda to establish its foothold in the area. He writes,

... the people were poor and easily lured by it [money]. In an area where there was no other employment, the influx of al-Qaeda money was just one more way by which tribesmen gained influence. Bin Laden's men distributed millions of dollars among the tribe elders in return for shelter. Local fighters, enlisted by al-Qaeda, received up to $250 each as monthly wages, many times more than the monthly wages of a government soldier ... Most of the al-Qaeda funds came through illegal and informal channels from Arab countries. While the tribesmen were familiar with the art of resistance, they had also learnt the art of extortion from outsiders who tried to buy them.[30]

With increased movement across the border, the United States started to exert more pressure on Pakistan to take control of its side of the border and to stop hit-and-run attacks on the U.S. and NATO forces. Pakistan reiterated that it has to be recognized that the FATA area was a kind of "no man's land," where the law of Pakistan remained minimal. It became a difficult proposition for the government to take any effective measures against the tribesmen, until an all-out assault was conducted against the insurgents of South Waziristan in 2009.

Initially, Pakistan made efforts by applying such conventional means of conflict management like holding of *jirgas*, raising *Lashkers*, imposing economic embargos, and offering to enlist the settled foreign militants under the Pakistani registration system. In the early stages, the Waziri tribes agreed to cooperate with the Pakistani government to protect their political and economic interests, but because of the lack of firm governmental commitment, repeatedly went back on their words by supporting and harboring the militants, thus challenging governmental authority in the area. Ultimately, Pakistani patience was eroded and the government was compelled to take military action against these tribes. This occurred for the first time in 2003 when the Waziri sub-tribe Akakhel in North Waziristan assisted al-Qaeda in attacking a U.S. army camp in Afghanistan.

The Pakistani government declared victory in 16 small and large military operations which had taken place in the FATA and nearby regions. This was followed by a peace agreement with the militants and the Taliban who had later emerged as an organized militant group, under the leadership of Baitullah Mehsud. Although, the peace agreement was intended to bring tranquility to the area and pacification of the tribes, it became a type of "peace gap" for the militants. It gave the militants enough time to regroup, recruit, and prepare for a future attack against Pakistani military installations. In the initial stages of the conflict, the government and the military visualized the Taliban as a temporary phenomenon, seeing it as ideologically and politically motivated political movement rather than an insurgence group. It can be said that before 2009, the various military operations in the area lacked conviction and commitment as the troops were spearheaded by local militias, who were hesitant to fight against their fellow tribesmen. The ordinary Pakistani soldier failed to understand the rationale of warfare against fellow Muslims, especially when they were trained to perceive India as the real enemy. The public sentiment was also against this approach and it was termed as a "war fought for the United States against our own people and soil." It was only when the civilian population was targeted by Waziristan-based militants through suicide bombings and their hard-line based *fatwas* that the public opinion turned against the Taliban and the military started to seriously consider the tribal activity in the area as a full-blown insurgency.

MILITARY OPERATIONS AND PEACE AGREEMENTS

To makes matters worse, South Waziristan became a host to al-Qaeda and the Taliban leadership when they sought refuge from the U.S. attacks on Afghanistan, in the aftermath of the events of 9/11.

In June–July of 2002, the Pakistan army entered FATA, for first time since the creation of Pakistan in 1947. The intention was to block the borders from Afghan intruders. Basically, the army had deployed a division into two adjoining Agencies, Khyber and Khurram. Later, the troops entered the Shawal Valley in North Waziristan. The army strategy at that time was to avoid a direct confrontation with the tribes of the area, as there was an extensive tradition of goodwill between the army, the Pakistani government, and the tribes. During Pakistan's tensions with Afghanistan, the tribes of FATA not only sided with Pakistan, but also provided useful logistic support to the troops. Thus, before the troops entered the area, lengthy negotiations were held between the leaders of the tribes and the army generals. The tribal chiefs were promised the introduction of extensive developmental projects in the area. However, later it was seen by some Waziri sub-tribes to be more of an attempt to subjugate them. In spite of extensive pressures, the Pakistani government of General Musharraf failed to handover the remnants of al-Qaeda, who had sought refuge with the hostile tribes. The tensions over this issue increased and by 2004, a full-scale undeclared war had started between the tribesmen and the Pakistani government. The Pashtun tribes could not comprehend that the same situation which was justified and encouraged in the past by the Pakistan agencies, i.e., to fight the foreigners (Soviets) in Afghanistan, has now become an unacceptable feat. They could not make a distinction between the two diverse situations and consider the U.S. and NATO forces as much foreigners as the Russians.

The fugitives from Afghanistan were not only the Pashtuns of Afghanistan, but Uzbeks, Tajik, and Chechen hardcore fighters as well. These non-Pashtun fighters proved to be more brutal and had a staunch extremist ideology with a universal agenda. There were also small groups of Arabs and some Westerners. All of these nationalities were introduced in the region by U.S. and Pakistani intelligence agencies during the Soviet occupation of Afghanistan. Army sources said that about 28,000 soldiers were in place to take on an estimated 10,000 hardcore Taliban. The Taliban forces included about 1,000 Uzbek militants, who have a reputation for being ruthless fighters, Chechens, al-Qaeda Arabs, and even a handful of militants from Western countries. These military operations came as an unwelcome surprise for the tribes and were resisted on more than one occasion. The actions, "were deeply unpopular and met with widespread resistance," and visualized, "as a violation of the promise by Pakistan's founding father, Muhammad Ali Jinnah, not to send troops into the FATA for any operation and instead to resolve dispute through negotiations and jirgas."[31]

After failing to convince the local tribal leaders to hand over al-Qaeda extremists, the army with a combination of 6,000 paramilitary and regular army troops went for a military option in South Waziristan (with headquarters in Wana) in March 2004. The objective of this armed action was to overcome about 500 Uzbeks, Chechens, and Arabs, who previously fought alongside the Taliban in the Afghanistan War. These Uzbeks were given shelter by Baitullah Mehsud when they were exiled by Molvi Nazir, as he wanted to abide by the peace agreement with the Pakistani government, which was violated by the Uzbeks in Wana. This move estranged Mehsud and Molvi Nazir into two groups and also became a cause of intra-militant group rivalry in Waziristan. In their armed conflict with the army, the Uzbeks sided with the TTP of the Baitullah faction, while Molvi Nazir sided with the army.

This operation was ill-planned, and the conviction, motivation, and the will to fight was lacking among the troops, mostly comprised of the local tribesmen. As a consequence, the army suffered heavy casualties in such militant strongholds as Angoor Adda, Shin Warsak, Kaloosha, and Shakai. Athough the war theater was made inaccessible to the media, news that came out from various clashes suggested that the army suffered serious setbacks. In less than two weeks, more than 50 members of the Pakistan forces were killed. "The intensity of the fighting shocked the military authorities, who had boasted that the operation would be completed in a matter of weeks."[32] The militants knew the area well as well as its escape routes while the army at that time was not well-versed in counter-insurgency and were no match for "a much stronger and better trained force than they had anticipated, comprising both militants from the local tribes and a large contingent of foreigners."[33] To make matters worse, the paramilitary forces, which belonged to local tribes, refused to fight back against their fellow tribal members and deserted by the hundreds. The foreign militants remained in place and the tribes continued to provide them with sanctuaries and active support.

THE "SHAKAI DEAL"

Just after a month of fighting, on April 24, 2004, the Pakistani government entered into the first of the three peace agreements which would become a part of the army strategy to take control of the affairs of South Waziristan and adjoining Agencies. As part of the deal with the tribal chief Nek Muhammad, a local leader of the militant group, five tribal elders surrendered to the Pakistani military authorities and in return, promised loyalty to the government of Pakistan. On its part, the government released 155 of the captured tribesmen. It also gave a month for the foreigners to surrender and in return, receive amnesty. While addressing the gathering, Nek Muhammad remarked that "tribesmen were like [an] atom bomb so it was up to the government whether to use them against the enemies or against itself."[34] He went on to say that he had no differences with the Pakistani authorities unless they are pushed to take up arms.

The Shakai deal took place with expectations that it would create conditions similar to that of pre-2002 level. There was sufficient evidence in the past that such arrangements had worked and had brought relative peace in the region, as it has been a traditional manner in a land where the government ruled through minimum interference in the local affairs of the agencies. This deal was also expected to restore the lack of trust between the tribesmen and the government. Unlike previously, the militant Taliban and the foreign extremists had taken control of the tribal areas, destroying centuries-old social, cultural and administrative institutions. It was not a surprise that on this occasion, the Taliban were quick to reveal their intentions by invoking a *Mujahideen Shura* soon after the deal for administrative management of South Waziristan. On his part, Nek Muhammad had declared soon after the deal that he would not attack the Pakistani forces, but would fight against the foreign occupation in Afghanistan. The supporters of this deal were of the view that it would be helpful to disassociate the local tribesmen from foreigners of al-Qaeda.

The main purpose of the deal, which was to stop border attacks, also was not abided by the local tribesmen. The security situation began to worsen when on June 9, 2004, Nek Muhammad killed 25 people, which included 17 security guards. Soon after, he himself was killed by a U.S. missile and the fighting resumed. It was argued in some circles that the tribesmen were not given enough opportunities to maintain the agreement. It is also said that the United States did not approve of the peace policy of the Pakistani government, therefore Nek Muhammad's killing was designed to force the Pakistani army into a conflict in South Waziristan, as the tribesmen were supporters of the Afghanistan Taliban. It was in U.S. interest to widen the conflict on the Pakistani side as well. A journalist who visited his village, soon after the killing of Nek Muhammad writes, "In death he became a legend, the tribesmen calling him a 'martyr of faith.' His mud grave in Shakai became a shrine, visited by scores of tribesmen every day. 'He lived and died like a true Pashtun,' read a banner on his grave."[35]

Sararogha Peace Deal

On February 7, 2005, a second deal was signed with Baitullah Mehsud, who had succeeded Nek Muhammad at Sararogha, a small settlement in South Waziristan. According to the provisions of the deal, Mahsud surrendered, layed down his arms, accompanied by his close comrades in a formal ceremony.

Apart from the same provisions of the Shakai deal, Mehsud agreed to stop his support for the foreign extremists and would maintain a ceasefire with government forces. In return, he was pardoned by the Pakistani government. This agreement held ground for few months as on July 27 of the same year, Mehsud resumed attacks on the military. His plea was that "the government has not kept the agreement with us. It is not holding anymore. . . . They have violated the agreement by arresting our Mujahiden." The Sararogha deal "replicated" in North Waziristan in September 2006 was the third and last deal between the militant tribesmen and the government of Pakistan, before the full-fledged military operation of 2009 in South Waziristan.

All the three peace deals were short-lived and did not achieved their main purpose, which was to dissuade the local tribesmen from assisting al-Qaeda and to provide military assistance and safe havens to the groups fighting against the U.S. and NATO troops in Afghanistan. Sirajuddin Haqqani, the leader of militant groups in Waziristan though vowed in June 2006 that his forces would not attack the Pakistani army and that his focus was against the U.S. troops in Afghanistan. Such diversity of focus and agendas among the Waziristan tribes further complicated the already tenuous relationship between Pakistan and the United States, as long as the strategic interests of both countries remained in the war theater of Afghanistan and the tribal belt of Pakistan with different perceptions and interests.

Apart from the historic, strategic, and tactical reasons to have peace deals with the tribesmen, the role of the Mutahidda Majlis-e-Amal (MMA)[36] government in the strategic province of NWFP cannot be underplayed. As a result of the 2002 national and provincial elections, the MMA was able to form a government in NWFP and became a coalition partner of the Musharraf-backed Pakistan Muslim League (Quaid-e-Azam), in Balochistan province. Its chief component, Jamiat-e-Ulema-e-Islam (JUI-Fazal-ur-Rehman Group), was a promoter of peace deals with the tribesmen of FATA. JUI leader Fazal-ur-Rehman has been a supporter of the Taliban and its Deobandi ideology. Many regard JUI as the political face of the militants as most of the recruits of major banned militant groups are somehow associated with the JUI. With 60 seats in the National Assembly and the Senate, JUI was in a position to provide comfort to Musharraf's ruling party. The General needed its support as he was in the midst of getting himself reelected and needed such legislations for his political legitimacy which went against the spirit of the 1973 Pakistani Constitution. Without JUI's support, Musharraf could not have achieved any of his agenda. In this scenario, it became a political necessity to go along with the peace deals to appease Fazal-ur-Rehman. "It is important to note that the three Deobandi groups are the most powerful and influential within the coalition; the death of hundreds of Pashtuns as a result of the American "Operation Enduring Freedom" led to growing support for the Deobandi factions and in turn, the founding of the MMA. Contrary to widespread belief, ousting the Taliban from Afghanistan did not mean the end of the Taliban regime or al=Qaeda. Instead, it simply moved large parts of its organization across the border to Pakistan,"[37] where large number of *madrasas* operate as the main cells to promote staunch Deobandi ideology among the youth of Pakistan.

OPERATION RAH-E-NIJAT (PATH TO SALVATION): 2009

After much hesitancy and debate within various divisions of the Pakistani government, on October 17, 2009, the army finally entered South Waziristan with full force. The final decision was taken in a well-attended meeting in Islamabad under the chairmanship of the Prime Minister, in which top military commands and most of the opposition parties' leaders participated, thus building a national consensus in favor of the South Waziristan war. Action against the militants could not be delayed, especially "after a spate of attacks, including (South Waziristan based) terror assault teams striking at the Army General Headquarters in Rawalpindi and three police centers in Lahore."[38]

There has been a myth in Pakistan and elsewhere that South Waziristan is invincible, as demonstrated by history. It has a more difficult terrain due to its geography and traditions than Swat and its residents are extremely hardy and exceptional marksmen. There were many risks involved in the operation by the

army and the political leadership, and a setback could have been disastrous for
Pakistani security interests, and its counterinsurgency and anti-terrorism measures. However, the Pakistani army's victory in Swat against the militants, the
killing of Baitullah Mehsud[39] in a drone attack in early August, and infighting
within the Taliban ranks provided an opportunity for the army to prove that it
was capable of dealing with all kinds of security challenges, including insurgencies and that its expertise was not confined to conventional warfare alone.
Another factor which was in military's favor was that by taking advantage of
differences between tribal factions, it was able to win over the Maulvi Nazir
group in Wana (South Waziristan) and Hafiz Gul Bahadur in North Waziristan,
thus isolating the militants into a weaker position. Another tribal commander
Misbahuddin had a grudge with Baitullah and had "assisted the law-
enforcement agencies in pointing out militants belonging to the Baitullah group
even in Islamabad and Karachi."[40] The participants of the high-level meeting
came to the conclusion that "a recent spate of suicide bombings in different parts
of the country had roots in South Waziristan and suicide bombings and terrorist
attacks could not be curbed without crushing terrorists hiding in tribal areas."[41]

As 8,000 families moved from South Waziristan to Dera Ismail Khan, a nearby
town of NWFP, the military launched an attack from three sides, with the help of
the air force on the known strongholds of Tehrik-i-Taliban Pakistan (TTP). The target areas were Makeen, Jandola, and Tiraza where 28,000–30,000 soldiers took part
in the operation supported by the air force. The main focus of interest was centered
on 1036 square kilometers (400 square miles) out of 6605 (2,550 square miles) of
the total area covering South Waziristan. This designated area of operation was considered to be a stronghold of the TPP. It was believed that an estimated 10,000–
15,000 extremists of all types had taken refuge here, out of which it was estimated
2,000 were of non-Pashtun elements, mainly Uzbeks. The obvious objective was
to affect the ability of the Mehsud tribe and to eliminate the armed capability of
the Tehrik-i-Taliban. The army had made it clear that their offense was to achieve
victory against those elements that were engaged in suicidal attacks against military
installations and other governmental facilities. The events since 2007 have showed
that nearly every suicidal terrorist attack in Pakistan has had a signature of the FATA
area in general and South Waziristan in particular. In this respect, it was also made
obvious that initially, the army desired to establish a foothold in the area and then,
in stages, expand the rule of the state into other parts of FATA.

Before the attack began, the Pakistan military, having learned from its experience with Swat and other insurgency-laden places, devised a strategy to soften
the target by taking the following steps: 1) Civilian population removal from
the conflict area; 2) Economic blockade of South Waziristan; and 3) Air strikes
on selected Taliban targets. The repatriation of the people had begun before
the main military operation, encouraging as many people as possible to leave
the area, as the expected onslaught was designed to flush out the extremists from

safe houses and prevent them from taking refuge among the population. While the economic blockade of South Waziristan started in June of 2009, the army blocked all possible routes to and from the area, but could not do the same with secondary routes, which are traditionally used for smuggling, because of the difficult terrain and vastness of the area. In addition, the military occupied the high elevations, setting up garrisons in the bigger population centers. The intention was to starve, freeze, and bomb out the Taliban and their extremist allies. The army made a good use of air power as from the beginning of the operation, militant targets were softened by repeated air strikes and helicopter gunships. There is no doubt that the Pakistani air force played a major role in destroying the militant hideouts and their resolve.

The military devised a comprehensive war strategy of pre- and post-operation, as part of a larger counter-insurgency plan. It was a three-pronged operational strategy, "1) seize control of communication infrastructure, clear the adjoining settlements and village, as well as destroy the command and control structure of the Taliban militants; 2) mop up operations aimed at the remaining terrorist infrastructure in far flung areas; 3) reconstruction of the area and rehabilitation of the internally displaced persons (IDPs)."[42] Finally, on December 12, 2009, the Pakistani army declared victory against the Taliban and the extremists in South Waziristan. This success came under difficult circumstances, especially since the extremists had been in control of the territory since 2004 and had sufficient time to prepare for an expected war with the Pakistani forces. As part of their preparation, they had "dispersed ammunition and weapons caches, built bunkers and fighting positions, and seeded the region with mines (IEDs). The Taliban have fought on this ground and know it well; they have defeated the Pakistani Army in four separate engagements since 2004."[43] In fact, army tactics have "beaten the Taliban on their own ground—descend from the ridges, command the heights and do not advance via roads . . . and the arms the militants left behind betray a flight in panic rather than a tactical withdrawal."[44]

Ever since the massive military attack against the extremists in South Waziristan,

a retaliatory terrorism spree has ripped through every large Pakistani city, including Peshawar, Islamabad, Rawalpindi, Lahore and Multan. Over 500 have been killed and thousands injured, mostly by suicide-blasts executed by indoctrinated young Mehsuds. Senior army officers, who have lofty status in a country ruled by them for half its history, have been among the dead. Among 40 killed in a commando-style attack on a crowded mosque in Rawalpindi last month was the only son of Lieutenant-General Masood Aslam, commander of Pakistan's north-western campaign.[45]

TOWARDS COUNTERINSURGENCY MEASURES

The unanimous opinion expressed in Pakistan is that the army's victory in South Waziristan signals a defining success against the overall war against terrorism in the country and that "the Waziristan counterterrorism model could be applied to other areas where the Taliban have strongholds and wreak havoc on the lives of innocent people. But still lot is needed to eradicate the influence of the extremists in the area."[46] The myth of Waziristan as an invincible region has been negated by the Pakistani army.

The counterinsurgency measures in Waziristan can broadly be divided into three categories: 1) the military defeat of insurgents; 2) a massive economic improvement; 3) the induction of locals into mainstream political process. The Pakistani army overwhelmed the insurgents in South Waziristan, but military defeat is only one step towards eradicating the wave of Talibanization in Pakistan. To eliminate the tendencies of intolerance and extremism, it is essential to win the hearts and minds of the general population of South Waziristan. Although over 400,000 Internally Displaced Persons (IDPs) have returned to their homes, there are still much apprehension about the prospects of a "permanent peace."[47] Permanent peace can only be insured through rapid economic development and the inclusion of the people into the Pakistani social, economic, and political mainstream. The second stage of the anti-insurgency involves massive and rapid economic development and addressing rampant poverty in the area. Another daunting task for the government is to implement administrative reforms by establishing concrete structures, so that such civic functions like education, health facilities, and a transportation system can occur. Citing the lack of seriousness in this regard, it is argued that,

> Pakistan's federal and provincial bureaucracies have failed to provide development and other aid to conflict-afflicted areas, offer adequate assistance to internally displaced persons, or engage in other efforts to secure the support of locals for the government and military operations. This has exacerbated the army's reliance on heavy force and concomitant destruction in places such as South Waziristan, Bajaur and Swat, which has alienated some locals and fostered anger throughout Pakistan.[48]

It is expected that the federal government will address the serious and chronic issues of poverty, health, and education in order to improve the social fabric of FATA, bringing to it a culture of moderation. Community participation can provide an environment for the locals to take part in the political process, thus becoming part of the system which the Taliban and other extremist groups so jealously despise. One of the most important tasks is to reform the Frontier Crimes Regulations (FCR) which were imposed upon the people during the British colonial times and have since outlived their utility. Moreover, Article 247(7) of the Pakistan Constitution states that the jurisdiction of provincial high courts and the Supreme Court does not include FATA. This reflects the alienation of FATA from the main structures of the Pakistani government. An integrated system of governance and justice thus becomes necessary to insure the rule of the government and state.

The functioning of national political parties without hindrance can also be a good step in the integration of the people into the mainstream political process of the country, thus isolating the extremists still further. In August 2009, as part of the reform package, a law was passed which allowed the once-forbidden political parties to operate in the tribal region. This was in spite of the fact that there are 12 seats allocated to FATA in the National Assembly and 8 in the Senate.[49] Based on the will of the people, there is a desperate need for reforms of all kinds in the FATA area, including South Waziristan. A report by Shaun Gregory suggests that,

> the political way forward in outline seems clear for the FATA. In the June 2007 FATA Reform Consultative Dialogue polling indicated that 20% of FATA residents favoured [sic] merging with the NWFP, 35% wanted the FATA to be a separate province, 13% preferred the status quo, while 29% wanted reform but also to keep the present dispensation. In sum therefore 55% wanted some form of provincial status, while 87% sought reform of some sort.
>
> The means to achieve these desired ends are broadly clear and include political enfranchisement through the extension of the Political Parties Act [PPA]; assertion of the rule of law through the reform of the Frontier Crimes Regulations [FCR] and the full inclusion of the FATA in Pakistan's legal frameworks; and a development strategy based on providing economic opportunity, investment in infrastructure and, above all, investment in education.[50]

At the beginning of this war, Pakistan had hardly any experience with a counter-insurgency. The Pakistani army was more inclined to fight a conventional war against India rather than fight militants within its own borders. Due to this reason, the initial military operations in Waziristan were more or less "cordon and search" operations. As stakes in the conflict increased, so did the military's commitment. Then suicide attacks, bomb blasts, and subversive attacks on the major cities like Lahore, Peshawar, and Islamabad created a sense of lawlessness in the country. These circumstances made military operation inevitable and the army reprioritized its strategy for the first time after 2008. Counterinsurgency measures were adopted in Swat, South Waziristan, Bajure Khyber, and Kurram agencies. The army concentrated on destroying militant networks and installations. It also focused on securing and retaining control of major cities and towns in possession of militant groups. Military operations became easier due to favorable public opinion.

CONCLUSION

Pakistan needs to follow a more indigenous strategy rather than reacting to foreign desires for its security needs. It is now required to keep public opinion on board in these matters, especially those of people in the affected area. As shown from military operations in South Waziristan and Swat, both proper planning and backing of the people bears effective results. An important permanent aspect of these successes will be guaranteed if the militants are not allowed to come back to the "cleared" areas, under one pretext or the other. Once the military operation is concluded, it becomes the responsibility of the civil administration to rehabilitate the affected people as quickly as it can, in order to avoid any resentment among the effected population.

According to a report by *The Economist*,

Many young Waziristanis are hungry for the political freedoms enjoyed, alas fitfully, by the rest of the country—as their enthusiasm for an abortive effort to introduce local government in 2005 showed. Even the Wazir maliks assembled in Wana, prime beneficiaries of the old order, admitted this. "Our youngsters want reform, adult franchise, no collective punishments," admitted one of the old men, Bizmillah Khan. "But they also want our culture, our traditions and our freedom to remain intact." [51]

By the end of the day, there remains no doubt that South Waziristan, along with other FATA agencies, will remain restive unless peace comes to Afghanistan and U.S. and NATO troops leave the area.

NOTES

1. Quoted in *Pakistan's Tribal Areas: Appeasing the Militants*; Asia Report N°125–December 11, 2006 (Brussels: International Crises Group, 2006), p. 13.

2. Mohammad Amir Rana, *The Seeds of Terrorism* (London: New Millennium, 2005), p. 236.

3. *Causes of Rebellion in Waziristan*, A study by Regional Institute of Policy Research & Training, Peshawar, 2007, p. 22.

4. Olaf Caroe, *The Pathans 550 B.C.A.D.*, (Oxford, Karachi, 1975), p. 409.

5. Mohammad Amir Rana, op. cit, p. 253.

6. Ibid.

7. "Pakistan Taleban kill 22 rivals," *BBC News*, June 25,2008, http://news.bbc.co.uk/2/hi/south_asia/7472612.stm

8. Ibid.

9. The Mahsuds are further divided into Alizai, Shaman Khel, and Bahlolzai sub-tribes. The Mashsud population mostly live in the villages of Kaniguram and Makin. While the other populous tribe, the Wazirs are divided into two sections, the Utmanzai and the Ahmadzai. Apart from these, there such smaller groups as Dottanis, Bhittanis, Ghaljis, and Urmurs.

10. "Government of Pakistan. "1998 Census Report of South Waziristan Agency, 24-5," as quoted in Mathew W. Williams, *The British Colonial Experience in Waziristan and its Applicability in the Current Operations;* School of Advance Military Studies United States Command and General Staff College, p. 8., http://www.dtic.mil/cgi-bin/GetTRDoc?Location=U2&doc=GetTRDoc.pdf&AD=ADA436296

11. "Another worrying aspect is the lack of students in government schools. For example in government high school Datta Khel in North Waziristan the total number of students is 96 as compared with more than 200 students in the Datta Khel madrassa. Interestingly, another nearby madrassa in Datta Khel, which teaches English and computer science the number of students, is about 600. One reason for the poor attendance in government schools is the fee of Rs. 100 per month charged as compared with free education in madrassas and Rs. 50 per month in community schools." *Causes of Rebellion in Waziristan,* op. cit., p. 30.

12. *Constitutional Status of FATA: The Way Forward*; First Consultative Dialogue, March 19–20 (Islamabad: Community Appraisal & Motivation Programme, 2010), pp. 5–6.

13. "In 1893, . . . the British began a concerted effort to buy off tribal elders, or maliks. In egalitarian Pushtun [*sic*] society, where prestige is won in battle, these grey-beards initially had limited authority. But through British patronage it grew, creating for the colonialists a pliable tribal elite. With this toehold established, the British then took a firmer grip on the area,

developing a system of indirect rule that has hardly changed since." "Waziristan: The last frontier," *The Economist*; http://www.economist.com/node/15173037/print

14. Syed Minhaj ul Hassan, "Tribal Areas of NWFP: Politics of Survival," in *Pakistan: Unresolved Issues of State and Society*, eds. Syed Farooq Hasnat and Ahmad Faruqui (Lahore: Vanguard, 2008), pp. 220–221.

15. "The real power in the tribal agencies has historically rested with the political agents, who represent the federal government and maintain control through the colonial-era FCR. The regulations allow the political agent to impose collective punishment for crimes committed by an individual and to deliver prison sentences without due process or right of appeal. . . . Individual tribesmen have limited rights while the political agents wield vast administrative and funding powers and collect and distribute revenue." Interview, Rahimullah Yusufzai, Executive Editor, *The News*, November, 2006; quoted in Shabana Fayyaz, *Towards a Durable Peace in Waziristan*; Brief Number 10 (Bradford: Pakistan Security Research Unit (PSRU), April 23, 2007); http://www.scribd.com/doc/38663590/Towards-a-Durable-Peace-in-Waziristan

16. Thomas H. Johnson, "On the Edge of the Big Muddy: The Taliban Resurgence in Afghanistan," *China and Eurasia Forum Quarterly*, Volume 5, No. 2 (2007), p. 121; http://www.silkroadstudies.org/new/docs/CEF/Quarterly/May_2007/Johnson.pdf

17. Shahid A. Afsar and Christopher A. Samples, "The Evolution of the Taliban," Master of Science Thesis, in *Defense Analysis from the Naval Postgraduate School*, Monterey, California, June 2008, pp. 27–29.

18. "Expert: Afghan War Needs New Strategy," *United Press International*, May 21, 2007, http://www.upi.com/Security_Terrorism/Briefing/2007/05/21/expert_afghan_war_needs_new _strategy/485 1, (accessed November 28, 2007).), quoted in Ibid, p. 27.

19. Owais Tohid and Scott Baldauf, "Pakistani Army must Go through the Pashtuns," *The Christian Science Monitor*, June 25, 2004, http://www.csmonitor.com/2004/0625/p07s 02-wosc.html (accessed September 4, 2007), quoted in Shahid A. Afsar and Christopher A. Samples, op.cit., pp. 28–29.

20. Kristin Mendoza, *Islam and Islamism in Afghanistan*, Islamic Legal Studies Program at Harvard Law School, Afghan Legal History Project; accessed date November 20, 2010, http://www.law.harvard.edu/programs/ilsp/research/mendoza.pdf

21. Robert Lane Sammon, "Mullas and Maliks: Understanding the Roots of Conflict in Pakistan's Federally Administered Tribal Areas," Master of Arts Thesis, The Lauder Institute, University of Pennsylvania, April, 2008, p. 10. (http://lauder.wharton.upenn.edu/pages/pdf/ Robert_Sammon_Lauder_Thesis_April_2008.pdf)

22. According to a national daily newspaper, "President Asif Ali Zardari announced . . . political, judicial and administrative reforms for the tribal areas, allowing political activities in Fata, setting up an appellate tribunal, curtailing arbitrary powers of political agents, giving people right to appeal and bail, excluding women and children from the territorial responsibility clause and envisaging audit of accounts by the auditor general." *Dawn*, August 14, 2009.

23. Paul Titus, "Honor the Baloch, Buy the Pushtun: Stereotypes, Social Organization and History in Western Pakistan," *Modern Asian Studies* 32, 3 (1998), p. 660.

24. Raja G. Hussain, *Badal: A Culture of Revenge: The Impact of Collateral Damage on Taliban Insurgency*, Master of Arts in National Security Studies Thesis, (Middle East, South Asia, Sub-Saharan Africa), The Naval Postgraduate School, Monterey, California, March 2008, p. 18.

25. It was reported in a magazine that a full-blown insurgency has started in Afghanistan, while the United States was busy with the Iraq conflict. The report said, "In their biggest show of strength in nearly five years, pro-Taliban fighters are terrorizing southern

Afghanistan—ambushing military patrols, assassinating opponents and even enforcing the law in remote villages where they operate with near impunity." Paul Wiseman, "Revived Taliban waging "full-blown insurgency'," *USA Today*, 6/20/2006, http://www.usatoday.com/news/world/2006-06-19-taliban-afghanistan-cover_x.htm

26. He remarried "after his wife and two children were killed during US attacks in Afghanistan," Safdar Sial, "Patterns of Talibanization in FATA," in Muhammad Amir Rana, Safdar Sial, and Abdul Basit, *Dynamics of Taliban Insurgency in FATA* (Islamabad: Pak Institute for Peace Studies [PIPS], 2010), p. 145.

27. Dr. Marvin G. Weinbaum, "Counterterrorism, Regional Security, and Pakistan's Afghan Frontier," in testimony to the U.S. House of Representatives Armed Services Committee, Washington, D.C., October 10, 2007, http://armedservices.house.gov/pdfs/FC101007/Weinbaum_Testimony101007.pdf (accessed 15 November, 2010), pp. 3–4.

28. Safdar Sial, op.cit., p. 151.

29. Muhammad Amir Rana, "Role of Arab Militants and Charities during and after Soviet-Afghan War," in Muhammad Amir Rana, Safdar Sial, and Abdul Basit, *Dynamics of Taliban Insurgency in FATA*, op. cit. p. 23.

30. Zahid Hussain, *Frontline Pakistan: The Struggle with Militant Islam* (New York: Columbia University Press, 2007), p. 148. *Newsline*, April, 2004, "The New Frontier." According to a *BBC News* report, "People interviewed in Mir Ali (North Waziristan) say the foreign fighters have paid huge sums of money in advance rents to their hosts which the latter may not be able to repay should they want to evict them. And there is the fear factor. Locals say the foreign militants could also resort to targeted killings in order to eliminate their enemies. The Pakistani government paid 32m rupees ($530,000) to four militant commanders in South Waziristan's Wana region to repay their debts to al-Qaeda militants following a peace deal signed in November 2004. But the result was just the opposite of what had been intended. The foreign fighters refused to leave. Instead, over the next two years, more than 150 local residents were assassinated while hundreds of others fled to the relative safety of North West Frontier Province (NWFP)." M. Ilyas Khan, "Fractious militants united by one thing," *BBC News*, http://news.bbc.co.uk/2/hi/south_asia/6423903.stm

31. Daniel Markey, *Securing Pakistan's Tribal Belt*; Council Special Report No. 36, (New York: Council on Foreign Relations, August 208), p. 11.

32. Zahid Hussain, *The Scorpion's Tail: The Relentless Rise of Islamic Militants in Pakistan—and how it Threatens the World* (New York: Free Press, 2010), p. 69.

33. Ibid.

34. Muhammad Amir Rana and Rohan Gunaratna, *Al-Qaeda Fights Back Inside Pakistani Tribal Areas* (Islamabad: Pak Institute for Peace Studies [PIPS], 2008), p. 66.

35. Ibid., p. 73.

36. In its fold are: Jamaat Islami (JI), Pakistan's oldest religious party, Jamiat Ulema-e-Pakistan (N), both factions of the pro-Taliban Jamiat Ulema-e-Islam [Jamiat Ulema-e-Islam (F) and Jamiat Ulema-e-Islam (S)], which represents the Deobandi school, Professor Sajid Mir's Jamiat-e-Ahle Hadith and Allama Sajid Naqvi's outlawed Shia group, Tehrik-e-Jafria Pakistan, which in its present incarnation is known as Pakistan Islami Tehrik.

37. Magnus Norell, "The Taliban and the Muttahida Majlis-e-Amal (MMA)," *The China and Eurasia Forum Quarterly*, Volume 5, No. 3 (August 2007), pp. 69–70; http://www.silk roadstudies.org/new/docs/CEF/Quarterly/August_2007/Norell.pdf

38. Bill Roggio, "What lies ahead in Waziristan," *The Long War Journal*, October 17, 2009, http://www.longwarjournal.org/archives/2009/10/analysis_what_lies_a.php (accessed 1 November, 2010)

39. Hakim Ullah Mehsood became the leader of TTP after the killing of Baitullah Meshood. Soon after, it was reported by Pakistan's Interior Minister Rehman Malik, in January 2010, that he too was either killed or injured in a U.S. drone attack. He also claimed that his possible successor, Qari Hussein might also have been killed in the same attack. However, these reports proved to be wrong. However, the Islamic Movement of Uzbekistan (IMU) Chief Tahir Yuldashev was killed in a drone attack in August 2009, thus depriving the extremists of a violent and fierce leader.

40. Sayed Bokhari, "The Battle for Waziristan," *Dawn*, October 18, 2009.

41. Those attending the meeting were also briefed by ISI Director General in which he said that "You cannot imagine how many people are on the hit list of terrorists. They are not only important personalities and politicians but some ordinary people in different professions," Syed Irfan Raza, "Waziristan Operation Given Go-Ahead," *Dawn*, October 17, 2009.

42. Syed Adnan Ali Shah Bukhari, *"New strategies in Pakistan's counter-insurgency operation in South Waziristan,"* Terrorism Monitor, Vol. VII, Issue 37 (December 3, 2009), p. 5, http://www.jamestown.org/uploads/media/TM_007_6b5e8c.pdf (accessed October 5, 2010)

43. Bill Roggio, op. cit.

44. "The task ahead," editorial, *Dawn*, November 6, 2009.

45. "Waziristan: The last Frontier," *The Economist,* Dec. 30, 2009; http://www.economist.com/node/15173037/print (accessed 12 January, 2010)Dennis C. Blair, Director of U.S. National Intelligence presented "Annual Threat Assessment of the U.S. Intelligence Community" for the Senate Select Committee on Intelligence, on February 2, 2010, in which his assessment about the South Waziristan attack and its fallout read as: "In the last three months of 2009, as Pakistan mounted new operations against the TTP stronghold in South Waziristan, Pakistan-based extremists and al-Qa'ida conducted at least 40 suicide terrorist attacks in major cities, killing about 600 Pakistani civilians and security force personnel. Al-Qa'ida, with the assistance of its militant allies, is trying to spark a more aggressive indigenous uprising against the government as it seeks to capitalize on militant gains and reorient Pakistan toward its extremist interpretation of Islam.," p. 20,http://www.dni.gov/testimonies/20100202_testimony.pdf (accessed 7 August, 2010).

46. Imtiaz Ali,"Military Victory in South Waziristan or the Beginning of a Long War?" *TerrorismMonitor* Volume VII, Issue 38; December 15, 2009, p. 6. http://www.jamestown.org/uploads/media/TM_007_58a465.pdf (accessed 2 January, 2010)

47. *Dawn*, November 29, 2010.

48. C. Christine Fair and Seth G. Jones, *Survival*, Vol. 51 No. 6 (December 2009–January 2010), p. 182.

49. Benazir Bhutto had filed a constitution petition in the Supreme Court of Pakistan, "seeking enforcement of the Political Parties Act of 1962 in the Federally Administered Tribal Areas (Fata)." The petition further said, "FATA is a unit of the federation, but it has been handed over to religious parties operating from mosques and madrassahs." Manzoor Ali Shah, "Ending FATA's political isolation," *The Express Tribune*, May 5, 2010, http://tribune.com.pk/story/10926/ending-fatas-political-isolation/ (accessed Nov 2, 2010).

50. Shaun Gregory, "Towards a Containment Strategy in the FATA," *Pakistan Security Research Unit* (PSRU), Brief Number 43, 20 October, 2008, p. 6, http://www.scribd.com/doc/38664032/Towards-a-Containment-Strategy-in-the-FATA (accessed 8 September, 2010)

51. "Waziristan: The last Frontier," op. cit.

CHAPTER 7

A Triangle of Security Concerns: Pakistan, the United States, and Afghanistan

INTRODUCTION

Pakistan's relations with the United States as a close ally were established and progressed during the rigid Cold War period. Pakistan had joined two security pacts sponsored by the United States during this period. However, with the lessening of the hostility between the two adversary superpowers, the United States and the Soviet Union, together with the elimination of mutual utility for each other, this closeness lost its symmetry and a variety of issues started to dominate the differing interests of each country. In this regard, the two alliance partners moved from a place of comfort to that of mutual suspicion and had to endure the tedious exercise of damage control a number of times.

This particular complexity of cooperation and divergent trends between the two countries established a framework of mutual distrust. A number of issues like the Pakistani desire to develop an atomic bomb, in reaction to India's capability in this field; Pakistan's tense relations with India and U.S. efforts to prompt India to act as a balance to the growing Chinese influence in South Asia, made the relations between the two countries ever more problematic and challenging. These and other matters created a feeling of mutual distrust, but the events in Pakistan's neighbor Afghanistan twice (1979 and 2001) provided an opportunity for dwindling U.S. interests in Pakistan to correct themselves and put things in the right perspective. These advances presented solutions as well as problems for the policymakers of both Pakistan and the United States.

The Pakistani over-reliance on the United States for practically all its problems and requirements created a wedge between the thinking processes of the rulers

and the people of Pakistan. This was vehemently demonstrated during the
October 2009 visit of the U.S. Secretary of State Hillary Rodham Clinton in
the aftermath of a stiff opposition by the Pakistani population against the U.S.
aid legislation known as the "Enhanced Partnership with Pakistan Act of 2009"
(Kerry–Lugar Bill). The $7.5 billion aid package was designated, over a period
of five years, mostly for the Pakistani social sector, with lots of strings attached.[1]
The bill had exposed a wide gap between the rulers and their perception of
Pakistan–U.S. relations and the civil society of Pakistan. The people saw this
aid as a compromise on their sovereignty and micro-management of the finances
and administration and other affairs. It was not an anti-American outburst, but
rather a protest against the manner in which the Pakistani political elite handled
the issues of Pakistan, which was seen within the context of an extreme form of
"dependency" on the United States.

A sharp rejection of the Kerry–Lugar Bill had sent a strong message to Washington that the views presented by Pakistani bureaucrats and politicians did not
synchronize with the "real Pakistan." Although the visit of the high official of
the Obama administration was intended to be an exercise in public diplomacy,
it turned out to be more of a damage control measure than anything else.
According to a commentary on the complications of the U.S.–Pakistan relationship, and the Pakistani domestic perspective,

Although the visit (of Secretary Clinton) was scheduled much earlier, it came when the Pakistani decision makers were in the midst of a crises laden disconnect with the people, on a variety of issues, Most of it relating to security and strategic questions, especially those of perceptions or misperceptions about the American external policies. The U.S. is accused of treating Pakistan as a matter of expediency—and nothing more than that. Examples of arms embargo after the 1965 war, leaving Afghanistan in disarray after the Soviet withdrawal in 1989 and demonizing Pakistan after 9/11, although none of the hijackers were from this land, are quoted in this regard. These and other questions emerge prominent in the minds of a great number of the general public. There is a general belief that whenever an occasion arose Pakistan came to the assist the Americans, but it was never reciprocated in kind—U.S. administrations preferred India over Pakistan, although the Indians were allies of the Soviets during the cold war and staunch supporters of the Soviet occupation of Afghanistan.[2]

The questions raised by various sections of the Pakistani society were focused on the past relationship between the two countries, on the drone attacks, and on the Kashmiri and U.S. relations with India, including the preference of that country on civilian nuclear cooperation.

During this visit, the Secretary of State spelled out in detail the whole spectrum of on-going Pakistani–U.S. ties by recognizing that there was a need for better understanding between the people of Pakistan and the U.S. administration. In this context, Clinton agreed that the U.S. policy towards Pakistan/Afghanistan, as it existed during the first half of the Obama administration, both in terms of policy and strategy, must take into consideration Pakistan's sensitivities. The Obama administration had admitted that the past policy of ignoring Pakistan, after a certain objective of U.S. had been fulfilled, should be avoided. At the same time, it was argued by U.S. policymakers that trust is a two-way street; they have accused the Pakistani establishment a number of times of not doing enough to undertake serious measures against the al-Qaeda leadership, which they believe is located now in the border areas of Pakistan.

It is further contended by the U.S. side that the Pakistani military is going after only those groups who threaten Pakistan's security, while doing little to eliminate groups that are a security threat to U.S. interests in Afghanistan, like the North Waziristan-based (Miramshah area in particular) network of Jalaluddin Haqqani (a former anti-Soviet commander) who is now accused of operations against U.S. troops in eastern Afghanistan. According to an analyst, "The Haqqanis are closely allied to al Qaeda and the Taliban, led by Mullah Omar. The Haqqani family runs the Manba Ulom madrassa in the village of Danda Darpa Khel, a hub of activity for the terror group."[3] In reiteration, U.S. drones have attacked suspected targets in the FATA region with regular frequency, killing numerous civilians in the process.[4] These cross-border attacks, although they are carried out with the approval and assistance of the Pakistani government, are disapproved by a majority of the population and it has become increasingly difficult for the Pakistani government to defend itself. These concerns became an irritant in Pakisanti–U.S. relations, when it came to public sentiment. In such a charged setting, it became difficult for both countries to create long-term strategic understanding.

It was after the events of September 11, 2001 that the whole structure of Pakistani–U.S. relations underwent a series of revisions. President George W. Bush, in a "revengeful" mood to punish the attackers of the Twin Towers and the Pentagon, issued a warning to the world by saying that "either you are with us or otherwise. . . ." There was no middle ground in his position. General Pervez Musharraf admitted that his decision to extend "unstinted support" to the United States against Afghanistan was taken under tremendous pressure. He further revealed that the "U.S. authorities had asked (him) to reply in definite terms whether Pakistan was a friend or foe of the United States." The United States had requested extensive support, including the use of Pakistan's air-space, logistics, and intelligence information. According to a leading newspaper of Pakistan, "Sources close to the government said the U.S. had left the president with no option other than extending the fullest support to Washington's endeavours [sic] against the Taliban."

The measures that Washington wanted Islamabad to take included allowing U.S. troops to use naval facilities and airspace and the sharing of all intelligence reports about Osama bin Laden's movements inside Afghanistan. Otherwise, President Musharref told the politicians, Washington had warned that it would treat Pakistan as a country harboring terrorists. In that case, Musharraf said, no strategic installations would have remained safe. Sources quoted Musharraf as having said that he could risk his life, but that he could not put the whole country at risk.

Soon after, sanctions were lifted one after another as the U.S. administration, ignoring the nature of regime in Pakistan, desperately sought Pakistan's help in their war against Afghanistan. On September 22, 2001, the United States took a first step by removing the nuclear-related sanctions. On September 29, President Bush applied another waiver when he lifted democracy sanctions installed after the October 1999 military takeover.

When the U.S. military operations started, the divergence of basic interests of the two countries widened, both in content and in strategy. On at least three counts, the United States ignored Pakistani policy positions on Afghanistan. First, the President of Pakistan had repeatedly pleaded for a "targeted bombing" in Afghanistan so that the innocent Afghan people could be spared. To the contrary, U.S. planes bombed indiscriminately, killing innocent civilians and even allowing the massacre by the Northern Alliance of prisoners of war (POWs) in places like Qila-e-Jangi prison. That act sent waves of resentment through the tribal areas of Pakistan. Second, while both leaders stood side-by-side in front of the international electronic media, President Bush announced that as desired by Pakistan, the Northern Alliance forces would not enter Kabul. Third, the

Pakistani government asked that the bombing would pause during the month of Ramazan. General Musharraf in all his earnestness said: "One also needs to give serious consideration to having operations ceased during Ramazan because one should be very clear that it will have its negative fallout," on the Pakistani side of the border. On all of these counts, the Pakistani positions were ignored. As an added problem, on November 3, 2001, Inter Services Public Relations Director General Major General Rashid Qureshi told journalists that the United States "was not disclosing details of its operational and tactical plans to Pakistan."

Even before the United States started military operations against al-Qaeda and Taliban militants in Afghanistan, U.S. circles expressed deep apprehension regarding the real intensions of the Pakistani establishment. Michael A. Sheehan, Coordinator for Counterterrorism, while testifying before the House International Relations Committee in July 2000 stated: "Pakistan has a mixed record on terrorism. Although it has cooperated with the United States and other countries on the arrest and extradition of terrorists, Pakistan has tolerated terrorists living and moving freely within its territory."

In spite of all the accusations and suspicion about Pakistan's intensions, by 2004 it was recognized by the U.S. administration and the U.S. Congress that the difficult war in Afghanistan required Pakistan's cooperation and a close coordination in logistics, especially in the field of ground intelligence. As a gesture to woo dejected Pakistan, President George W. Bush, in a statement on June 17, 2004, declared Pakistan to be a "major non-NATO ally of the United States for the purposes of the Arms Export Control Act." A *BBC* commentary explained that this move

> is in recognition of Islamabad's contribution in the fight against al-Qaeda, and is being seen as Washington's way of saying thank-you. Pakistan will now enjoy a special security relationship with the US . . . Pakistan's new status means that it is now eligible for a series of benefits in the areas of foreign aid and defence [*sic*] co-operation, including priority delivery of defence [*sic*] items. . . . (but this) symbolism is more important than the substance.

On a number of issues, the perceptions of the Pakistani public differ from that of the U.S. public, especially when it comes to India, Afghanistan, and Pakistan's nuclear program. There is a strongly held view in Pakistan that the U.S. administration feels more comfortable with military dictators than with the elected governments. The Pakistani public has long held a view that the ruling elite easily give way to U.S. pressures and for their legitimacy, look towards the support of Washington. These views have been confirmed by the recent revelations of WikiLeaks. While on the other hand, the U.S. public perceives Pakistani–U.S. relations from a regional/global perspective, where realpolitik overcomes all other considerations.

Ever since numerous military operations in the FATA region bordering Afghanistan, (since 2001) the ties established by the Pakistani tribes with the

Afghan Taliban have been a cause of serious strategic concern for NATO and U.S. forces in Afghanistan. That is the reason why numerous and contradictory policies have been adopted by the United States to handle the delicate situation in Afghanistan, along with its fallout in Pakistan. The main U.S. objective has been to establish a reasonable peace in Afghanistan and then leave. That "reasonable peace" cannot be achieved unless the Pashtun tribes have a say in any future "national government" and for that to happen, Pakistan-based militant groups have to be on-board and Pakistan's cooperation is required. There have been various strategies adopted and time tables given by the U.S. administration, and every new date adds more complications to the situation, sending contradictory messages to the various stakeholders.

These extensions are taken by some as a sign of U.S. weakness, implying that U.S. forces are unable to gain control of the ground situation and that even after an extensive tenure, the Karzai government is unable to bring all the ethnic groups, Pashtuns in particular into the process of decision making; thus, the national unity government has failed to materialize. To make matters worse, the Karzai government has been unable to build a national army and other security-related services. The failure of this government has encouraged the Taliban to carry on their subversive activities. It also becomes an incentive for the Pakistani Taliban to shy away from any conciliatory moves attempted by the Pakistani government. It was expected that the second Afghan presidential elections held in August 2009 would bring at least a form of stability, thus allowing sufficient space for U.S. forces to withdraw, but that did not happen. To make matters worse, the influence of corrupt warlords has remained dominant in every sphere of life, and "the expectations of building new Afghanistan have been shattered."[5]

In spite of all efforts by the military and the recent "surge" in forces, the resurgent Taliban are able to preserve their infrastructure, although the al-Qaeda leadership has been minimized. The Pakistan army was able to successful launch a military campaign in 2009 to effectively curtail the effectiveness of the Pakistani Taliban in the tribal belt, especially in South Waziristan, mainly due to Pashtun tribal infighting which was growing because of their difference over the presence of foreigners and al-Qaeda Uzbeks. The Pakistani Taliban had grown in both effectiveness and reach when they carried out suicidal attacks in the far corners of Pakistan, with the assistance and coordination of the vicious and lethal sectarian Punjabi terrorists. But once they over-stretched themselves and challenged the security forces and the intelligence agencies, who allegedly had nourished them during the Soviet occupation of Afghanistan, they have undergone retaliation by the state since 2007, thus blunting their capabilities.

BACKGROUND

Pakistan and Afghanistan have scores of common features and interests that link the two societies. The Pashtuns, a warlike ethnic group lives on both sides of the border and are important minorities with considerable influence in both countries. The Afghan Pashtuns number around 12.5 million and are the largest single ethnic entity in the country, while their fellow Pashtuns in Pakistan make up 16 percent of the total population of Pakistan and number 26 million. According to the 1998 Pakistan census, in the North-West Frontier Province (NWFP), Pashtuns make up 80 percent of the population, while in the Federal Administrative Tribal Areas (FATA), they are 99 percent of the population. The Pakistani Pashtuns, in particular, are an important part of mainstream economic, military, administrative, and political systems and many have held high positions in the government and in business corporations.

The Pashtun tribes, especially those residing in the Federally Administrative Tribal Areas (FATA) have a close affinity with their Afghan ethnic cousins. They share common familial, religious, cultural, and trade traditions and above all, feelings of tribal solidarity. Any harm that comes to the Pashtuns of Afghanistan is deeply felt by their counterparts in Pakistan. The mountainous border which is 2,575 kilometers (1,600 miles) long, crosses one of the most difficult terrains in the world and has been historically a safe haven for fugitives, and is now a sanctuary for the Taliban and al-Qaeda leadership.

Fallout of Afghan Militancy on Pakistan

It must be accepted, as previously mentioned, that during the Taliban rule (1996–2001), Pakistani tribesman had very little to do with Afghanistan's domestic affairs. The Pakistani establishment, in spite of pressure from the Bush administration, refrained from starting a conflict with the tribes, well aware of their warlike nature. They were also concerned that any premature action might trigger a wider ethnic-related conflict in the Pashtun areas of Pakistan, and beyond. Even after the Soviet withdrawal, Pakistan had continued to present itself as a front-line state, not by its ability to perform an effective role in the Afghan crisis, but because of the fact it is a geographic neighbor of that country.

Pakistan's involvement with Afghanistan and its subsequent role as part of the war against international terrorism has a history. Foreign volunteers from various nationalities went to Afghanistan, convinced by the Taliban leadership that their hosts were fighting a *jihad* against evil forces. In the case of the Pakistanis, the leaders of "Talibinized" religious groups provided support to the Taliban militia. This section of the semi-educated Pakistani clergy was responsible for the slaughter of thousands of youths, who went to Afghanistan at their request. In many cases, their parents were not even aware of the real intensions of those who taught them at the *madrasas*. The principal violator in this tragedy was the Amir of Tehrik-I-Nifaz-Shariat (TNSM), Maulana Sufi Muhammad who was instrumental in leaving behind (all in the name of fighting a *jihad* against the United States) more than 8,000 young people in Afghanistan, while he returned to Pakistan, fleeing for his life. He was later arrested and jailed for three years by the Pakistani authorities.

In the days following 9/11, at least two high-powered Pakistani delegations visited Kandhar, apparently requesting that Mullah Umar to listen to reason and take appropriate steps to defuse the situation. The delegation of September 29th was assigned to convince the Taliban to take notice of the requirements of changing global realities. Demands also included releasing the arrested aid workers. None other than Mullah Umar's teacher formed a part of the good-will delegation from Pakistan. Upon their return, one of the members of the ten-member delegation said, "We did not discuss Osama. Osama was not on our agenda." The Afghan Council in Karachi explained, "It is not possible that clerics of such a caliber would make such irresponsible demands, because without evidence the Americans would never give up a person, so why should we be expected to do that?"[6] Even a list presented of 40 Pakistani terrorists who had taken refuge in Afghan territory was not addressed. The visit of the Pakistani delegation and the reaction of its members generated more suspicion than anything else towards the already hostile international environment against terrorism.

It took General Musharraf more than three months after 9/11 to admit that the Taliban-backed Pakistani extremists were responsible for harming and creating divisions within Pakistani society, through a series of sectarian killings. He said during his address to the nation,

> They (extremists) are indulging in fratricidal killings. There is no tolerance among them … Look at the damage they have caused. They have murdered a number of our highly qualified doctors, engineers, civil servants and teachers who were pillars of our society … These extremists did not stop here. They started killing other innocent people in mosques and places of worship.[7]

General Musharraf's pronouncement was not made as a matter of concern for Pakistani society, but as a result of international pressure, led by the anti-terrorism campaign of President Bush's administration. The problem of extremism in the region had existed since 1996, with the advent of the Taliban in Afghanistan. Even during the midst of the post 9/11 fallout, the Foreign Office and various sections of the ruling elite felt that Pakistan must obstruct any settlement, which would dislodge the Taliban from Kabul and they regarded it as a perfect model for preserving Pakistan's security interests.

It is against this backdrop of misperception and misjudgment that a former Foreign Minister, had to express his apprehension in these words,

A word of advice to Pakistan: difficult days are ahead for us. There is no need for us to panic. But let us be clear where we stand. While America simmers with rage, Washington will be less tolerant towards us. There are those in the US who have indicated that parts of Pakistan can be hit. The hawks must be advising Bush to hit Pakistan's missile and nuclear installations. Washington will be in no mood to accept Islamabad's explanations and reasons.[8]

However, the reality was far from that which the Pakistani elite perceived. As a direct result of interfering in Afghan affairs, Pakistan society had to confront at least two evils: one in the form of aligning themselves with the terrorists and the other related to the ideological decay of the society. The first evil is reflected in the world-wide and regional suspicion of Pakistan's involvement in international terrorism, thus isolating the country in regional as well as in international environments. Most dangerous of all, Pakistani status as a responsible nuclear power came under strict scrutiny. In an October 2001 interview, Dr. Stephen Cohen, an expert in Pakistani affairs, accused Pakistan of following a policy of colonization in Afghanistan.

The Pakistani establishment's "fixation" with the Taliban regime in Afghanistan presented grave consequences for the country. It spoiled Pakistan's relationship with its traditional allies such as Iran, Turkey, the larger Middle East, and the Central Asian Republics. At one stage, even China became apprehensive about the pro-Taliban posture and its fallout in Xinjiang province bordering Pakistan and Afghanistan. The most negative effect of "Talibanization" in Pakistan occurred when India got the opportunity to propagate and effectively neutralize Middle Eastern opinion and the indigenous Kashmir freedom struggle was "linked" with extremist elements in Pakistan via Taliban Afghanistan.

However, Islamabad's connections with the Taliban remained one-sided. At least on two vital occasions, the Afghan government ignored Pakistani requests. One occasion was the safety of Iranian diplomats in Herat in September 1998, where nine Iranians were killed, in spite of the fact that "on the day of the attack, Pakistani diplomats had relayed to Teheran an assurance from the Taliban that the safety of the Iranian consulates and diplomats in Mazar-i-Sharif would be guaranteed."[9] The other occasion dealt with the unwarranted demolition of centuries-old Buddha statues in March 2001. These incidents damaged Pakistan's credibility still further, creating more suspicion about its dubious dealings with the Afghan regime. It also proved how little leverage the country exercised on Kabul, while no concrete steps were taken by the military rulers to distance them-selves from the Taliban.

In some circles in Pakistan, a non-friendly government in Kabul was regarded as a setback for Pakistan's security, but given the landlocked nature of the country, any government in Kabul, as in the past, has little choice but to rely on Pakistan for its land route to the Arabian Sea. Among the regional nations, Pakistan had or could provide a significant helping-hand for this conflict-ridden land, in a number of ways:

- It has the longest border with Afghanistan and thus, the capacity to provide needed logistic support to the landlocked country.
- Afghanistan owes its trade and social support to the liberal passage policies of its eastern neighbor.
- Pakistan has close religious and ethnic links with Afghanistan.
- Pakistan provided a safe haven to the 3 million Afghan refugees that fled after the Soviet invasion; the Afghan *mujahideen* were provided with Pakistani passports and the borders were kept open for those who wanted to seek asylum in Pakistan.
- All Afghan leaders were given extensive Pakistani support during the Soviet invasion and they operated from Pakistani territory, thus subjecting Pakistan to frequent Soviet bombardment and sabotage activities in which thousands of Pakistani citizens lost their lives.

Pakistan Dragged into the Regional Conflict

Since the 1980s, Afghanistan has been linked with Pakistan in a number of ways. The basis being that no matter what happens in Afghanistan, it has a direct implication for Pakistani society, whether as a result of regional or Pakistani establishment desires. The many attacks on Afghan government troops and the U.S. military deployments during the months of June and July 2005, raised many new questions. These were not only in regard to Afghanistan's internal security, but also in regard to the fragile relations between the two neighboring countries. At least, as a part of a policy pronouncement, Kabul recognized that its security was closely allied with that of Pakistan. On the eve of Prime Minister Shaukat Aziz's official visit to Kabul on July 24, 2005, these sentiments were reflected in an Afghan Foreign Ministry statement which stated that "friendly relations between Pakistan and Afghanistan were in the national interest of both countries and an essential component to promote stability in the region." On several occasions, similar statements had also been made in the past. However, whenever there were Pashtun related conflicts of varying nature, it had fallout on the Pakistan tribal belt, and the relationship between the two countries deteriorated and both parties had to start once again to reestablish normal ties. The Afghan government continued to suspect Pakistan for being supportive of the militants in their country and in the present circumstances, there was little chance that Kabul could be convinced otherwise. The focal point of these relations centered on the conflict between the security organization of Taliban and the Afghan state. Pakistan is thus dragged into the Afghan dilemma when it fails to manage the operations of Afghan-related militant groups in its own society.

Therefore, when it comes to Afghan militancy, part of the problem comes from within Pakistan. Musharraf's government was seen by many as ineffective, as well as indulging in dubious policies, whether sectarian or otherwise. In his address to the nation on July 21, 2005, he vowed to eradicate militancy in Pakistan, but his address was regarded by observers as nothing more than his declaration on January 12, 2002 to take charge of extremism and militancy in the country. This "awakening" of Musharraf was attributed to the July 7, 2005 London bombings, in which the suicide bombers were alleged to have visited a Pakistani *madrasa*.

On its part, Afghan society always presents itself in a package of dynamics and variables, which most of the time are difficult to manage by any normal means. Past experience shows that the Afghans have yet to learn how to solve their conflicts and accommodate the other point of view while running government affairs. They have no experience in the modern concepts of legislative bodies, political parties, or a structured judicial system. Whatever little they experience they do have, is confined to the capital Kabul. In sum, there does not exist a political culture on whose foundations a modern society could be constructed. Even more so with the "brain drain" since 1979 that went on unabated in the following years, Afghan society lacks an indigenous expertise to manage their country. History has proved that a divided Afghanistan, devoid of any functional institutions, is incapable of reaching any political solutions.

With the resurgence of Taliban, there was an increase in Afghan militancy in 2005, and with that came a volley of direct and indirect denunciation of Pakistan. Included in that rhetoric were the statements of Afghan-American U.S. Ambassador to Afghanistan, Zalmay Khalizad, who was reacting to the arrest of three Pakistanis in June by Afghan forces who had been charged of plotting to kill the U.S. Ambassador to Afghan. He vehemently said that Mullah Omar and Osama bin Laden were somewhere in Pakistan, but he could not however substantiate his allegations with details and evidence. Ambassador Khalizad's charge was followed by statements by Afghan government officials, the officially controlled news media, and President Karzai, himself. In Pakistan, the reaction was sharp and forthcoming. Apart from a strong statement from government, the media started to question the rationale of Pakistan's complete commitment towards the war against terrorism in this part of the world. An editorial in one of the leading Pakistani daily newpapers remarked, "It's time Pakistan should rethink its policy of cooperating in the War on Terror and being rewarded only with slurs." The reasons for the resurgence of 2005–2006 terrorist acts was explained by a *BBC* commentary as,

> The powerful drugs trade is undoubtedly intertwined with the current (2006) violence. Local power drugs trade is undoubtedly intertwined with the current violence.
>
> Local power holders who feel marginalized may find themselves allied to the Taleban [*sic*], at least in the short term. In some areas it's difficult to distinguish between attacks by the Taleban [*sic*] and those by other radical Islamic groups or individuals. These include Hezb-e Islami, headed by former Prime Minister Gulbuddin Hekmatyar, or those loyal to Jalaluddin Haqqani, a former *mujahideen* leader who also served in the Taleban [*sic*] government. The situation is further complicated by a complex web of shifting allegiances, tribal, ethnic and local rivalries and feuds within Afghan society.

Afghans have been known to denounce rivals or enemies as members of the Taleban [*sic*] for political or economic gain.[10]

The then-ongoing crisis between Pakistan and Afghanistan was defused with the intervention of President George W. Bush, who persuaded both countries to focus more on the war against terrorism, than on finding fault with each other. These developments further confirmed that bilateral ties between the two neighboring countries had become a matter of triangular relations (now with the involvement of the United States), aggravated by the spread of global terrorism and becoming more problematic with every reversal. Pakistani–Afghan relations remained a matter of serious concern for U.S. strategic planners, and will be as long as militancy continues to dominate the region.

In 2004, Pakistan had deployed more than 80,000 troops to the tribal and adjoining areas with Afghanistan and by September 2008, the number was increased to 120,000. The borders were effectively sealed with latest reconnaissance devices and the Taliban entering Afghanistan in any organized manner became difficult. The main weakness remained with the Afghan security apparatus itself. A glaring example is the escape of four most-wanted al-Qaeda prisoners in July, 2005 from Bagram Prison, a facility that is heavily guarded and is under the direct control of U.S. troops. The escape was not possible without the cooperation of the Afghan soldiers on duty. Until now there has been no trace of the escapees, who were known for their hardened ideology and considered extremely dangerous. A U.S. defense official remarked, "It is embarrassing and amazing at the same time, (and). . . . it was a disaster."[11]

Again in 2008, around 1,100 detainees escaped from *Sarposa* Prison in Kandahar after an attack by the Taliban. It became easier for the Afghan administration to blame Pakistan for their security lapses, as little effort was made by Kabul administration to establish its control in areas that are beyond the city of Kabul. Apart from that, the Pashtun population is kept alienated by the Tajik-Uzbak alliance in the government and that generated resentment among the ignored tribes. All of the Taliban might be Pashtuns, but not all Pashtuns confer to the ideology of the Taliban. In the closely knit tribal society of Afghanistan, it is difficult to make a clear distinction between the two groups. Sometimes, it is done so deliberately to keep the majority of the Pashtuns who are the largest single ethnic group out of mainstream politics.

The noted aspect is that Pakistan had lost its creditability to perform any meaningful role in the divided and volatile Afghan society. Because of intense past interference in the Afghan factional conflict, Pakistan had conceded most of its neutral ground and was branded as an active partner in the cross-border Afghan militancy. In fact, the Pakistani establishment was visualized as a major part of the problem. This view was shared by some U.S. officials, who regarded Musharraf as not doing enough to stop the recruitment of Taliban cadres.

Through the efforts of Bush administration, a joint Pakistan-Afghanistan peace (Grand) *jirga* was called in Kabul in August, 2007. This idea originated when President Karzai suggested to President Bush in 2006 to call a meeting of a wide-range of individuals and groups from the two countries on one platform. The *jirga* had a broad representation, ranging from parliament members of the two countries to political parties, religious scholars, and business community and tribal elders. According to Pakistan's former foreign secretary, "after a telephone call or two from Washington and some undisclosed reappraisal in Islamabad, the general (President Musharraf) . . . went and delivered a speech urging the two Muslim neigbours [*sic*] to overcome their mutual mistrust."[12]

The 700 participants of the *jirga* issued a joint declaration calling for the exchange of anti-terrorism intelligence and a "strict monitoring of the Pak-Afghan border areas . . . and promotion of economic and social ties,"[13] between the two neighboring countries. At the same meeting, it was agreed to form a "mini-*jirga*, consisting of 50 members, equally representing Pakistan and Afghanistan, to talk to the Afghan groups, involved in insurgency and acts of violence."[14] Doubts were raised about the effectiveness of this exercise as the Pashtun tribes were not unified enough to conduct a joint effort to address the militancy in Afghanistan, as well as the tribal areas of Pakistan. First, there was also a conspicuous absence of 40 participants from the FATA area who gave the reason for their absence as their concern about the fighting in their areas, so establishing peace in Afghanistan is of secondary nature for them.[15] Second, the members attending this *jirga* had little or no contact with the Taliban and other belligerent groups, nor were these groups taken into confidence before this *jirga*. Expressing skepticism on the issue of unconditionally approaching the militants, Pakistan's newspaper *Dawn*, in its editorial, wrote:

> With no delegates from Pakistan's tribal areas attending the Kabul *jirga*, how will it be ensured that the insurgents will accept these conditions? The accord reached by the Pakistan government with the insurgents in Waziristan came to nothing while it gave time to the Taliban to regroup. What could produce results is joint action by Pakistan and Afghanistan to clip the wings of the extremists and then enter into a dialogue with them. If Kabul and Islamabad act jointly, they may be able to achieve what they have failed to attain separately.[16]

Such *jirgas* and gatherings had lost their significance as the insurgents were in no mood to enter into dialogue with the Afghan government in the presence of foreign troops. An additional factor of weaknesses within the Karzai government also made such gestures ineffective. This government had failed to prove that it was in command of law and order and that their reliance on foreign troops would decrease in the future. It also lacked the ability to build social/economic and administrative institutions in Afghanistan. Rampant corruption made the matters still more complicated, as the Taliban exploited the lack of popular support for the Karzai regime,[17] which was supported by many notorious and corrupt Afghan warlords.

PAKISTAN'S ONSLAUGHT AGAINST THE MILITANTS

Newly elected Prime Minister of Pakistan, Yousaf Raza Gillani declared that his government would no longer tolerate the activities of the insurgents. He emphasized that, "We will not bow down before terrorists and extremists and force them to lay down arms."[18] A spokesman for the Pakistani armed forces made it clear that military action against the militants in Swat was in the national interest of Pakistan and had nothing to do with the pressure of external powers, meaning the United States.[19] He explained that in spite of foreign (U.S. and NATO) pressure, efforts were made by the government to reconcile with the militants and full opportunity was provided, "to establish peace . . . (The) militants stood fully exposed now. . . . The operation will continue till its logical conclusion and complete elimination of extremists from the area."[20]

In 2009, within a short span of about three months, 12,000 to 15,000 Pakistani army personnel effectively overcame some 4,000 insurgents, who were largely locals but included some cross-border militants including Tajiks and Uzbeks in the Malakand Division, especially in the Swat and Buner areas. In just three months, more than 1.3 million displaced persons started returning to their homes, where near normal life had returned. Pakistan had faced 6,210 terrorist attacks in 2007, which decreased to 3,258 in 2008 and there was yet a further decrease of such incidents in 2009.[21] This presents a different scenario from Afghanistan during this time period where the fighting has gone on for years with no end in sight. More important of all, in spite of all the criticism and condemnation, while the Pakistani army fights its internal war, the Afghan government is entirely dependent on foreign troops to curtail the insurgents, with adverse repression.

Even after the exit of Musharraf in August, 2008, there was a large section of public opinion, including that of members of legislature, who believed that they were being dragged into a war which was not that of Pakistan's doing. They argued that the Afghanistan conflict was a U.S. war and that Pakistan should not be drawn into that "messy" affair. They believed that the Pakistani government must find ways to negotiate with angry tribes who were upset because of the U.S. and NATO military assaults on the Afghan people, including the Taliban.

Public opinion started to shift later in the beginning of 2009 when the tribesman became more radicalized and militant religious groups in settled areas like Swat and other parts of Malakand Division of NWFP started daring attacks, targeting the army, police, and public places. High-profile suicide terrorist attacks took place on a police training facility near Lahore, and on the Sri Lankan cricket team. There was also the June 12, 2009 assassination of the highly respected religious scholar Dr. Sarfraz Hussain Naeemi in his *madrasa* named Jamia Naimia in

Lahore by a 17-year-old suicide bomber. Naeemi was a vocal advocate of sectarian unity and had declared that suicide attacks were against the principles of Islam and he had led a group of over 20 religious groups against the activities of the Taliban. An editorial of a widely read Pakistani newspaper said,

> The attack [against Dr. Naeemi] is also a very grim reminder that contrary to trumpets declaring victory in Swat and Buner, and ISPR's often-positive sounding and optimistic press briefings, the war against the Taliban and their Al Qaeda allies, and indeed against militancy, obscurantism and terrorism, is far from over. In fact, as has been predicted often in these columns, it is just the beginning and the battlefront is not going to be Malakand division or Swat but indeed the better part of the whole country, and it is now clearly shifting to the cities as well. That said, the fight will have to be carried to its logical conclusion, and in this ordinary Pakistanis who comprise civil society will need to bring unity in their ranks to realize and understand that they all have a common enemy. If they do not stand with other organs/institutions of state and society to fight it and defeat it, it will devour them.[22]

These attacks helped to foster a near unanimous opinion among the people of Pakistan, the army, and political leadership that the Pakistani Taliban and other militant groups are harming the state and must be eliminated by force. Pakistan's second largest political party, the Muslim League (Nawaz group), which was hesitant in the past to take a clear stand against the terrorist groups, now declared that it supported the military action to eliminate the Taliban and other militant groups. Those who had favored dialogue with the militants also changed their standpoint. For the first time, U.S. and Pakistani strategic interests coincided. Now, the U.S. drone attacks were no longer seen as a violation of Pakistani territory and sovereignty. In fact, many were relieved whenever a drone killed a suspected Taliban or al-Qaeda leader.[23] Reflecting Pakistan's change of attitude, a Lahore-based newspaper editorial wrote, "One clear difference is that Pakistan is now less confused about what to do with its own Taliban than ever in the past. It has decided to take on the warlords of its Tribal Areas, and the world clearly sees that it is fighting them in real earnest, killing the terrorists and losing its own soldiers in the process."

The United States and the AfPak Strategy

President Barak Obama announced on March 27, 2009 his roadmap for the AfPak strategy. This strategy was in specific reference to confront the remnants of al-Qaeda and the resurgent Taliban in Afghanistan, along with the growing militant groups in the Pakistani tribal belt. The Obama administration lumped together Afghanistan and Pakistan in this strategy as it presumed that both the countries had similar features and requirements. According to the new strategy, it was conceived to design a similar plan to defeat the terrorists and the insurgents.

This change, of course, was "in the cards" as soon as Obama assumed office in January of that year. During the presidential debates, candidate Obama had made it clear that Afghanistan and the tribal areas of Pakistan would be his priority as al-Qaeda and the Taliban leadership is present there and active. He was critical of the Bush administration for diverting funds and troops to Iraq at the expense of Afghanistan. Obama made his point in the first presidential debate held in October, 2008 when he said, "The question is, was this wise [to leave Afghanistan]? We have seen Afghanistan worsen, deteriorate. We need more troops there. We need more resources there."[24] He explained further,

> [In Iraq] we have four times more troops there than we do in Afghanistan. And that is a strategic mistake, because every intelligence agency will acknowledge that al Qaeda is the greatest threat against the United States and that Secretary of Defense Gates acknowledged the central front—that the place where we have to deal with these folks is going to be in Afghanistan and in Pakistan. So here's what we have to do comprehensively, though. It's not just more troops. We have to press the Afghan government to make certain that they are actually working for their people. And I've said this to President Karzai.
>
> No. 2, we've got to deal with a growing poppy trade that has exploded over the last several years.
>
> No. 3, we've got to deal with Pakistan, because al Qaeda and the Taliban have safe havens in Pakistan, across the border in the northwest regions, and although, you know, under George Bush, with the support of Senator McCain, we've been giving them $10 billion over the last seven years, they have not done what needs to be done to get rid of those safe havens. And until we do, Americans here at home are not going to be safe.[25]

Departing from the previous policy of President George W. Bush, the Obama administration promised to concentrate on the al-Qaeda leadership and its Taliban allies which were thought to be present in southwest Afghanistan and the tribal areas of Pakistan, especially in Waziristan.[26]

President Obama's new policy announcement was accompanied by the White House "White Paper," which spelled out the objectives and recommendations for the new policy. The main features of the Pakistan-related objectives are:

- Disrupt, dismantle, and defeat al-Qaeda and its save havens in Pakistan, preventing their return
- Assistance for a civilian control and a democratic government
- Help build up the economic structures
- Conditional assistance for the military, depending on their willingness to eliminate al-Qaeda and other terrorist groups
- Engage Pakistani people on long-term commitment[27]

After the so-called AfPak strategy was announced, the U.S. administration and its military leadership struggled with a generally agreed-upon strategy for Afghanistan. This confusion came with the report of assessment by General

Stanley McChrystal, Commander of the U.S. and NATO forces in Afghanistan. The report painted a doomsday picture of Afghanistan and asked for more troops. It was further complicated by the rigged Afghan presidential elections, as mentioned before, where the Karzai government lost its legitimacy and credibility among the Afghan people.[28]

General McChrystal asked for 40,000 more troops, raising the total number to 110,000, close to the number of Soviet troops in Afghanistan in the 1970s. On the other hand, Vice President Joe Biden and other civilian members of the Obama administration supported reducing the U.S. military presence in Afghanistan, talking to certain Taliban groups, and going after the leadership of al-Qaeda, especially in Pakistan. In a White House meeting held on October 1, 2009 by the Obama National Security Team to review Afghan policy, there was a split among those in attendance. According to a report,

> Secretary of State Hillary Rodham Clinton and special Afghan and Pakistan envoy Richard Holbrooke appeared to be leaning toward supporting a troop increase. . . . White House chief of staff Rahm Emanuel and Gen. James Jones, Obama's national security adviser, appeared to be less supportive. Vice President Joe Biden, who attended the meeting, has been reluctant to support a troop increase, favoring a strategy that directly targets al-Qaida fighters who are believed to be hiding in Pakistan. . . . Adm. Mike Mullen, chairman of the Joint Chiefs of Staff, and Gen. David Petraeus, the top commander for the wars in Iraq and Afghanistan, both support McChrystal's strategy. . . . Defense Secretary Robert Gates is on the fence.[29]

As a result of the changing circumstances in Afghanistan, President Obama was confronted with a dilemma to define a final strategy for the country, i.e., away from the AfPak strategy launched in March, 2009. In a *CNN* interview, he said, "I don't want to put the resource question before the strategy question. . . . There is a natural inclination to say, 'If I get more, then I can do more.' But right now, the question is—the first question is—are we doing the right thing? Are we pursuing the right strategy?"[30]

Many in Pakistan do not feel comfortable with the neologism of "AfPak," as it signifies placing together the security interests of Pakistan and Afghanistan. It also means that the U.S. defense establishment will design a policy that would jointly deal with these two countries, as if they are two parts of a same nation and that their structures, polity, and defense and political interests are at similar level of development and magnitude. From a Pakistani perspective, it is wrong to presume that the strategic interests of Pakistan and Afghanistan are tied together. Both of these countries do have a variety of commonalities, but at the same time, they have divergent perceptions about their security needs. A former Chief of the Pakistan Army, General Aslam Beg wrote that AfPak has presented many challenges for Pakistan as "Afghanistan has been reversed on Pakistan resulting into a running battle from Swat to Dir, to Waziristan and possibly Balochistan in the very near future (and) the occupation forces surge in Helmand province of Afghanistan is causing spillover effects on the ongoing operations in Pakistan."[31]

Aslam Beg and others have long held this view that the presence of U.S. and NATO troops in Afghanistan and the drone attacks on the Pakistani tribal areas have caused the Pashtun tribe to become aggressive, defiant, and militant. They believe that it was the presence and attacks of U.S forces on the tribal belt of Pakistan and General Musharraf's policies of belligerence that ignited suicide bombers and other terrorist activities. Jamaat-e-Islami (JI) Chief Qazi Hussain Ahmad said in a public speech, "I guarantee if the government withdraws the army from the Tribal Areas and leaves the restoration of peace to the local *jirgas*, normalcy will return to the region."[32] He also stressed that "dialogue, not force, was the solution to the FATA problem."[33] Former Chair of Senate Foreign Relations Committee, Mushahid Hussain has held the view that "some people in the United States were using Pakistan as a 'scapegoat' to hide their failure in Afghanistan."[34] There is also a third view held by the conspiracy theorists, who are many in Pakistan and who should be taken seriously, as it helps to build a certain type of opinion in the society, no matter how farfetched it might be. Ahmed Quraishi, a former journalist at the Pakistan Television Corporation, represents this view as the following,

> In less than two years, the United States has successfully managed to drop from news headlines its failure to pacify Afghanistan. The focus of the Anglo-American media—American and British—has been locked on Pakistan. In order to justify this shift, multiple insurgencies and endless supply of money and weapons has trickled from U.S.-occupied Afghanistan into Pakistan to sustain a number of warlords inside Pakistan whom the American media calls 'Taliban' but they are actually nothing but hired mercenaries with sophisticated weapons who mostly did not even exist as recently as the year 2005.[35]

In the past, both the United States and Pakistan had followed different patterns of regional policies that suited their respective interests. Firstly, the United States abandoned Afghanistan after the Soviets left (1988–1989) and took no measures to monitor the foreigners who were, in the first place, encouraged by the United States to come to Afghanistan to participate in the "international *jihad*" against the infidel Russians. Pakistan, on the other hand, diligently interfered in the domestic affairs of its neighbor, choosing its allies, the last of them being the wrong choice of the Taliban.

Secondly, while Pakistan was condemned for talking to militant tribesmen who had been converted by the Pakistani Taliban, British and U.S. government officials in July 2009, reiterating President Obama's policy statement of March 27, declared that they were ready to accommodate the "moderate" Taliban. British Foreign Secretary David Miliband and International Development Secretary Douglas Alexander hinted that there was a possibility of a "reconciliation," between the Afghan government and those Taliban who were ready to talk. It was reported in the British press that "for more than a year, British intelligence officers have been instigating contacts with Taliban commanders and their entourage. But their task has been very delicate given the sensitivities of the Karzai administration in Kabul."[36] Earlier, while presenting a new strategy for Afghanistan and Pakistan, President Obama had said that he would start a "reconciliation process" with those Afghan Taliban who are willing to do so.[37] This clearly showed that the occupying forces consider the Afghan Taliban as a separate entity from the Pakistani militant situation and that is why two different standards are being applied. Teresita C. Schaffer, a former senior State Department official with extensive Pakistan experience, admits that the U.S. and Pakistan's concerns on war against the militants differs, "While the United States and Afghanistan are particularly concerned about the Taliban crossing back and forth across the Pakistan border, Pakistan is more concerned with stopping internal terrorism caused by suicide bombings and the seizure of territory within the country by insurgents."[38]

CONCLUSION

A Pakistani retired army general, who held important positions in the government and was closely associated with Afghan affairs during Zia-ul-Haq's rule, advises Pakistan to keep away from the domestic affairs of Afghanistan. His presumptions are based on the lessons learned from past history of Pakistan-Taliban relations, which ultimately led to Pakistan's present difficulties. The general writes,

> Pakistan must give up its previous policy and strictly adhere to a policy of non-interference in the internal affairs of Afghanistan. Islamabad should try to have friendly relations with whichever government the Afghans choose for themselves. Regular meetings of the Tripartite Commission, comprising senior military and diplomatic representatives of the three countries (US; Pakistan and Afghanistan) jointly fighting the war against terrorism are needed. The Karzai administration should be wholeheartedly supported. Pakistan should play a positive role in the rehabilitation and reconstruction of Afghanistan, within its limited resources. Close coordination with Iran on the developments in Afghanistan would avoid any misunderstanding between the two Muslim neighbours [sic]. Make use of the presence of the Pakistan army in the Tribal Areas for the economic development of that part of Pakistan.[39]

The long-term Pakistani fear of Indian influence in Afghanistan was confirmed by General McChrystal's September 2009 report in which was said,

> Indian political and economic influence is increasing in Afghanistan, including significant development efforts and financial investment. In addition, the current Afghan government is perceived by Islamabad to be pro-Indian. While Indian activities largely benefit the Afghan people, increasing Indian influence in Afghanistan is likely to exacerbate regional tensions and encourage Pakistani countermeasures in Afghanistan or India.[40]

This assessment from the American general will reinforce the opponents of AfPak strategy that there are more than one interest and country involved in Afghanistan and therefore, it is not logical to place Afghanistan and Pakistan together exclusively for the purposes of strategic policy.

The strategic requirements of Pakistan are a world apart from those of Afghanistan. It is true that events in Afghanistan had a bearing upon Pakistan, at least twice in recent history in 1978 and then in 2001, but that was because of choice and the improvised policies of Islamabad. Otherwise, Pakistan could have stayed out of the events in Afghanistan with little strategic impact on its own society. The meddling in Afghan affairs had its negative repercussions, which not only involved the tribal areas of Pakistan but other parts of the country were radicalized, as well. It wreaked havoc upon the centuries-old liberal and accommodating Pakistani society, by inducting alien cultures of bigotry, extremism, and fanaticism. Because of a vicious series of suicidal bomb attacks by the FATA-based Taliban, a near consensus has now developed in Pakistan that the armed forces and the government should eradicate the terrorist groups, but it is equally desired that Pakistan's security concerns are different from those of Afghanistan and that Pakistan should stay out of its internal affairs.

Skeptics in Pakistan see an unwritten understanding in the new policy of inducting India by "regional diplomacy involving all key players in South Asia." Encouraged by Afghan President Hamid Karzai, India is already playing a considerable role in Afghanistan, expending its influence through reconstruction and developmental contracts. Pakistan has held the view that the Indians have more consulates in Afghanistan than they require and that these are being used for spying on Pakistan. Many in the Pakistan government believe that "Kabul is being run by a puppet government put up by the Americans,"[41] and that the Indians are being promoted to establish its hegemony in Afghanistan and in the region. It is also considered as an established fact that Kabul supports Baloch secessionist leaders who are being protected by Karzai regime. These facts can become a hindrance in the effectiveness of war against terror in Afghanistan.

The positive aspect of the AfPak strategy lies in the economic part of the agenda and the building of its civil institutions. The Obama administration's promise to have oversight and auditing over the dispersal of aid is a welcome sign. In the past, billions of U.S. aid dollars were squandered by Pakistani bureaucrats and army generals, and it never reached the needy, nor was institutional-building taken seriously. Education, health, and other essential services in present-day Pakistan are in shambles and need immediate attention. A Pakistani lawyer who commented on the U.S. aid package and its conditionality wrote, "Not many will disagree with this approach of giving aid for the people's welfare. In fact, given past allegations of the diversion of funds, the US government will, rightly so, put in checks to ensure that these funds are not diverted for military purposes."[42] The key to success of Obama's new strategy depends on the swift upgrading of literacy and the reduction of poverty especially in FATA and other underdeveloped regions of the country. On the Pakistan side, there is near consensus that the elected government of Prime Minister Gillani should take stern measures to curtain militancy in the country, it is equally accepted that Pakistan's security concerns are different from that of Afghanistan.

NOTES

1. Senator John Kerry, one of the co-authors of the Bill gave a list of eight Pakistani "myths" regarding this financial legislation. In the same documents, he responded to each "myth," saying that the Pakistani perception was not true.

> Myth 1: The $7.5 billion authorized by the bill comes with strings attached for the people of Pakistan.

> Myth 2: The bill impinges on Pakistan's sovereignty.

> Myth 3: The bill places onerous conditions on U.S. military aid to Pakistan that interfere in Pakistan's internal affairs and imply that Pakistan supports terrorism and nuclear proliferation.

> Myth 4: The bill requires U.S. oversight on promotions and other internal operations of the Pakistani military.

> Myth 5: The bill expands the Predator program of drone attacks on targets within Pakistan.

> Myth 6: The bill funds activities within Pakistan by private U.S. security firms, such as Dyncorp and Blackwater/Xe.

> Myth 7: The bill aims for an expanded U.S. military footprint in Pakistan.

> Myth 8: The United States is expanding its physical footprint in Pakistan, using the bill as a justification for why the U.S .Embassy in Islamabad needs more space and security. For the American response, see "Myths and facts about Kerry-Lugar bill," *Dawn*, October 10, 2009.

2. Syed Farooq Hasnat, "Hillary Converse with Real Pakistan," *The Nation*, November 15, 2009.

3. Bill Roggio, "US hits Haqqani Network in North Waziristan, kills 8," *The Long War Journal*, February 24, 2010, (accessed October 06, 2010); http://www.longwarjournal.org/archives/2010/02/us_hits_haqqani_netw_1.php

4. The American drone (unmanned aircraft) attacks, which began in 2004 increased to 117 in 2010. In 2008, there were 35 such attacks, while in 2009, 53 drones hit the Taliban and al-Qaeda sanctuaries inside the FATA region. So far, (until January 7, 2011) there have been a total of 219 such attacks, of which 158 were in North Waziristan. These attacks have killed some key leaders of the terror organization, but at the same time, numerous civilians have lost their lives, including women and children. Created by Bill Roggio and Alexander Mayer, "Charting the data for US airstrikes in Pakistan, 2004–2011," *The Long War Journal*; (accessed January 8, 2011); http://www.longwarjournal.org/pakistan-strikes.php

5. Syed Farooq Hasnat, "The Flawed Afghan Elections," *The Nation*, September 12, 2009.

6. *The News*, September 29, 2001.

7. Daily *Nawa-e-Waqt*, January 12, 2002; Translation from Urdu by the author.

8. Sardar Aseff Ahmad Ali, "A Defining Moment for the US," *Dawn*, September 16, 2001.

9. Douglas Jehl, "Iran Holds Taliban Responsible for 9 Diplomats' Deaths," *The New York Times*, September 11 1998.

10. Pam O'Toole, "Who are the militants in Afghanistan?" *BBC News*, August 18, 2006, http://news.bbc.co.uk/2/hi/south_asia/4801303.stm

11. http://www.nytimes.com/2005/12/04/international/asia/04escape.html

12. Tanvir Ahmad Khan, "A jirga under alien shadow," *Dawn*, August 20, 2007, http://www.dawn.com/2007/08/20/op.htm#1

13. *The News*, August 13, 2007, http://thenews.jang.com.pk/print3.asp?id=9565

14. The text of Pak-Afghan Peace *jirga*, held in Kabul from August 9 to August 12 laid down guiding principles of future relations between the two countries. For details of the Declaration, see *Daily Times*, August 13, 2007, http://www.dailytimes.com.pk/default.asp?page=2007\08\13\story_13-8-2007_pg7_48

15. Ashfaq Yusufzai "Pakistan-Afghanistan: Kabul Peace Jirga Falls Short," *IPS* (Inter Press Service News Agency), August 14, 2007, http://ipsnews.net/print.asp?idnews=38884

16. *Dawn*, August 14, 2007, "Decisions at the grand Jirga," http://www.dawn.com/2007/08/14/ed.htm#2

17. Shanthie Mariet D'Souza, "Afghanistan: Continuing Violence," in D. Suba Chandran and P.R. Chari (eds), *Armed Conflicts in South Asia, 2008: Growing Violence* (New Delhi: Routledge, 2008), p. 46.

18. *Dawn*, May 8, 2009, http://www.dawn.com/wps/wcm/connect/dawn-content-library/dawn/the-newspaper/front-page/army-told-to-crush-swat-militants-militants-mistook-govts-sincerity-for-weakness-women-subjected-to-discrimination-pmln%2C-anp%2C-jup-back-operation-rs1bn-859

19. *The News*, May 9, 2009, http://thenews.jang.com.pk/arc_default.asp

20. Ibid.

21. http://www.cnn.com/2009/WORLD/asiapcf/04/30/terrorism.report/index.html

22. "Jamia Naeemia attack," editorial, *The News*, June 13, 2009, http://thenews.jang.com.pk/print1.asp?id=182695

23. *Daily Times*, July 20, 2009, http://www.dailytimes.com.pk/default.asp?page=2009\07\20\story_20-7-2009_pg3_1

24. http://www.cnn.com/2008/POLITICS/09/26/debate.mississippi.transcript/

25. Ibid.

26. Syed Farooq Hasnat, "Pakistans Strategic Interests, Afghanistan and the Fluctuating U.S. Strategy," *Journal of International Affairs*, Vol. 63, No. 1 (Fall/Winter, 2009), p. 150.

27. "White Paper of the Interagency Policy Group's Report on U.S. Policy toward Afghanistan and Pakistan." March 27, 2009, http://thecable.foreignpolicy.com/posts/2009/03/27/white_house_white_paper_on_us_policy_to_afghanistan_and_pakistan

28. Syed Farooq Hasnat, "Pakistan's Strategic Interests, Afghanistan and the Fluctuating U.S. Strategy," op. cit., p. 151.

29. Philip Elliott, "Council split complicates Obama's Afghan decision," *Associate Press*, October 1, 2009, http://www.google.com/hostednews/ap/article/ALeqM5iqyaFh_efr-brDq0rMLF1hkop0tgD9B2B5G00

30. Elizabeth Williamson and Henry J. Pulizzi, "Obama Questions Plan to Add Forces in Afghanistan," The Wall Street Journal, September 21, 2009, http://online.wsj.com/article/SB125345323201025705.html

31. General Aslam Beg, "AfPak strategy and Pakistan," *The Nation*, July 14, 2009.

32. *Daily Times*, January 24, 2009.

33. Ibid.

34. *Dawn*, January 27, 2007.

35. Quoted in Robert Mackey, "A Grand Conspiracy Theory From Pakistan," *The Lede* (The New York Times News Blog), May 12, 2009, http://thelede.blogs.nytimes.com/2009/05/12/a-grand-conspiracy-theory-from-pakistan/

36. Richard Norton-Taylor, "Britain and US prepared to open talks with the Taliban," *Guardian*, July 28, 2009, http://www.guardian.co.uk/world/2009/jul/27/britain-us-talks-taliban-afghanistan

37. "A New Strategy for Afghanistan and Pakistan," March 27, 2009, http://www.whitehouse.gov/blog/09/03/27/A-New-Strategy-for-Afghanistan-and-Pakistan/

38. "Pakistan and United States: Two Different Priorities," interview with Teresita C. Schaffer, Director, South Asia Program, Center for Strategic and International Studies, Washington, D.C. Bernard Gwertzman, Consulting Ed., Council on Foreign Relations is the interviewer, June 26, 2008, http://www.cfr.org/publication/16639/pakistan_and_united_states.html

39. Kamal Matinuddin, "Post-9/11 Afghanistan," *South Asian Journal*, Issue 3 (January/March, 2004), http://www.southasianmedia.net/Magazine/Journal/post_nineeleven.htm

40. COMISAF Initial Assessment (Unclassified), *The Washington Post*, September 21, 2009, http://www.washingtonpost.com/wp-dyn/content/article/2009/09/21/AR2009092100110_pf.html

41. *Daily Times*, July 20, 2009, op.cit.

42. Ahmer Bilal Soofi, "US aid: some legal aspects," *Dawn*, July 15, 2009.

APPENDIX

Chronology

1948	First border war with India over Kashmir.
October, 1951	Pakistan's first Prime Minister Liaquat Ali Khan assassinated.
October, 1958	Constitution abrogated and Martial Law declared by Army Commander Ayub Khan.
April, 1965	Rann of Kutch border war with India.
September, 1965	Second all-out war with India over Kashmir, followed by Tashkent Agreement.
March, 1969	General Ayub Khan resigned after widespread and consistent mass movement for democracy. Army Chief General Yahya Khan declared Martial Law.
December, 1971	Third all-out war with India; as a consequence, the independent state of Bangladesh emerged.
July, 1972	Simla Peace Agreement with India, with a recognition that Kashmir dispute is an unsettled issue.
1973–1977	Insurgency and military action in Balochistan, triggered by dismissal of the provincial government by Prime Minister Bhutto.
July, 1977	General Zia-ul-Haq dismissed Prime Minister Zulfiqar Ali Bhutto's government and later declared Martial Law.
April, 1979	Zulfiqar Ali Bhutto hanged by Zia regime.
August, 1988	General Zia, the U.S. ambassador, and top Pakistan army officials killed in air crash.
August, 1990	Benazir Bhutto's first government dismissed on corruption charges.

April, 1993	Nawaz Sharif's first government dismissed on corruption charges. Later restored by Supreme Court, but Sharif resigned along with the President, as a compromise deal.
November, 1996	Benazir Bhutto's second government dismissed on corruption charges.
May, 1998	Pakistan conducted nuclear tests, in retaliation for earlier India tests.
February, 1999	Lahore Declaration signed during the visit of Indian Prime Minister Vajpayee to Lahore. First major agreement to normalize relations after 1972 Simla Peace Agreement.
May–July, 1999	Border war with India on Kargil. Prime Minister Sharif was unaware of the military action by Army Chief General Musharraf.
October, 1999	Prime Minister Nawaz Sharif's government overthrown and Martial Law imposed by Army Chief General Musharraf.
September, 2001	Musharraf supports the United States on war against terrorism in Afghanistan.
December, 2001	Terror attack on Indian Parliament is blamed on Pakistan-based groups. As a consequence, amassing of troops by India on Pakistan border and beginning of standoff, the largest since 1971.
January, 2002	Musharraf banned two militant groups: Lashkar-e-Toiba and Jaish-e-Mohammad, under U.S. pressure.
April, 2002	Musharraf won five years in office in a flawed referendum.
May, 2002	Pakistan test-fired three medium-range missiles capable of carrying nuclear warheads.
November, 2002	National Assembly elected Mir Zafarullah Jamali, a member of Musharraf's party to head a coalition government, after rigged elections.
	A group of religious parties opposed to the U.S. presence in Afghanistan form a government in NWFP province, bordering Afghanistan.
December, 2003	Two assassination attempts on General Musharraf traced to Waziristan.
2004	Military operations in FATA against al-Qaeda militants.
April, 2004	Shakai Peace Deal with South Waziristan militant Nek Muhammad Wazir, after fierce fighting. He was soon killed by a U.S. air strike for his ties with al-Qaeda.
February, 2005	Sara Rogha Peace Deal with Pakistani Taliban leader Baitullah Mehsud, in South Waziristan, after fierce fighting with Pakistan army.
August, 2005	Pakistan test-fired nuclear-capable cruise missile.
August, 2006	Security forces killed prominent Balochistan tribal leader, Nawab Akbar Bugti.
February, 2007	Sixty-eight Lahore-bound Pakistani passengers killed by train bomb blasts in India.
March, 2007	Tribesmen of FATA fought against foreign Uzbek militants (al-Qaeda).
May, 2007	Several killed in Karachi during rival demonstrations over arrival of dismissed Chief Justice Chaudhry.

July, 2007	Military action against radical group of Red Mosque in Islamabad.
	Army under attack in Waziristan by militants.
October, 2007	Suicide terror attack on Benazir Bhutto's welcome procession in Karachi, killed more than 150 people.
November, 2007	General Musharraf declared emergency rule (Martial Law) and dismissed Chief Justice of Supreme Court and other judges, putting them under house arrest, along with a media blackout of private TV channels.
December, 2007	Benazir Bhutto assassinated after election rally in Rawalpindi.
January, 2008	Operation Zalzala ("Earthquake") by army against Baitullah Mehsud's militants, followed by a peace agreement.
August, 2008	Under impeachment threat by two main parties, Musharraf resigned as President.
September, 2008	Armed tribesmen in FATA challenged the militants.
	Islamabad Marriott Hotel devastated in a suicide truck bombing attack.
November, 2008	India blamed Pakistan for Mumbai terrorist attack.
March, 2009	Gunmen in Lahore attacked Sri Lankan cricket team bus. Seven players injured.
	Terrorists attacked police training facility in Lahore, killing 40 people.
April, 2009	Military operation (Rah-e-Rast—"Righteous Path") against militants in Swat Valley.
August, 2009	Baitullah Mehsud killed by U.S. drone. He was replaced by Hakimullah Mehsud, as Pakistan Taliban leader.
October, 2009	Army started a large-scale offensive (Rah-e-Nijat—"Salvation Path") in South Waziristan against the Taliban.
July, 2010	Twin suicide attacks at Muslim shrine of a popular saint, Data Ganj Bakhsh in Lahore, killing 44 people. Punjabi Taliban with sectarian leaning was blamed.
September, 2010	Triple blasts, two suicides, and one grenade targeted Yaum-e-Ali Shia procession in Lahore, killing 30 people. Sectarian terror group was accused.
	After increasing U.S. drone attacks in FATA, Pakistan temporarily suspended NATO supply into Afghanistan.
October, 2010	Karachi under a spate of target killings ascribed to ethnic and sectarian reasons.

Bibliography

BOOKS

Abbas, Hassan, *Pakistan's Drift into Extremism: Allah, the Army, and America's War on Terror* (Armonk, NY: M.E. Sharpe, 2005).

Adeney, Katharine, *Federalism and Ethnic Conflict Regulation in India and Pakistan* (New York: Palgrave Macmillan, 2007).

Ahmad, Mushtaq, *Pakistan at the Crossroads* (Karachi: Royal Book Co., 1985).

Ahmad, Shamshad, *Dreams Unfulfilled*, revised & enlarged ed. (Lahore: Jahangir Books, 2010).

Ahmad, Waheed, (ed.) *Quaid-i-Azam Mohammad Ali Jinnah: The Nation's Voice towards Consolidation–Speeches and Statements, March 1935 –March 1940* (Karachi: Quaid-i-Azam Academy, 1992).

Ahmed, Akbar S., *Resistance and Control in Pakistan* (London: Routledge, 2004).

Ahmed, Akbar S., *Religion and Politics in Muslim Society: Order and Conflict in Pakistan* (Cambridge: Cambridge University Press, 2003).

Ahsan, Aitzaz, *The Indus Saga and the Making of Pakistan* (Karachi: Oxford University Press, 1996).

Ali, Chaudhri Muhammad, *The Emergence of Pakistan*, 6th Imp. (Lahore: Research Society of Pakistan, 1988).

Ali, Shaheen Sardar and Javaid Rehman, *Indigenous Peoples and Ethnic Minorities of Pakistan Constitutional and Legal Perspectives* (Richmond, surrey: Curzon Press, 2001).

Amin, Shahid M., *Pakistan's Foreign Policy: A Reappraisal* (Karachi: Oxford University Press, 2003).

Awan, A. B., *Baluchistan: Historical and Political Processes* (London: New Century Publishers, 1985).

Axmann, Martin, *Back to the Future; the Khanate of Kalat and the Genesis of Baloch Nationalism, 1915–1955* (New York: Oxford University Press, 2008).

Aziz, Sartaj, *Between Dreams and Realities: Some Milestones in Pakistan's History* (Karachi: Oxford University Press, 2009).

Blank, Stephen J., *Natural Allies*? Regional Security in Asia and Prospects for Indo-American Strategic Cooperation, The Strategic Studies Institute (U.S. Army War College, 2005).

Bugti, Professor Aziz Muhammad, (Urdu) *Balochistan: Sayasi Culture aur Qabale Nizam, (Balochistan: Political Culture and Tribal System)* (Lahore: Function House, 1995).

Burki, Shahid Javed, *Historical Dictionary of Pakistan* (Lanham, Maryland: The Scarecrow Press, Inc., 2006).

Cloughley, Brian, *A History of the Pakistan Army: Wars and Insurrections* (Karachi: Oxford University Press, 1999).

Cohen, Stephen P., *The Idea of Pakistan* (Lahore: Vanguard Books, 2005).

Faruqui, Ahmad, *Rethinking the National Security of Pakistan* (Burlington, VT: Ashgate, 2003).

Gartenstein-Ross, Daveed and Clifford D. May, eds., *The Afghanistan-Pakistan Theater: Militant Islam, Security and Stability* (Washington, D.C.: FDD Press, 2010).

Gilani, Yousaf Raza, *Chah-e-Yousaf Ki Sada, in Urdu (Reflections from Yousaf's Well)* (Lahore: Nigarshat Publishers, 2006).

Gul, Imtiaz, *The Al Qaeda Connection: The Taliban and the Terror in Pakistan's Tribal Areas* (New Delhi: Viking, 2009).

Gul, Imtiaz, *The Most Dangerous Place: Pakistan's Lawless Frontier* (London: Penguin Books, 2010).

Gunaratna, Rohan and Khuram Iqbal, *Pakistan: Terrorism Ground Zero* (London: Reaktion Books Ltd, 2011).

Haq, Dr. Inam ul and Professor Anwar Ruman, (Urdu) *Balochistan Aazadi ke Bade (1947–1997) (Balochistan after Independence: 1947–1997)* (Quetta: Mushawara Talime Tahqaq, 1997)

Haqqani, Husain, *Pakistan: Between Mosque and Military* (Washington, D.C.: Carnegie Endowment for International Peace, 2005).

Hashmi, Makhdoom Muhammad Javed, *Han! Mee Baghi Hu (Yes! I Am a Rebel)* (Lahore: Saghar Publishers, 2005).

Hasnat, Syed Farooq and Pelinka, Anton, eds., *Security for the Weak Nations: A Multiple Perspective*; *A Joint Project of Pakistani and Austrian Scholars* (Lahore: Izharsons, 1986).

Hasnat, Syed Farooq and Ahmad Faruqi, eds., *Pakistan: Unresolved Issues of State and Society* (Lahore: Vanguard, 2008).

Hussain, Zahid, *Frontline Pakistan: The Struggle with Militant Islam* (New York: Columbia University Press, 2007).

Hussain, Zahid, *The Scorpion's Tail: The Relentless Rise of Islamic Militants in Pakistan–and How It Threatens the World* (New York: Free Press, 2010).

Jaffrelot, Christophe, ed., *Pakistan: Nationalism without Nation* (New Delhi: Manohar Publishers & Distributors, 2002).

Jones, Owen Bennett, *Pakistan: Eye of the Storm* (New Haven and London: Yale University Press, 2002).

Khan, Adeel, *Politics of Identity: Ethnic Nationalism and the State in Pakistan* (New Delhi: Sage Publications Pvt. Ltd., 2005).

Khan, Hamid, *Constitutional and Political History of Pakistan* (Karachi: Oxford University Press, 2004).

Khan, Mir Ahmad Yar, *Inside Balouchistan: A Political Autobiography of His Highness Baiglar Baigi Khan-e-Azam XIII* (Karachi: Royal Book Company, 1975).

Khan, Rais Ahmad, (ed.), *Forty Years of Pakistan-United States Relations: In Search of Peace and Security* (Karachi: Royal Book Company, 1990).

Kukreja, Veena, *Contemporary Pakistan: Political Process Conflicts and Crises* (New Delhi: Sage Publications Inc., 2003).

Kukreja, Veena and M. P. Singh (eds.), *Pakistan: Democracy, Development and Security Issues*, (New Delhi: Sage Publications, 2005).

Madalena, Maria L., Carvalho-Fischer and Matthias Fischer, *Pakistan Under Siege: Pakistan after September 11th, 2001* (Lahore: Vanguard Books, 2004).

Malik, Hafeez (ed.), Soviet-*American Relations with Pakistan, Iran and Afghanistan* (London: MacMillan, 1987).

Malik, Hafeez, *US Relations with Afghanistan and Pakistan: The Imperial Dimension* (Karachi: Oxford University Press, 2008).

Malik, Iftikhar H., *State and Civil Society in Pakistan: Politics of Authority, Ideology and Ethnicity* (Hampshire: Palgrave Macmillan, 1997).

Malik, Iftikhar H., *The History of Pakistan* (Westport, CT: Greenwood Press, 2008).

Marri, Dr. Shah Muhammad, (Urdu) *Baloch Quam: Qadeem Ahad se Asr Hazar Tak* (*Baloch Nation: From Ancient Era to Present Times)* (Lahore: Takhliqat, 2000).

Matheson, Sylvia A., The *Tigers of Baluchistan*; with a new Introduction by Paul Titus (New York: Oxford University Press, 1997).

Matinuddin, Kamal, *Taliban Phenomenon: Afghanistan, 1994–1997;* Fourth Imp. (Karachi: Oxford University Press, 2002).

Mazari, Sherbaz Khan, *A Journey to Disillusionment* (Karachi: Oxford University Press, 2000).

Mir, Amir, *The Fluttering Flag of Jehad*, foreword by Khalid Ahmed, (Lahore: Mashal Books, 2008).

Mir, Amir, *Talibanization of Pakistan from 9/11 to 26/11* (New Delhi: Pentagon Security International, 2009).

Musharraf, Pervez, *In the Line of Fire: A Memoir* (New York: Free Press, 2006)

Nawaz, Shuja, *Crossed Swords: Pakistan, its Army, and the Wars Within* (New York: Oxford University Press, 2008).

Owtadolajam, Dr. Mohammad, *A Sociological Study of the Hazara Tribe in Balochistan* (An Analysis of Socio-cultural Change), (Quetta: Hazaragi Academy; [Tanzeem Nasle Nau Hazara Mughal], 2006).

Paul, T. V., ed., *The India-Pakistan Conflict: An Enduring Rivalry* (Cambridge: Cambridge University Press, 2005).

Rahman, Tariq, *Language and Politics in Pakistan* (Karachi: Oxford University Press, 1999).

Rana, Mohammad Amir, *The Seeds of Terrorism* (London: New Millennium, 2005).

Rana, Muhammad Amir and Rohan Gunaratna, *Al-Qaeda Fights Back Inside Pakistani Tribal Areas*, 2nd ed. (Islamabad: Pak Institute for Peace Studies [PIPS], 2008).

Rana, Muhammad Amir, *translated* Saba Ansari, *A to Z of Jehadi Organizations in Pakistan* (Lahore: Mashal, 2009).

Rana, Muhammad Amir, Safdar Sial and Abdul Basit, *Dynamics of Taliban Insurgency in FATA* (Islamabad: Pak Institute for Peace Studies [PIPS], 2010).

Rengel, Marian, *Pakistan: A Primary Source Cultural Guide* (New York: PowerPlus Books, 2004).

Rizvi, Hasan-Askari, *Pakistan and the Geostrategic Environment: A Study of Foreign Policy* (London: The Macmillan Press, 1993).

Rizvi, Hasan-Askari, Military*, State and Society in Pakistan* (New York: St. Martin's Press, Inc., 2000).

Sattar, Abdul, *Pakistan's Foreign Policy: 1947–2005, a Concise History* (Karachi: Oxford University Press, 2007).

Shah, Mehtab Ali, *The Foreign Policy of Pakistan: Ethnic impacts on Diplomacy, 1971–1994* (London: I. B. Tauris & Co Ltd., 1997).

Siddiqa, Ayesha, *Military Inc.: Inside Pakistan's Military Economy* (London: Pluto Press, 2007).

Suskind, Ron, *The Way of the World: A Story of Truth and Hope in an Age of Extremism* (New York: HarperCollins, 2008).

Tahir-Kheli, Shirin, *The United States and Pakistan: The Evolution of an Influence Relationship* (New York: Praeger, 1982).

Talbot, Ian, *Pakistan: A Modern History* (Hampshire: Palgrave Macmillan, 2005).

Titus, Paul, *Marginality and Modernity: Ethnicity and Change in Post-Colonial Balochistan* (New York: Oxford University Press, 1997).

Weaver, Mary Anne, *Pakistan: In the Shadow of Jihad and Afghanistan* (New York: Farrar, Straus and Giroux, 2002).

Weiner, Myron and Banuazizi, Ali, eds., *The Politics of Social Transformation in Afghanistan, Iran, and Pakistan* (Contemporary Issues in the Middle East) (Syracuse: Syracuse University Press, 1994).

Weiss, Anita M., and S. Zulfiqar Gilani, *Power and Civil Society in Pakistan* (Karachi: Oxford University Press, 2001).

Wilcox, Wayne Ayres, *Pakistan: The Consolidation of a Nation*; third printing (New York: Columbia University Press, 1966).

Wirsing, Robert G., *Pakistan's Security under Zia, 1977–1988* (New York: St. Martin's Press, 1991).

Woodward, Bob, *Obama's Wars* (New York: Simon & Schuster, 2010).

Zahid, Hussain, *Frontline Pakistan: The Struggle with Militant Islam* (New York: Columbia University Press, 2007).

Ziring, Lawrence, *Pakistan in the Twentieth Century: A Political History* (Karachi: Oxford University Press, 1997).

Ziring ,Lawrence, *Pakistan: At the Crosscurrents of History* (Lahore: Vanguard, 2004).

RESEARCH PAPERS AND ARTICLES

Aftab, Safiya "Poverty and Militancy," *Pips Journal of Conflict and Peace Studies*, Vol. 1, Issue 1 (Oct.–Dec., 2008).

Ahmad, Eqbal, "A mirage mis-named strategic depth," *Al-Ahram* Weekly online, August 27–September 2, 1998, http://weekly.ahram.org.eg/1998/392/foc12.htm

Ashraf, Tariq M., "Terrorism in Pakistan: Emerging Trends," http://www.grandestrategy.com/2009/03/terrorism-in-pakistan-emerging-trends.html

Barracca, Steven, "Military Coups in the Post-Cold War Era: Pakistan, Ecuador and Venezuela," *Third World Quarterly*, Vol. 28, No. 1 (2007): 137–154.

Baxter, Craig, "Constitution Making: The Development of Federalism in Pakistan," *Asian Survey*, Vol. 14, No. 12 (December, 1974).

Bhutto, Benazir, "Only Democracy will Break Pakistan's Terror Link," *New Perspectives Quarterly*, Vol. 23, No. 4 (Fall, 2006): 19–21.

Braun, Dieter, "Pakistan's Balancing Act—Factors Determining its Foreign and Security Policy," translated from *Europa—Arc/n'v*, Bonn, No. 15/1985 (August 10, 1985).

Bukhari, Syed Adnan Ali Shah, "New strategies in Pakistan's counter-insurgency operation in South Waziristan," *TerrorismMonitor*, Vol. VII, Issue 37 (December 3, 2009); http://www.jamestown.org/uploads/media/TM_007_6b5e8c.pdf

Cheema, Pervaiz Iqbal, "The Afghanistan Crisis and Pakistan's Security Dilemma," *Asian Survey*, Vol. 23, No. 3 (March, 1983): 227–243.

Cohen, Stephen Philip, "America and Pakistan: Is the Worst Case Avoidable?" *Current History*, March (2005): 131–136.

Cole, Juan, "Pakistan and Afghanistan: Beyond the Taliban, *Political Science Quarterly*, Vol. 124, No. 2. (Summer 2009): 221–249.

D'Souza, Shanthie Mariet, "Afghanistan: Continuing Violence," in D. Suba Chandran and P.R. Chari (eds.), *Armed Conflicts in South Asia, 2008: Growing Violence* (New Delhi: Routledge, 2008).

Fair, C. Christine, "Militant Recruitment in Pakistan: Implications for Al Qaeda and other organizations," *Studies in Conflict and Terrorism*, Vol. 27, No. 6 (Nov.–Dec., 2004): 489–504.

Fair, C. Christine, et al., "Demographics and Security: The Contrasting Cases of Pakistan and Bangladesh," *Journal of South Asian and Middle Eastern Studies*, Summer (2005): 53–76.

Farooq, Umer, "Pakistani Madrasahs . . . Heated Debate Rages," *The Journal of Turkish Weekly*, August 6, 2005, http://www.turkishweekly.net/news.php?id=16926

Gera, Nina, "Food Security under Structural Adjustment in Pakistan," *Asian Survey*, Vol. 44, No. 3 (May–June, 2004): 353–369.

Gregory, Shaun, "The ISI and the War on Terrorism," *Studies in Conflict and Terrorism*, Vol. 30, No. 12 (December, 2007): 1013–1032.

Haider, Ziad, "Baluchis, Beijing, and Pakistan's Gwadar Port," *Georgetown Journal of International Affairs*, Vol. 6, No. 1 (Winter/Spring 2005): 95–103.

Hasnat, Syed Farooq, "Bureaucracy, Political Process and Nation-Building: The Case of Pakistan, 1947–1977," in S. A. H. Haqqi, ed., *Democracy, Pluralism and Nation Building* (Delhi: N.B. O. Publishers' Distributors, 1984): 126–139.

Hasnat, Syed Farooq, "Environmental Typologies of Pakistan's Security," Pakistan Horizon. Vol. XL (1987): 51–64.

Hasnat, Syed Farooq, "Pakistan's Vital Environment: The Middle East Region," in Leo E. Rose and Kamal Matinuddin, (eds.),*Beyond Afghanistan: The Emerging U.S.–Pakistan Relations*; Research Papers and Policy Studies (Berkeley, Cal: Institute for East Asian Studies, University of California, 1989): 228–251.

Hasnat, Syed Farooq, "Pakistan's Strategic Interests, Afghanistan and the Fluctuating U.S. Strategy," *Journal of International Affairs*, Vol. 63, No. 1 (Fall/Winter, 2009): 141–155.

Hasnat, Syed Farooq, "The Flawed Afghan Elections", *The Nation*, September 12, 2009.

Hasnat, Syed Farooq, "Hillary Converse with Real Pakistan," *The Nation*, November 15, 2009.

Haqqani, Husain, "Pakistan and the Islamists," *Current History*, April (2007): 147–152.

Haqqani, Irshad Ahmad, "Failure of Democracy in Pakistan?," *The Muslim World*, April (2006): 219–232.

Hassan, Syed Minhaj ul, "Tribal Areas of NWFP: Politics of Survival," in *Pakistan: Unresolved Issues of State and Society*, Syed Farooq Hasnat and Ahmad Faruqui (eds.) (Lahore: Vanguard, 2008).

Kennedy, Charles H., "Pakistan in 2004: Running Very Fast to Stay in the Same Place," *Asian Survey*, Vol. 45, No. 1 (Jan.–Feb., 2005): 105–112.

Kennedy, Charles H., "Pakistan in 2005: Surviving Domestic and International Tremors," *Asian Survey*, Vol. 46, No. 1 (Jan.–Feb., 2006): 125–131.

Khan, Adeel, "Pakistan in 2006: Safe Center, Dangerous Peripheries," *Asian Survey*, Vol. 47, No. 1 (Jan.,–Feb., 2007): 125–132.

Kennedy, Charles H., "Pakistan in 2007: More Violent, More Unstable," *Asian Survey*, Vol. 48, No. 1 (Jan.–Feb., 2008): 144–153.

LaPorte, Jr., Robert, "Succession in Pakistan: Continuity and Change in a Garrison State," *Asian Survey*, Vol. 9, No. 11 (November, 1969): 842–861.

Lieven, Anatol, "A Difficult Country: Pakistan and the Case for Developmental Realism," *The National Interest*, (Spring, 2006): 43–49.

Marten, Kimberly, "Misunderstanding Pakistan's Federally Administered Tribal Area?" *International Security*, Vol. 33, No. 3 (Winter 2008/2009): 180–189.

Matinuddin, Kamal, "Post-9/11 Afghanistan," *South Asian Journal*, Issue 3 (January/March, 2004), http://www.southasianmedia.net/Magazine/Journal/post_nineeleven.htm

McPastner, Stephen and Carroll, "Adaptations to State-Level Politics by the Southern Baluch," in Lawrence Ziring, Ralph Braibanti, and W. Howard Wriggins, (eds.) *Pakistan: The Long View* (Durham, N.C.: Duke University Press, 1977).

Nasr, S. V. R., "Islam, the State and the Rise of Sectarian Militancy in Pakistan," in Christophe Jaffrelot, (ed.), *Pakistan: Nationalism without a Nation?*, (New Delhi: Manohar Publishers & Distributors, 2002).

Norell, Magnus, "The Taliban and the Muttahida Majlis-e-Amal (MMA)," *The China and Eurasia Forum Quarterly*, Vol., No. 3 (August, 2007) http://www.silkroadstudies.org/new/docs/CEF/Quarterly/August_2007/Norell.pdf

Rahman, Khalid, Syed Rashad Bukhari, "Pakistan: Religious Education and Institutions," *The Muslim World*, (April, 2006): 323–339.

Rais, Rasul B., "Pakistan in the Regional and Global Power Structure," *Asian Survey*, Vol. 31, No. 4 (April, 1991): 378–393.

Riedel, Bruce, "Armageddon in Islamabad," *The National Interest*, July/August 2009, (retrieved on Dec. 12, 2010), http://nationalinterest.org/print/article/armageddon-in-islamabad-3148

Rizvi, Hasan-Askari, "Electoral Process in Pakistan," in *Pakistan: Unresolved Issues of State & Society*, Syed Farooq Hasnat, and Ahmed Faruqui, (eds.) (Lahore: Vanguard Books, 2008).

Sokefeld, Martin, "From Colonialism to Postcolonial Colonialism: Changing Modes of Domination in the Northern Areas of Pakistan," *Journal of Asian Studies*, Vol. 64, No. 4 (November, 2005): 939–973.

Titus, Paul, "Honor the Baloch, Buy the Pushtun: Stereotypes, Social Organization and History in Western Pakistan," *Modern Asian Studies,* Vol. 32, No. 3 (1998): 657–687.

Wirsing, Robert G., "Pakistan's Security in the 'New World Order': Going from Bad to Worse," Asian *Affairs*, Vol. 23, No. 2 (Summer, 1996): 101–126.

Wright, Jr., Theodore P., "Center-Periphery Relations and Ethnic Conflict in Pakistan: Sindhis, Muhajirs, and Punjabis," *Comparative Politics*, Vol. 23, No. 3 (April, 1991): 299–312.

Yousuf, Mohammed, "The Historical Roots of Islamic Militancy in Pakistan and Current Scenario: Amicus," *The Journal of Turkish Weekly*, May 19, 2005, http://www.turkishweekly.net/articles.php?id=68

Zaidi, Syed Manzar Abbas, "The United States and the Counterinsurgency: the Peace Process in Pakistan," *American Foreign Policy Interests*, Vol. 31, No. 3: 149–165.

Index

About the Author

SYED FAROOQ HASNAT is Adjunct Scholar at the Middle East Institute, Washington, D.C. He completed his Ph.D. in Regional Security Affairs from University of South Carolina and University of the Punjab, Lahore. He was Professor/Chair of the Department of Political Science, University of the Punjab, Lahore. Dr. Farooq Hasnat was appointed to Pakistan Chair at the Center for Strategic Studies at University of Jordan, Amman for four years. He also served as Deputy Chief of the Political Affairs Wing of Cabinet Division (Prime Minister's office), government of Pakistan, Islamabad. He took up a position as in charge of the Middle Eastern section of Islamabad Institute for Strategic Studies. Professor Hasnat was also a visiting Researcher in the Department of Political Science at University of Innsbruck, Austria. He is author of *Security Problems of the Persian Gulf: Conflicts and their Resolution* and *The Sikh Question: From Constitutional Demands to Armed Conflict*. He is a co-editor of *Security for the Weak Nations: A Multiple Perspective* and *Pakistan: Unresolved Issues of State and Society*. He has published extensively on Pakistan and the Middle East Region in research journals and newspapers of Pakistan, Iran, Jordan and the United States.